HOLT SCIENCE & TECHNOLOGY

Animals

HOLT, RINEHART AND WINSTON

A Harcourt Education Company

Orlando • **Austin** • New York • San Diego • Toronto • London

Acknowledgments

Contributing Author

Jennie Dusheck
Science Writer
Santa Cruz, California

Inclusion Specialist

Ellen McPeek Glisan
Special Needs Consultant
San Antonio, Texas

Safety Reviewer

Jack Gerlovich, Ph.D.
Associate Professor
School of Education
Drake University
Des Moines, Iowa

Academic Reviewers

Christopher B. Boyko, Ph.D.
Research Associate
Division of Invertebrate
    Zoology
American Museum of
    Natural History
New York, New York

Michael Carleton, Ph.D.
Curator of Mammals
Smithsonian Museum
    of Natural History
Washington, D.C.

William Grisham, Ph.D.
Lecturer
Psychology Department
University of California,
    Los Angeles
Los Angeles, California

Jamie Kneitel, Ph.D.
Postdoctoral Associate
Department of Biology
Washington University
St. Louis, Missouri

John Krenz, Ph.D.
Associate Professor
Biological Sciences
Minnesota State
    University
Mankato, Minnesota

Gerald J. Niemi, Ph.D.
*Professor and Center
    Director*
Biology and Center
    for Water and the
    Environment
Natural Resources
    Research Institute
University of Minnesota
Duluth, Minnesota

Laurie Santos, Ph.D.
Assistant Professor
Department of
    Psychology
Yale University
New Haven, Connecticut

Richard P. Vari, Ph.D.
*Research Scientist and
    Curator*
Division of Fishes
National Museum of
    Natural History
Washington, D.C.

Teacher Reviewers

Diedre S. Adams
Physical Science Instructor
West Vigo Middle School
West Terre Haute,
    Indiana

Sarah Carver
Science Teacher
Jackson Creek Middle
    School
Bloomington, Indiana

Hilary Cochran
Science Teacher
Indian Crest Junior
    High School
Souderton, Pennsylvania

**Debra S. Kogelman,
    MAed.**
Science Teacher
University of Chicago
    Laboratory Schools
Chicago, Illinois

Augie Maldonado
Science Teacher
Grisham Middle School
Round Rock, Texas

Helen P. Schiller
Instructional Coach
The School District of
    Greenville County
Greenville, South
    Carolina

Stephanie Snowden
Science Teacher
Canyon Vista Middle
    School
Austin, Texas

Larry A. Weber, M.S.
Science Teacher
Marshall School
Duluth, Minnesota

Angie Williams
Teacher
Riversprings Middle
    School
Crawfordville, Florida

Lab Development

Diana Scheidle Bartos
Research Associate
School of Mines
Golden, Colorado

Carl Benson
General Science Teacher
Plains High School
Plains, Montana

Charlotte Blassingame
Technology Coordinator
White Station
    Middle School
Memphis, Tennessee

Marsha Carver
*Science Teacher and
    Department Chair*
McLean County
    High School
Calhoun, Kentucky

Kenneth E. Creese
Science Teacher
White Mountain Junior
    High School
Rock Springs, Wyoming

ISBN 0-03-025534-1

5 6 7 048 08 07

B Animals

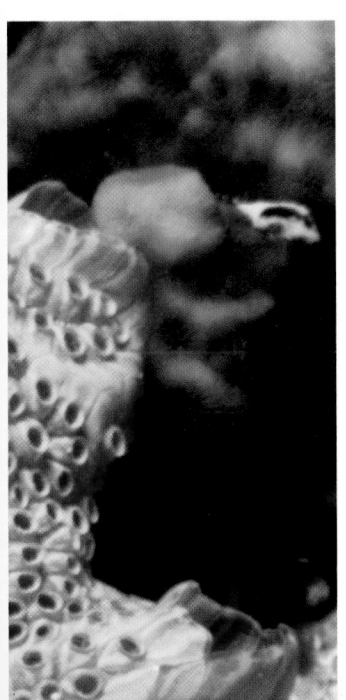

Labs and Activities

MATH PRACTICE

Science in Action

LabBook

How to Use Your Textbook

Your Roadmap for Success with Holt Science and Technology

Reading Warm-Up

A Reading Warm-Up at the beginning of every section provides you with the section's objectives and key terms. The objectives tell you what you'll need to know after you finish reading the section.

Key terms are listed for each section. Learn the definitions of these terms because you will most likely be tested on them. Each key term is highlighted in the text and is defined at point of use and in the margin. You can also use the glossary to locate definitions quickly.

STUDY TIP Reread the objectives and the definitions to the key terms when studying for a test to be sure you know the material.

Get Organized

A Reading Strategy at the beginning of every section provides tips to help you organize and remember the information covered in the section. Keep a science notebook so that you are ready to take notes when your teacher reviews the material in class. Keep your assignments in this notebook so that you can review them when studying for the chapter test.

SECTION 1

Simple Invertebrates

Humans and snakes have them, but octopuses and butterflies don't. What are they? Backbones!

Animals that don't have backbones are called **invertebrates** (in VUHR tuh brits). They make up about 96% of all animal species. So far, more than 1 million invertebrates have been named. Most biologists think that millions more have not been identified yet.

Invertebrate Characteristics

Invertebrates come in many different shapes and sizes. Grasshoppers, clams, earthworms, and jellyfish are examples of invertebrates. They are all very different from each other. Some invertebrates have heads, and others do not. Some invertebrates eat food through their mouths. Others absorb food particles through their tissues. But all invertebrates are similar because they do not have backbones.

Invertebrates have three basic body plans, or types of *symmetry*. Symmetry can be bilateral (bie LAT uhr uhl) or radial (RAY dee uhl). Some animals have no symmetry at all. Animals that don't have symmetry are *asymmetrical* (AY suh MEH tri kuhl). Most animals have bilateral symmetry. **Figure 1** shows examples of each kind of symmetry.

READING WARM-UP

Objectives
- Describe the body plans, nervous systems, and guts of invertebrates.
- Explain how sponges get food.
- Describe three cnidarian traits.
- Describe the three kinds of flatworms.
- Describe the body of a roundworm.

Terms to Learn

invertebrate gut
ganglion coelom

READING STRATEGY

Reading Organizer As you read this section, create an outline of the section. Use the headings from the section in your outline.

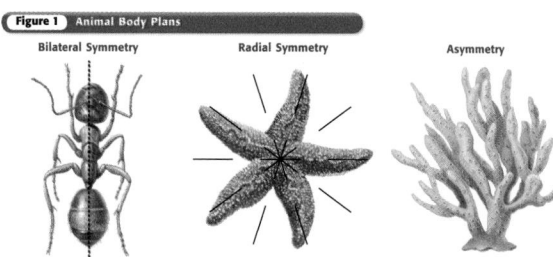

Figure 1   Animal Body Plans

Bilateral Symmetry | Radial Symmetry | Asymmetry

This ant has **bilateral symmetry.** The two sides of its body mirror each other. On each side of its body, the ant has one eye, one antenna, and three legs.

This sea star has **radial symmetry.** Its body is organized around the center, like spokes on a wheel.

This sponge is **asymmetrical.** You cannot draw a straight line to divide its body into two or more equal parts. Its body is not organized around the center.

380   Chapter 15   Invertebrates

Be Resourceful—Use the Web

SCILINKS®

Internet Connect boxes in your textbook take you to resources that you can use for science projects, reports, and research papers. Go to scilinks.org, and type in the SciLinks code to get information on a topic.

go.hrw.com

Visit go.hrw.com

Find worksheets, **Current Science®** magazine articles online, and other materials that go with your textbook at **go.hrw.com.** Click on the textbook icon and the table of contents to see all of the resources for each chapter.

Nerves

All animals except sponges have special tissues that make fibers called *nerves*. Nerves allow animals to sense their environment. Nerves also carry messages around the body to control an animal's actions. Simple invertebrates have nerves arranged in networks or in nerve cords. *Nerve cords* are packs of nerves that carry messages along a single path.

In some invertebrates, many nerve cells come together as ganglia (singular, *ganglion*). A **ganglion** (GANG glee uhn) is a concentrated mass of nerve cells. Each ganglion controls different parts of the body. Ganglia are connected by nerve cords. In complex invertebrates, ganglia are controlled by a brain. The *brain* is an organ that controls nerves throughout the body.

Guts

Almost all animals digest food in a gut. A **gut** is a pouch lined with cells that release chemicals that break down food into small particles. The cells in the gut then absorb the food particles. In complex animals, the gut is inside a coelom (SEE luhm). A **coelom** is the body cavity that surrounds the gut. The coelom contains many organs, such as the heart and lungs. But these organs are separated from the gut. This arrangement keeps other body processes from disturbing the gut. **Figure 2** shows an earthworm's coelom.

✔ **Reading Check** How is the coelom related to the gut? (*See the Appendix for answers to Reading Checks.*)

Sponges

Sponges are the simplest invertebrates. They are asymmetrical and have no tissues, gut, or nerves. Adult sponges move only millimeters per day—if they move at all. In fact, sponges were once thought to be plants! But sponges can't make their own food. That's one reason they are classified as animals. **Figure 3** shows a spo[...]

invertebrate an animal that does not have a backbone

ganglion a mass of nerve cells

gut the digestive tract

coelom a body cavity that contains the internal organs

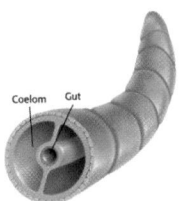

Coelom   Gut

Figure 2 Earthworms have a coelom that contains the gut.

Use the Illustrations and Photos

Art shows complex ideas and processes. Learn to analyze the art so that you better understand the material you read in the text.

Tables and graphs display important information in an organized way to help you see relationships.

A picture is worth a thousand words. Look at the photographs to see relevant examples of science concepts that you are reading about.

Answer the Section Reviews

Section Reviews test your knowledge of the main points of the section. Critical Thinking items challenge you to think about the material in greater depth and to find connections that you infer from the text.

STUDY TIP When you can't answer a question, reread the section. The answer is usually there.

Do Your Homework

Your teacher may assign worksheets to help you understand and remember the material in the chapter.

STUDY TIP Don't try to answer the questions without reading the text and reviewing your class notes. A little preparation up front will make your homework assignments a lot easier. Answering the items in the Chapter Review will help prepare you for the chapter test.

SECTION Review

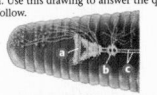

Summary

- Invertebrates are animals that do not have a backbone. Most invertebrates have nerves and a gut. The gut is located in the coelom.
- Almost all animals have radial or bilateral symmetry. But some animals, including sponges, are asymmetrical.
- Sponges filter food from water with collar cells. Collar cells also digest food. Sponges can regenerate body parts. They are classified by the kinds of skeletons they have.
- Cnidarians have stinging cells and have two body forms: the medusa and the polyp. Hydrozoans, jellyfish, and sea anemones and corals are cnidarians.
- Planarians, flukes, and tapeworms are three classes of flatworms. Planarians have eyespots and sensory lobes. Flukes and tapeworms are parasites.
- Roundworms are tiny worms that break down dead plant and animal tissue. Some roundworms are parasites.

Using Key Terms

Complete each of the following sentences by choosing the correct term from the word bank.

invertebrate   gut
ganglion   coelom

1. A(n) ___ is a mass of nerves that controls an animal's actions.

2. A(n) ___ does not have a backbone.

3. The ___ is a special space in an animal's body that surrounds the ___ and other organs.

Understanding Key Ideas

4. Which of the following is a trait shared by all invertebrates?
   a. having no backbone
   b. having radial symmetry
   c. having a brain
   d. having a gut

5. What do sponges use to digest food?
   a. an osculum
   b. pores
   c. collar cells
   d. a gut

6. Describe cnidarian body forms and stinging cells.

7. How is a roundworm similar to a piece of spaghetti?

Interpreting Graphics

All invertebrate nervous systems are made up of some or all of the same basic parts. The drawing below shows the nervous system of a segmented worm. Use this drawing to answer the questions that follow.

8. The letters in the drawing point to nerve cords, a ganglion, and a brain. Which letter points to the brain? How can you tell?

9. How is the brain connected to the ganglion?

Critical Thinking

10. **Making Inferences** Explain why it would be important for a parasite that its host survive.

SCI LINKS.   NSTA
Developed and maintained by the National Science Teachers Association

For a variety of links related to this chapter, go to www.scilinks.org

Topic: Sponges; Roundworms
SciLinks code: HSM1443; HSM1332

387

SAFETY FIRST!

Exploring, inventing, and investigating are essential to the study of science. However, these activities can also be dangerous. To make sure that your experiments and explorations are safe, you must be aware of a variety of safety guidelines. You have probably heard of the saying, "It is better to be safe than sorry." This is particularly true in a science classroom where experiments and explorations are being performed. Being uninformed and careless can result in serious injuries. Don't take chances with your own safety or with anyone else's.

The following pages describe important guidelines for staying safe in the science classroom. Your teacher may also have safety guidelines and tips that are specific to your classroom and laboratory. Take the time to be safe.

Safety Rules!

Start Out Right

Always get your teacher's permission before attempting any laboratory exploration. Read the procedures carefully, and pay particular attention to safety information and caution statements. If you are unsure about what a safety symbol means, look it up or ask your teacher. You cannot be too careful when it comes to safety. If an accident does occur, inform your teacher immediately regardless of how minor you think the accident is.

If you are instructed to note the odor of a substance, wave the fumes toward your nose with your hand. Never put your nose close to the source.

Safety Symbols

All of the experiments and investigations in this book and their related worksheets include important safety symbols to alert you to particular safety concerns. Become familiar with these symbols so that when you see them, you will know what they mean and what to do. It is important that you read this entire safety section to learn about specific dangers in the laboratory.

Eye protection

Clothing protection

Hand safety

Heating safety

Electric safety

Chemical safety

Animal safety

Sharp object

Plant safety

x

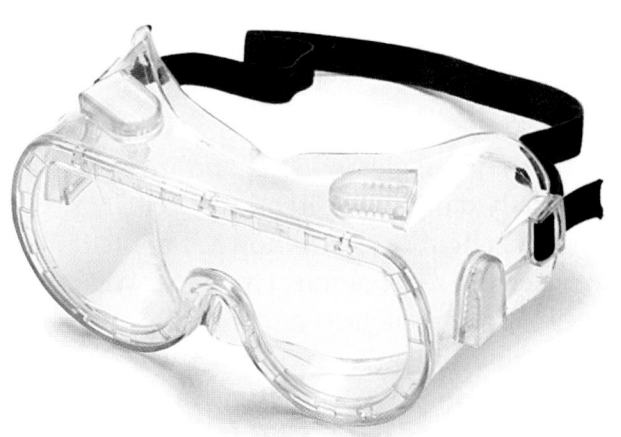

Eye Safety

Wear safety goggles when working around chemicals, acids, bases, or any type of flame or heating device. Wear safety goggles any time there is even the slightest chance that harm could come to your eyes. If any substance gets into your eyes, notify your teacher immediately and flush your eyes with running water for at least 15 minutes. Treat any unknown chemical as if it were a dangerous chemical. Never look directly into the sun. Doing so could cause permanent blindness.

Avoid wearing contact lenses in a laboratory situation. Even if you are wearing safety goggles, chemicals can get between the contact lenses and your eyes. If your doctor requires that you wear contact lenses instead of glasses, wear eye-cup safety goggles in the lab.

Safety Equipment

Know the locations of the nearest fire alarms and any other safety equipment, such as fire blankets and eyewash fountains, as identified by your teacher, and know the procedures for using the equipment.

Neatness

Keep your work area free of all unnecessary books and papers. Tie back long hair, and secure loose sleeves or other loose articles of clothing, such as ties and bows. Remove dangling jewelry. Don't wear open-toed shoes or sandals in the laboratory. Never eat, drink, or apply cosmetics in a laboratory setting. Food, drink, and cosmetics can easily become contaminated with dangerous materials.

Certain hair products (such as aerosol hair spray) are flammable and should not be worn while working near an open flame. Avoid wearing hair spray or hair gel on lab days.

Sharp/Pointed Objects

Use knives and other sharp instruments with extreme care. Never cut objects while holding them in your hands. Place objects on a suitable work surface for cutting.

Be extra careful when using any glassware. When adding a heavy object to a graduated cylinder, tilt the cylinder so the object slides slowly to the bottom.

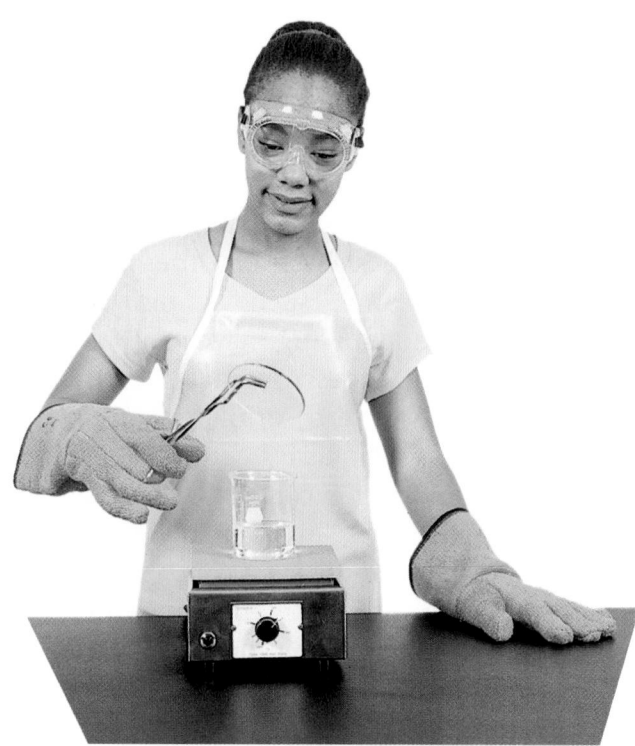

Chemicals

Wear safety goggles when handling any potentially dangerous chemicals, acids, or bases. If a chemical is unknown, handle it as you would a dangerous chemical. Wear an apron and protective gloves when you work with acids or bases or whenever you are told to do so. If a spill gets on your skin or clothing, rinse it off immediately with water for at least 5 minutes while calling to your teacher.

Never mix chemicals unless your teacher tells you to do so. Never taste, touch, or smell chemicals unless you are specifically directed to do so. Before working with a flammable liquid or gas, check for the presence of any source of flame, spark, or heat.

Heat

Wear safety goggles when using a heating device or a flame. Whenever possible, use an electric hot plate as a heat source instead of using an open flame. When heating materials in a test tube, always angle the test tube away from yourself and others. To avoid burns, wear heat-resistant gloves whenever instructed to do so.

Electricity

Be careful with electrical cords. When using a microscope with a lamp, do not place the cord where it could trip someone. Do not let cords hang over a table edge in a way that could cause equipment to fall if the cord is accidentally pulled. Do not use equipment with damaged cords. Be sure that your hands are dry and that the electrical equipment is in the "off" position before plugging it in. Turn off and unplug electrical equipment when you are finished.

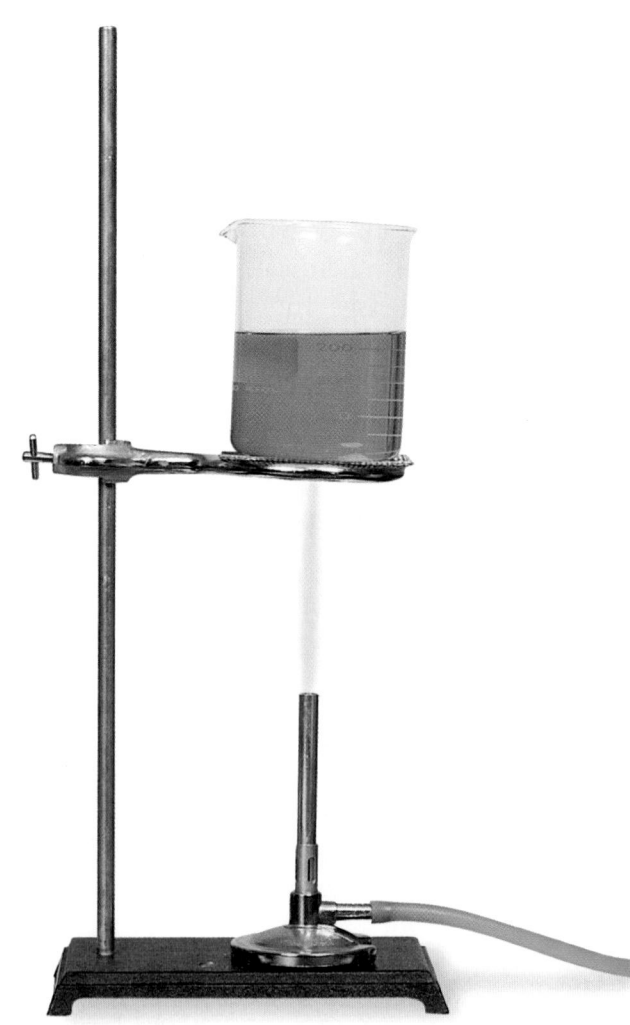

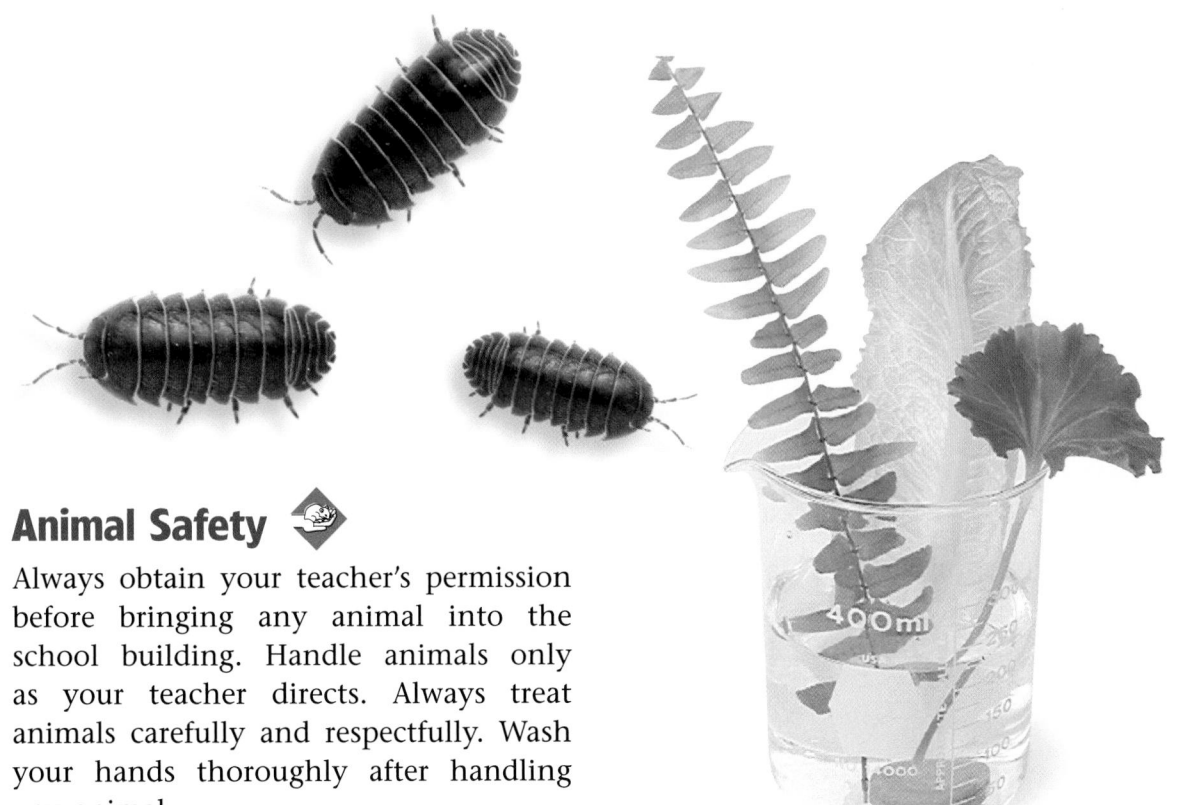

Animal Safety

Always obtain your teacher's permission before bringing any animal into the school building. Handle animals only as your teacher directs. Always treat animals carefully and respectfully. Wash your hands thoroughly after handling any animal.

Plant Safety

Do not eat any part of a plant or plant seed used in the laboratory. Wash your hands thoroughly after handling any part of a plant. When in nature, do not pick any wild plants unless your teacher instructs you to do so.

Glassware

Examine all glassware before use. Be sure that glassware is clean and free of chips and cracks. Report damaged glassware to your teacher. Glass containers used for heating should be made of heat-resistant glass.

Animals and Behavior

About the PHOTO

This spider needs to eat in order to survive. On the other hand, this hover fly needs to avoid being eaten in order to survive. How do the spider, the fly, and other animals get what they need to live? Animals use many behaviors to compete with each other for survival.

PRE-READING ACTIVITY

Graphic Organizer

Spider Map Before you read the chapter, create the graphic organizer entitled "Spider Map" described in the **Study Skills** section of the Appendix. Label the circle "Animal Behavior." Create a leg for each type of animal behavior. As you read the chapter, fill in the map with details about each type of animal behavior.

START-UP ACTIVITY

Go on a Safari!

You don't have to travel far to see interesting animals. If you look closely, you can find many animals nearby. **Caution:** Always be careful around wild or unfamiliar animals, because they may bite or sting. Do not handle wild animals or any animals that are unfamiliar to you.

Procedure

1. Go outside, and find **two different kinds of animals** to observe.

2. Without disturbing the animals, watch them quietly for a few minutes from a distance. You may want to use **binoculars** or a **magnifying lens.**

3. Write down everything you notice about each animal. Do you know what kind of animal each is? Where did you find them? What do they look like? How big are they? What are they doing? You may want to draw a picture of them.

Analysis

1. Compare the two animals that you studied. Do they look alike? Do they have similar behaviors?

2. How do the animals move? Did you see them communicating with other animals or defending themselves?

3. Can you tell what each animal eats? What characteristics of each animal help it find or catch food?

What Is an Animal?

What do you think of when you hear the word animal? You may think of your dog or cat. You may think about giraffes or grizzly bears. But would you think of a sponge?

The natural sponges that people use for washing are the remains of an animal. Animals come in many shapes and sizes. Some have four legs and fur, but most do not. Some are too small to be seen without a microscope, and others are bigger than a school bus. They are all part of the animal kingdom.

Animal Diversity

How many different kinds of animals do you see in **Figure 1**? You may be surprised to learn that feather stars and corals are animals. Spiders, fish, and birds are also animals. And slugs, kangaroos, and monkeys are animals, too. Scientists have named more than 1 million species of animals. Many species that exist have not yet been named. Some scientists estimate that more than 3 million species of animals live on the Earth.

Vertebrates

Most animals look nothing like humans. However, we share many characteristics with a group of animals called vertebrates (VUHR tuh brits). A *vertebrate* is an animal that has a backbone. Vertebrates include fishes, amphibians, reptiles, birds, and mammals. Humans are one of about 5,000 species of mammals.

Figure 1 *All of the living things in this picture are animals.*

Feather star

Fish

Coral

4

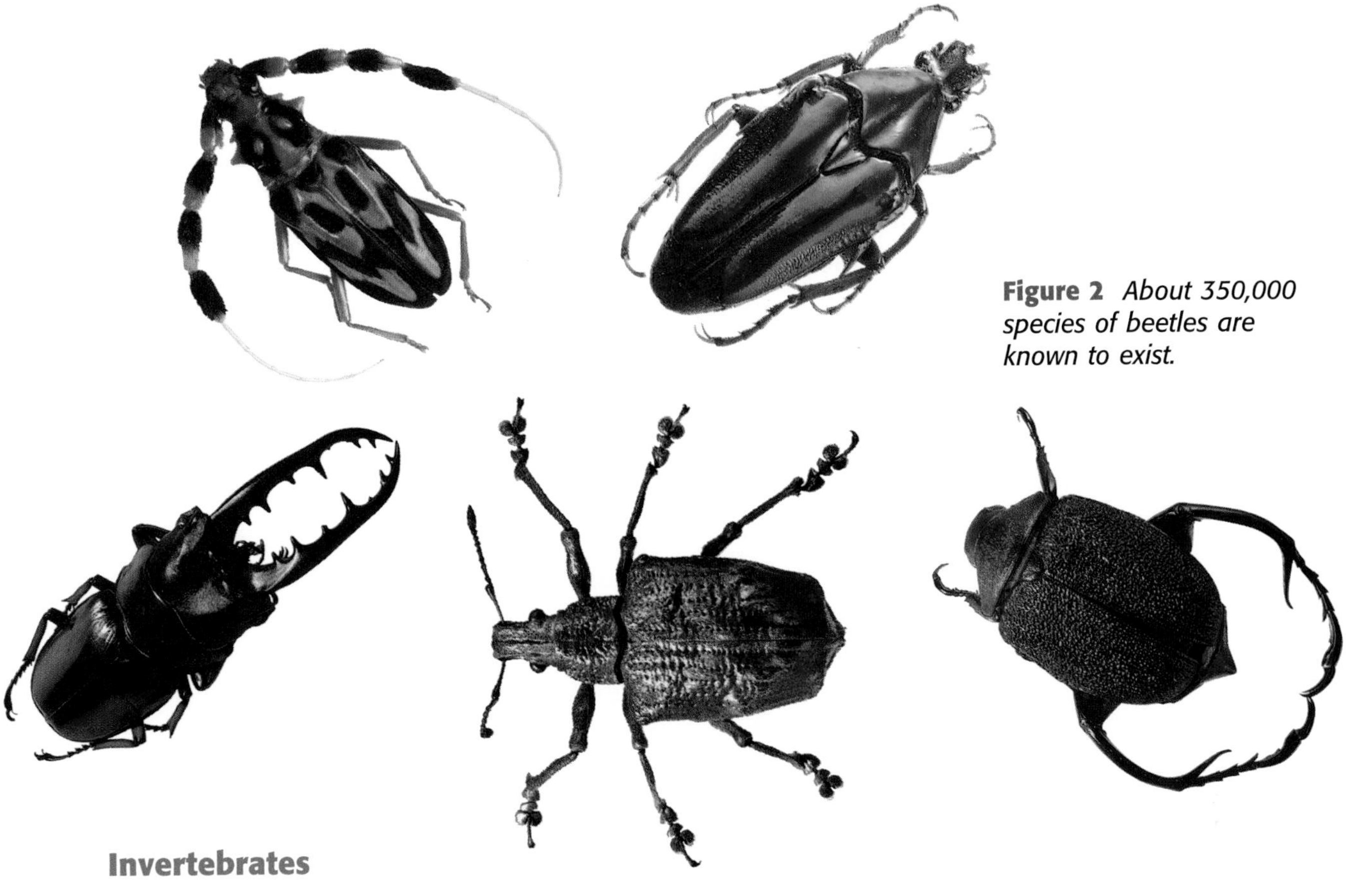

Figure 2 *About 350,000 species of beetles are known to exist.*

Invertebrates

You are probably more familiar with vertebrates than invertebrates, but vertebrates are definitely the minority among living things. Less than 5% of known animal species are vertebrates. Most animal species are insects, snails, jellyfish, worms, and other *invertebrates* (in VUHR tuh brits), or animals without backbones. In fact, beetles make up more than 30% of all animal species! **Figure 2** shows a few species of beetles.

Reading Check Are people vertebrates or invertebrates? (*See the Appendix for answers to Reading Checks.*)

Animal Characteristics

Sponges, worms, penguins, and lions are animals. But until about 200 years ago, most people thought sponges were plants. And worms don't look anything like penguins or lions. So why do we say all these things are animals? What determines whether a living thing is an animal, a plant, or something else? There is no single answer. But all animals share characteristics that set them apart from all other living things.

Multicellular Makeup

All animals are *multicellular*, which means they are made of many cells. Your own body has trillions of cells. Animal cells are *eukaryotic*, which means they have a nucleus. Unlike plant cells, animal cells do not have cell walls. Animal cells are surrounded by only cell membranes.

Explore Your Home

With your family, list all the animals that you find around your home. Do you have pets? Do any spiders spin webs outside your front door? Can you see any animals outside your window? Remember that cats, spiders, and birds are animals. When you have finished writing your list, make a poster about the animals you found.

Reproduction and Development

Almost all animals reproduce sexually. These animals make sex cells—eggs or sperm. When an egg and a sperm join during fertilization, they form the first cell of a new organism. This cell divides into many cells to form an embryo (EM bree OH). An **embryo** is an organism at an early stage of development. A mouse embryo is shown in **Figure 3.** Many stages of development follow the embryo stage as an animal grows.

A few animals can reproduce asexually. For example, hydras can reproduce by budding. In *budding,* part of an organism breaks off and develops as a new organism.

Many Specialized Parts

An animal's body has distinct parts that do different things. When a fertilized egg cell divides into many cells to form an embryo, the cells become different from each other. Some of the cells may become skin cells. Other cells may become muscle cells, nerve cells, or bone cells. These different kinds of cells form *tissues,* which are collections of similar cells. For example, muscle cells form muscle tissue, and nerve cells form nerve tissue.

Most animals also have organs. An *organ* is a group of tissues that carry out a special function of the body. Your heart, lungs, and kidneys are all organs. Each organ in an animal's body has a unique job. The shark shown in **Figure 4** has organs that allow the shark to digest food, pump blood, and sense the environment.

✓ Reading Check Name three organs that are inside your body.

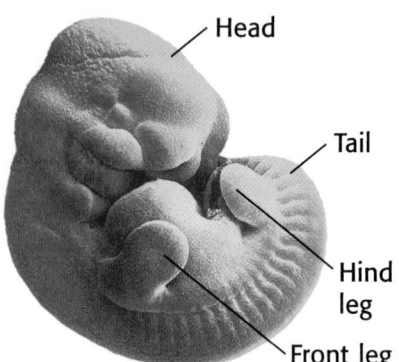

Figure 3 *Embryos are very small. When mouse embryos like this one are 10 days old, they are about 4.5 mm long.*

Head

Tail

Hind leg

Front leg

embryo a plant or animal at an early stage of development

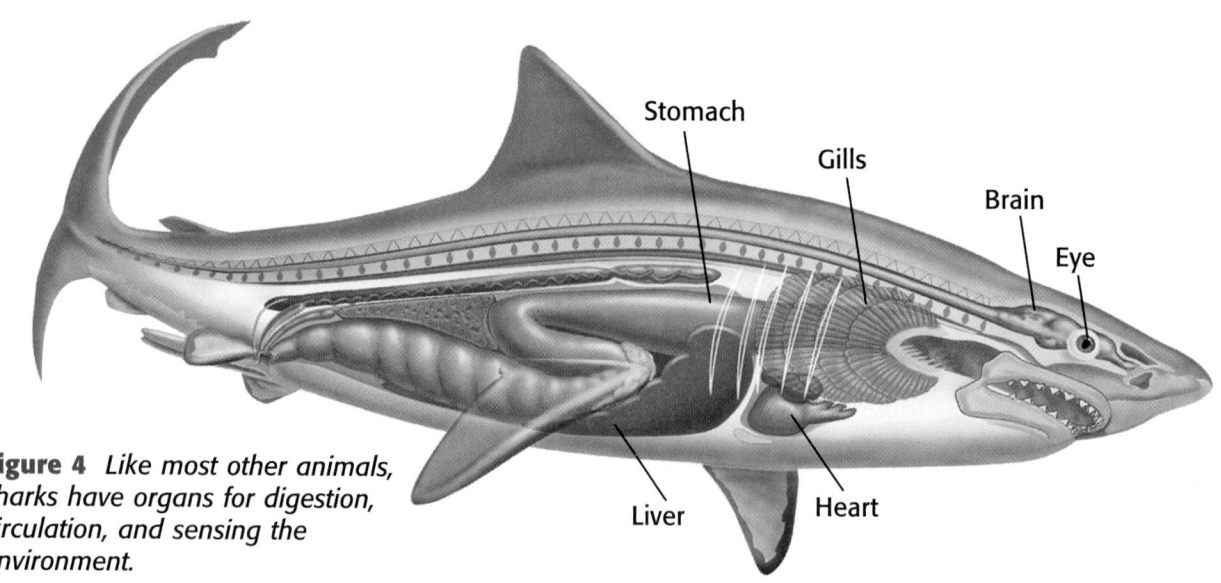

Figure 4 *Like most other animals, sharks have organs for digestion, circulation, and sensing the environment.*

Stomach

Gills

Brain

Eye

Liver

Heart

Movement

Most animals can move from place to place. They may fly, run, swim, or jump. Nearly all animals use movement to search for food, shelter, or mates at some stage of life. However, some animals are less active at certain stages of life than at other stages. For example, young sea anemones swim through the ocean to find their food. But adult sea anemones attach to rocks or the ocean floor and wait for food to arrive.

Consuming

Animals cannot make their own food. All animals survive by eating other organisms or parts and products of other organisms. In other words, animals are consumers. A **consumer** is an organism that eats other organisms. This trait sets animals apart from plants. Though there are a few exceptions, most plants do not eat other organisms. Plants make their own food.

Animals eat a great variety of foods. As shown in **Figure 5,** pandas eat bamboo. Spiders eat other animals. Mosquitoes drink blood. Butterflies drink nectar from flowers. All animals need to eat to survive.

Figure 5 *Pandas eat about 30 pounds of bamboo every day.*

consumer an organism that eats other organisms or organic matter

SECTION Review

Summary

- Scientists have named over 1 million animal species. Humans are vertebrates, but most animals are invertebrates.

- Animals are multicellular, reproduce sexually (usually), have many specialized parts, are able to move, and consume other organisms. Only animals have all of these characteristics.

Using Key Terms

1. In your own words, write a definition for each of the following terms: *embryo* and *consumer*.

Understanding Key Ideas

2. Which of the following must be true if a sponge is an animal?
   a. Sponges eat other organisms.
   b. Sponges make their own food.
   c. Sponges move all of the time.
   d. Sponges have a backbone.

3. What five characteristics distinguish animals from other organisms?

4. How are vertebrates different from invertebrates?

Math Skills

5. If a fish can swim short distances at 48 km/h, how long would the fish take to reach a smaller fish that is 3 m away?

Critical Thinking

6. **Applying Concepts** Choose an animal that interests you. Explain how you know that this organism is an animal.

7. **Identifying Relationships** Suppose that a certain fish tank contains the following: water, chemicals, fish, snails, algae, plants, and gravel. Which of these items are alive? Which are animals? Why aren't some of the living organisms classified as animals?

SCiLINKS

NSTA
Developed and maintained by the National Science Teachers Association

For a variety of links related to this chapter, go to www.scilinks.org

Topic: Vertebrates and Invertebrates
SciLinks code: HSM1603

Animal Behavior

Suppose that you look out a window and see a bird flying away from a tree. Could the bird be leaving a nest in search of food? Or could the bird be escaping from danger?

Though the bird's purpose may not be clear, the bird is flying away for a specific reason. Animals run from enemies, search for food, battle for territory, and build homes. All of these activities are known as *behavior*.

Kinds of Behavior

How do animals know when a situation is dangerous? How do they know where to find food? Sometimes animals instinctively know how to behave, but sometimes they learn how.

Innate Behavior

Behavior that doesn't depend on learning or experience is known as **innate behavior.** Innate behaviors are inherited through genes. Puppies inherit the tendency to chew, and bees inherit the tendency to fly. The male bird in **Figure 1** inherited the tendency to collect colorful objects for its nest. Some innate behaviors are present at birth. Newborn whales have the innate ability to swim. Other innate behaviors develop months or years after birth. For example, walking is innate for humans. But we do not walk until we are about one year old.

Learned Behavior

Innate behaviors can be modified. Animals can use learning to change a behavior. **Learned behavior** is behavior that has been learned from experience or from observing other animals. Humans inherit the tendency to speak. But the language we use is not inherited. We might learn English, Spanish, or sign language. Humans are not the only animals that change behaviors through learning. All animals can learn.

Figure 1 *The male bowerbird collected colorful objects for its nest to attract the female bowerbird to be his mate.*

Figure 2 *Chimpanzees make and use tools to get ants and other food out of hard-to-reach places.*

Survival Behavior

Animals depend on their behaviors to survive. To stay alive, an animal has to do many things. It must avoid being eaten, and it must find food, water, and a place to live.

Finding Food

Animals find food in many ways. Bees fly from flower to flower collecting nectar. Koala bears climb trees to get eucalyptus leaves. Some animals, such as the chimpanzee shown in **Figure 2,** use tools to get food. Many animals hunt for their food. For example, owls hunt mice.

Animals that eat other animals are known as *predators*. The animal being eaten is the *prey*. Animals that are predators can also be the prey for another animal. For example, a frog eats insects. So the frog is a predator. But a frog may be eaten by a snake. In this case, the frog is the prey.

✓ Reading Check What is the relationship between a predator and its prey? (*See the Appendix for answers to Reading Checks.*)

Marking Territory

Sometimes, members of the same species must compete for food and mates. Some animals claim territories to save energy by avoiding this competition. A **territory** is an area that is occupied by one animal or by a group of animals that do not allow other members of the species to enter. Some birds mark a territory by singing. The song lets other birds know not to enter the area. If other birds do enter the area, the first bird may chase them away. Animals use their territories for mating, raising young, and finding food.

innate behavior an inherited behavior that does not depend on the environment or experience

learned behavior a behavior that has been learned from experience

territory an area that is occupied by one animal or a group of animals that do not allow other members of the species to enter

For another activity related to this chapter, go to **go.hrw.com** and type in the keyword **HL5ANMW**.

Defensive Action

Defensive behavior allows animals to protect resources, including territories, from other animals. Animals defend food, mates, and offspring. Have you ever heard a pet dog growl when a person approached while it was eating? Many male animals, such as lions, fight violently to defend mates. Some birds use distraction to defend their young. When a predator is near, a mother killdeer may pretend to have a broken wing and move away from her young. This action distracts the predator's attention from the young so they will remain safe.

Defensive behavior also helps animals protect themselves from predators. One way animals avoid predators is to make themselves hard to see. For example, a rabbit often "freezes" so that its color blends into a background of shrubs or grass. But once a predator is aware of its prey, the prey needs another way to defend itself. Rabbits try to outrun predators. Bees, ants, and wasps inject a powerful acid into their attackers. As seen in **Figure 3,** skunks spray irritating chemicals at predators. Has an animal ever defended itself against you?

✓ **Reading Check** What are two ways a rabbit can defend itself?

Courtship

Animals need to find mates to reproduce. Reproduction is essential for the survival of an individual's genes. Animals have special behaviors that help them find a mate. These behaviors are referred to as *courtship*. Some birds and fish build nests to attract a mate. Other animals use special movements and sounds to attract a mate. **Figure 4** shows two cranes performing a courtship display.

Figure 3 *Skunks spray irritating chemicals at attackers to protect themselves.*

Figure 4 *These Japanese ground cranes use an elaborate courtship dance to tell each other when they are ready to mate.*

Figure 5 *Adult killer whales teach their young how to hunt in the first years of life.*

Parenting

Some animals, such as caterpillars, begin life with the ability to take care of themselves. But many young animals depend on their parents for survival. Some adult birds bring food to their young because they cannot feed themselves at hatching. Other animals, such as the killer whales in **Figure 5,** spend years teaching their young how to hunt for food.

Seasonal Behavior

Humans bundle up when it is cold outside. Many other animals have to deal with bitter cold during the winter, too. They may even face winter food shortages. Frogs hide from the cold by burrowing in mud. Squirrels store food to prepare for winter. Seasonal behaviors help animals adjust to the environment.

Migration

Many animals avoid cold weather by traveling to warmer places. These animals migrate to find food, water, or safe nesting grounds. To *migrate* is to travel from one place to another. Whales, salmon, bats, and even chimpanzees migrate. Each winter, the monarch butterflies shown in **Figure 6** migrate to central Mexico from all over North America. And each fall, birds in the Northern Hemisphere fly south thousands of kilometers. In the spring, they return north to nest.

If you were planning a trip, you would probably use a map. But how do animals know which way to go? For short trips, many animals use landmarks to find their way. *Landmarks* are fixed objects that an animal uses to find its way. Birds use landmarks such as mountain ranges, rivers, and coastlines to find their way.

Migration Mapping

1. Pair up with a classmate to draw a map of your school. Include at least five landmarks.

2. Use a **compass** to label North, South, East, and West on your map.

3. Draw the path you would travel if you were migrating from north to south.

4. Use the landmarks and compass directions to describe the path of your migration.

Figure 6 *When monarch butterflies gather in Mexico for the winter, there can be as many as 4 million butterflies per acre!*

11

Figure 7 *Bears slow down for the winter, but they do not enter deep hibernation.*

hibernation a period of inactivity and lowered body temperature that some animals undergo in winter as a protection against cold weather and lack of food

estivation a period of inactivity and lowered body temperature that some animals undergo in summer as a protection against hot weather and lack of food

circadian rhythm a biological daily cycle

CONNECTION TO Environmental Science

Do Not Disturb Many bats avoid food shortages during winter by hibernating in caves. Visiting a cave of hibernating bats may sound like fun, but people can endanger the bats by visiting their caves. The bats sleep with a lowered heart rate that allows them to save their energy until food is available. When people visit the caves, the bats may wake up. Waking up requires a lot of energy and makes it harder for the bats to survive until spring to find more food. If the bats lose too much energy, they can die. Make a poster that explains how people can help bats survive winters by avoiding their caves.

ACTIVITY

Slowing Down

Some animals deal with food and water shortages by hibernating. **Hibernation** is a period of inactivity and decreased body temperature that some animals experience in winter. Hibernating animals survive on stored body fat. Many animals hibernate, including mice, squirrels, and skunks. While an animal hibernates, its temperature, heart rate, and breathing rate drop. Some hibernating animals drop their body temperature to a few degrees above freezing and do not wake for weeks at a time. Other animals, such as the bear in **Figure 7,** slow down but do not enter deep hibernation. The bear's body temperature does not drop to just above freezing. Also, bears sleep for shorter periods of time than hibernating animals sleep.

Winter is not the only time that resources can be hard to find. Many desert squirrels and mice experience a similar internal slowdown in the hottest part of the summer, when they run low on water and food. This period of reduced activity in the summer is called **estivation.**

✓ Reading Check Name three animals that hibernate.

A Biological Clock

Animals need to keep track of time so that they know when to store food and when to migrate. The internal control of an animal's natural cycles is called a *biological clock*. Animals may use clues such as the length of the day and the temperature to set their clocks.

Some biological clocks keep track of daily cycles. These daily cycles are called **circadian rhythms.** Most animals wake up and get sleepy at about the same time each day and night. This is an example of a circadian rhythm.

Cycles of Change

Some biological clocks control long cycles. Seasonal cycles are nearly universal among animals. Many animals hibernate at certain times of the year and reproduce at other times. Reproducing during a particular season takes advantage of environmental conditions that help the young survive. Migration patterns are also controlled by seasonal cycles.

Biological clocks also control cycles of internal changes. For example, treehoppers, such as the one in **Figure 8,** go through several stages in life. They begin as an egg, then hatch as a nymph, and then develop into an adult. Finally, the adult emerges from the skin of its nymph form.

Figure 8 *The treehopper's biological clock signals the animal to shed the skin of its nymph form.*

SECTION
Review

Summary

● Behavior may be classified as innate or learned. The potential for innate behavior is inherited. Learned behavior depends on experience.

● Behaviors that help animals survive include finding food, marking a territory, defensive action, courtship, and parenting.

● Animals have internal biological clocks that control daily, seasonal, and internal natural cycles.

Using Key Terms

1. Use each of the following terms in a separate sentence: *territory, innate behavior,* and *circadian rhythm.*

2. In your own words, write a definition for each of the following terms: *hibernation* and *estivation.*

Understanding Key Ideas

3. An animal that lives in a hot, dry environment might spend the summer
   a. hibernating.
   b. estivating.
   c. migrating to a warmer climate.
   d. None of the above

4. Biological clocks control
   a. seasonal cycles.
   b. circadian rhythms.
   c. internal cycles.
   d. All of the above

5. How do innate behaviors and learned behaviors differ?

6. Do bears hibernate? Explain your answer.

7. Name five behaviors that help animals survive.

Math Skills

8. Suppose that an animal's circadian rhythms tell it to eat a meal every 4 h. How many meals will the animal eat each day?

Critical Thinking

9. **Applying Concepts** People who travel to different time zones often suffer from *jet lag.* Jet lag makes people have trouble waking up and going to sleep at appropriate times. Why do you think people experience jet lag? Explain.

10. **Making Inferences** Many children are born with the tendency to make babbling sounds. But few adults make these sounds. How could you explain this change in an innate behavior?

For a variety of links related to this chapter, go to www.scilinks.org
Topic: Animal Behavior; Rhythms of Life
SciLinks code: HSM0069; HSM1311

Developed and maintained by the National Science Teachers Association

Social Relationships

Have you ever noticed a pair of squirrels chattering and chasing each other through the branches of a tree? Though it may not be clear why they behave this way, it is clear that they are interacting.

Animals often interact with each other—in groups and one on one. They may work together, or they may compete. All of this behavior is called social behavior. **Social behavior** is the interaction among animals of the same species. Animals depend on communication for their social interactions.

Communication

Imagine what life would be like if people could not talk or read. There would be no telephones, no books, and no Internet. The world would certainly be different! Language is an important way for humans to communicate. In **communication,** a signal must travel from one animal to another, and the receiver of the signal must respond in some way. Animals do not use a language with complex words and grammar, but they communicate in many ways.

Communication helps animals survive. Many animals, such as the wolves in **Figure 1,** communicate to defend a territory from other members of the species. Animals also communicate to find food, to warn others of danger, to identify family members, to frighten predators, and to find mates.

✓ *Reading Check* **What are six reasons that animals communicate with each other?** (*See the Appendix for answers to Reading Checks.*)

social behavior the interaction between animals of the same species

communication a transfer of a signal or message from one animal to another that results in some type of response

Figure 1 *These wolves are howling to discourage neighboring wolves from invading their territory.*

Ways to Communicate

Animals communicate by signaling information to other animals through sound, touch, chemicals, and sight. Each of these methods can be used to convey specific information.

Sound

Many animals communicate by making noises. Wolves howl. Dolphins use whistles and complex clicking noises to communicate with other dolphins. Male birds may sing songs in the spring to claim their territory or to attract a mate.

Sound is a signal that can reach many animals over a large area. As described in **Figure 2,** elephants use low frequency rumbles to communicate with other elephants that are kilometers away. Humpback whales sing songs that can be heard for many kilometers. Both species use these sounds to convey information about their locations.

Figure 2 *Elephants communicate with low-pitched sounds that humans cannot hear. When an elephant is communicating this way, the skin on its forehead flutters.*

Touch

Animals may also use touch to communicate. For example, chimpanzees often groom each other. Grooming involves animals resting together while picking bits of skin from each other's fur. This activity is an important way for primates to communicate. Chimpanzees use grooming to calm and comfort one another. Through touch, they may communicate friendship or support.

pheromone a substance that is released by the body and that causes another individual of the same species to react in a predictable way

Chemicals

One way to communicate is through chemicals. The chemicals that animals use to communicate are called **pheromones** (FER uh MOHNZ). Ants and other insects secrete a variety of pheromones. For example, alarm chemicals can warn other ants of danger. Recognition chemicals announce which colony an ant is from to both friends and enemies.

Many animals use pheromones to find a mate. Amazingly, elephants and insects use some of the same pheromones to attract mates. Fire ants, such as the ones in **Figure 3,** use pheromones to control which colony members can reproduce.

Figure 3 *This fire ant queen can make pheromones that other ants in the colony cannot make.*

Figure 4 The Dance of the Bees

a A honeybee leader does a "waggle dance" to tell other bees where it has found food. Other worker bees—followers—gather closely around the dancing bee to learn the details about the food source.

Followers can tell what kind of food was found by smelling the pollen on the leader's body. Or the leader may spit out some nectar for the followers to smell.

b The leader dances a figure eight, beating its wings rapidly and waggling its abdomen. The wings make sounds that communicate information about the food's distance from the hive.

As the bee goes through the center, it waggles its abdomen. The number of waggles tells the other bees how far away the nectar is.

The direction of the center line of the figure eight tells the other bees the direction from the hive to the nectar.

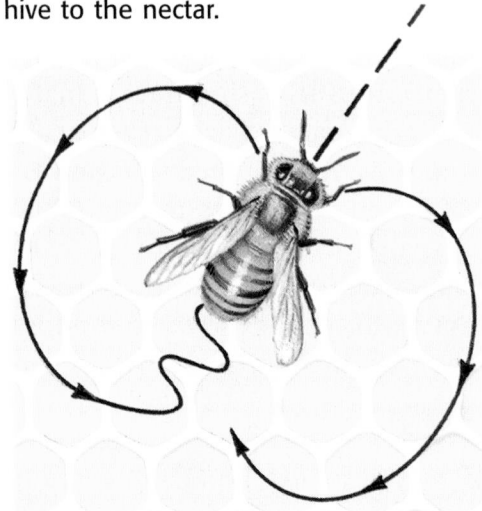

Sight

Animals also use visual communication. When we smile at a friend, we are sending a visual message with *body language*. As shown in **Figure 4**, bees use body language, along with other forms of communication, to spread news about food.

Body language can communicate many ideas. An animal that wants to scare another animal may ruffle its feathers to look bigger, or it may show its teeth as a threat. Visual displays are also used in courtship. For example, fireflies blink signals to attract each other. Animals also use body language when playing. The dog in **Figure 5** is play bowing to show that it wants to play.

✔ *Reading Check* How do honeybees use body language?

Living Together

Tigers live alone. Except for the time a mother tiger spends with her cubs, a tiger meets other tigers rarely. Yet the tiger's closest relative, the lion, is rarely alone. Lions live in groups called *prides*. The members of a pride sleep together, hunt together, and raise their cubs together. Why do some animals live in groups, while others live apart?

Figure 5 *When dogs want to play, they drop down on their forelegs.*

The Benefits of Living in Groups

Living in groups can be safer than living alone. Large groups can spot a predator quickly because they have so many pairs of eyes watching for danger. As shown in **Figure 6,** one animal can warn many others of danger. Also, groups can work together to defend themselves. For example, threatened musk oxen will circle their young with their horns pointed outward.

Living together can also help animals find food. Animals that hunt alone can usually kill only animals that are smaller than themselves. In contrast, predators such as lions and wolves, which hunt in groups, can kill larger prey.

The Downside of Living in Groups

Living in groups causes problems as well. Animals living in large groups must compete with each other for food and mates. An area that has enough food for one animal may not have enough food for a group of animals. In these cases, groups must move around in search of food. Also, animals in groups attract predators, so they must always be on the lookout. Living as a group can also help diseases spread.

Figure 6 *A ground squirrel whistles a loud alarm to alert other ground squirrels that danger is near.*

SECTION Review

Summary

- Animals communicate with each other. Communication must include both a signal and a response.
- Animals communicate through chemicals, touch, sound, and sight.
- Animals that live in groups can spot both prey and predators more easily. But living in a group increases competition for food and mates and attracts the attention of predators.

Using Key Terms

1. Use each of the following terms in a separate sentence: *social behavior* and *communication.*

2. In your own words, write a definition for the following term: *pheromone.*

Understanding Key Ideas

3. Which of the following is NOT an example of social behavior?
   a. a wolf howling at distant wolves to protect its territory
   b. a rabbit hiding from a predator
   c. a ground squirrel calling to signal danger to other squirrels
   d. a group of lions working together to hunt prey

4. Describe four ways that animals communicate with each other. Give an example of each type of communication.

5. Compare the costs and benefits of living in a group of animals.

Math Skills

6. How fast could a bee that flies 6 km/h reach a flower that is 1.2 km from the hive?

Critical Thinking

7. **Applying Concepts** Why do you think humans live together?

8. **Identifying Relationships** Language is not the only way that humans communicate. Describe how we use sound, touch, chemicals, and sight to communicate.

SCiLINKS®

NSTA
Developed and maintained by the National Science Teachers Association

For a variety of links related to this chapter, go to www.scilinks.org

Topic: Communication in the Animal Kingdom

SciLinks code: HSM0320

Plan a way to test bumblebee behavior.

Conduct your own experiment on bumblebees.

Describe materials that attract bumblebees.

• items to be determined by the students and approved by the teacher

Aunt Flossie and the Bumblebee

Last week Aunt Flossie came to watch the soccer game, and she was chased by a big, yellow-and-black bumblebee. Everyone tried not to laugh, but Aunt Flossie did look pretty funny. She was running and screaming, and she was wearing perfume and dressed in a bright floral dress, shiny jewelry, and a huge hat with a big purple bow. No one could understand why the bumblebee bugged Aunt Flossie and left everyone else alone. She told you that she would not come to another game until you figure out why the bee chased her.

Your job is to design and carry out an experiment that will determine why the bee was attracted to Aunt Flossie. You may simulate the situation by using objects that contain the same sensory clues that Aunt Flossie wore that day—bright, shiny colors and strong scents.

Ask a Question

1 Use the information in the story above to ask a question that would lead you to a hypothesis about the bee's behavior. For example, your question may be one of the following: What was Aunt Flossie wearing? What did she look like to a bumblebee? What scent was she wearing? Which characteristics may have affected the bee's behavior? What characteristic of Aunt Flossie affected the bee's behavior?

Form a Hypothesis

2 Form a testable hypothesis about insect behavior based on your observations of Aunt Flossie and the bumblebee at the soccer game. One possible hypothesis is the following: Insects are attracted to strong floral scents. Write out your own hypothesis.

Test the Hypothesis

3 Plan a procedure for your experiment. Be sure to follow the steps of the scientific methods. Design your procedure to answer specific questions. For example, if you want to know if insects are attracted to different colors, you might want to hang up pieces of paper of different colors.

4 Make a list of materials for your experiment. You may want to include colored paper, pictures from magazines, or strong perfumes as bait. You may not use living things as bait in your experiment. Your teacher must approve your experimental design before you begin.

5 Decide what safety procedures are necessary for your experiment. Add them to your written procedure.

6 Find a place to conduct your experiment. For example, you may want to place your materials in a box on the ground, or you may want to hang items from a tree branch.

7 Using graph paper or a computer, construct tables to organize your data. Be sure that your data tables fit your investigation.

8 Have your teacher approve your plans. Carry out your procedure using the materials and safety procedures that you selected. **Caution:** Be sure to remain at a safe distance from your experimental setup. Do not touch any insects. Have an adult help you release any insects that are trapped or collected.

9 When you are finished, clean and store your equipment. Recycle or dispose of all materials properly.

Analyze the Results

1 **Describing Events** Describe your experimental procedure. How did bumblebees and other insects behave in your experiment?

2 **Analyzing Results** Did your results support your original hypothesis? Explain.

Draw Conclusions

3 **Evaluating Results** Compare your results with those of your classmates. Which hypotheses were supported? What conclusions can you draw from the class results?

4 **Applying Conclusions** Write a letter to Aunt Flossie telling her what you have learned. Tell her what you think caused the bee attack. Invite her to attend another soccer game, and tell her what you think she should or should not wear!

Chapter Review

USING KEY TERMS

1 In your own words, write a definition for each of the following terms: *embryo, consumer,* and *pheromone.*

2 Use the following terms in the same sentence: *estivation, hibernation,* and *circadian rhythm.*

For each pair of terms, explain how the meanings of the terms differ.

3 *social behavior* and *communication*

4 *learned behavior* and *innate behavior*

UNDERSTANDING KEY IDEAS

Multiple Choice

5 Which of the following is a characteristic of all animals?

   a. asexual reproduction
   b. producing their own food
   c. having many specialized parts
   d. being unable to move

6 An innate behavior

   a. cannot change.
   b. must be learned from parents.
   c. is always present from birth.
   d. does not depend on learning or experience.

7 Migration

   a. occurs only in birds.
   b. helps animals escape cold and food shortages in winter.
   c. always refers to moving southward for the winter.
   d. is a way to defend against predators.

8 A biological clock controls

   a. circadian rhythms.
   b. defensive behavior.
   c. learned behavior.
   d. being a consumer.

9 For animals, living as part of a group

   a. is always safer than living alone.
   b. can attract attention from predators.
   c. keeps them from killing large prey.
   d. decreases competition for mates and food.

Short Answer

10 What is a territory? Give an example of a territory from your environment.

11 What landmarks help you find your way home from school?

12 What are five behaviors that animals may use to survive?

13 What do migration and hibernation have in common?

14 Describe the differences between vertebrates and invertebrates.

15 Describe four ways that an animal could communicate a message to other animals about where to find food.

CRITICAL THINKING

16 Concept Mapping Use the following terms to create a concept map: *animals, survival behavior, finding food, migration, defensive action, seasonal behavior, marking a territory, estivation, parenting, hibernation,* and *courtship.*

17 Analyzing Processes If you see a skunk raise its tail toward you while you are hiking and you turn around to take a different path, has the skunk communicated with you? Explain your answer.

18 Making Inferences Ants depend on pheromones and touch for communication, but birds depend more on sight and sound. Why might these two types of animals have different forms of communication?

19 Making Comparisons Dogs use visual communication in many situations. They may arch their back and raise their fur to look threatening. When they want to play, they may bow down on their front legs. How are these two visual signals different from each other? How do the different visual signals relate to the different information they are meant to communicate?

20 Analyzing Ideas People have internal biological clocks. However, people are used to keeping track of time by using clocks and calendars. Why do you think people use these tools if they have internal clocks?

21 Applying Concepts Imagine that you are taking care of a friend's cat for a few days but that the friend forgot to tell you where to find the cat food. When you arrive at the friend's house, the cat meows and runs to the door that leads to the garage. Where would you look for the cat food? What kind of communication led you to this conclusion?

INTERPRETING GRAPHICS

The diagram below shows some internal organs of a fish. Use the diagram below to answer the questions that follow.

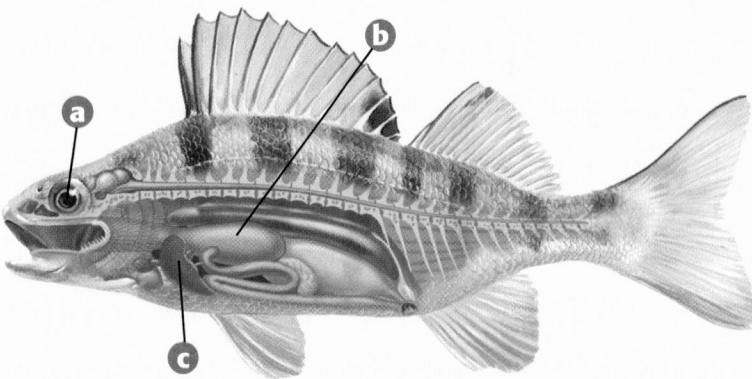

22 What characteristics suggest that this organism is an animal?

23 Which labels point to the animal's organs? Name any organs that you can recognize.

24 Do any labels point to the animal's tissues? Explain.

25 Is this animal a vertebrate or an invertebrate? Explain.

READING

Read each of the passages below. Then, answer the questions that follow each passage.

Passage 1 Competing, surviving, and reproducing are all part of life. And in some species, cannibalism (eating members of one's own species) is part of life. But how does cannibalism relate to competing, surviving, and reproducing? It turns out that sometimes competition for survival can lead to cannibalism. Young tiger salamanders eat zooplankton, aquatic insect larvae, and sometimes tadpoles. But if conditions in their small pond include <u>intense</u> competition with members of their own species, certain larger salamanders may begin to eat other salamanders!

1. In the passage, what does the term *intense* mean?

  A weak

  B strong

  C some

  D furious

2. Based on the passage, which of the following statements is a fact?

  F Large tiger salamanders sometimes eat other tiger salamanders.

  G Animals often use cannibalism to help themselves survive.

  H Female spiders sometimes eat male spiders.

  I Tadpoles do not practice cannibalism.

3. What do young salamanders eat?

  A other small salamanders

  B large salamanders

  C frogs and small fish

  D zooplankton, aquatic insect larvae, and tadpoles

Passage 2 Unlike many birds, most bat species in the northern and central parts of the United States don't fly south for the winter. Instead of migrating, many bat species go into hibernation. Hibernation is usually a safe way to pass the cold winter. However, if their deep sleep is disturbed too often, the bats may die. People visiting bat caves sometimes force hibernating bats to wake up. When the bats wake up, they use up their stored fat too quickly. For example, each time a little brown bat wakes up, it consumes stored fat that would have lasted for 67 days of deep sleep. And because few insects live in the caves during the winter, the bats cannot build up fat <u>reserves</u> during the winter.

1. According to the passage, what is one reason that it is harmful for people to visit bat caves in the winter?

  A Bats migrate south for the winter.

  B People wake up the bats, which forces the bats to use much of their stored fat.

  C People spread diseases to hibernating bats.

  D People may scare insects away from the bat caves and leave the bats with no food.

2. In the passage, what does the term *reserve* mean?

  F needs

  G days

  H supply

  I weight

3. Why do many bats from the northern and central parts of the United States hibernate?

  A to survive the winter

  B to store fat

  C to compete with birds

  D to be near people that visit their caves

The graphs below show the average high and low temperatures for 1 year at two locations. Use the graphs to answer the questions that follow.

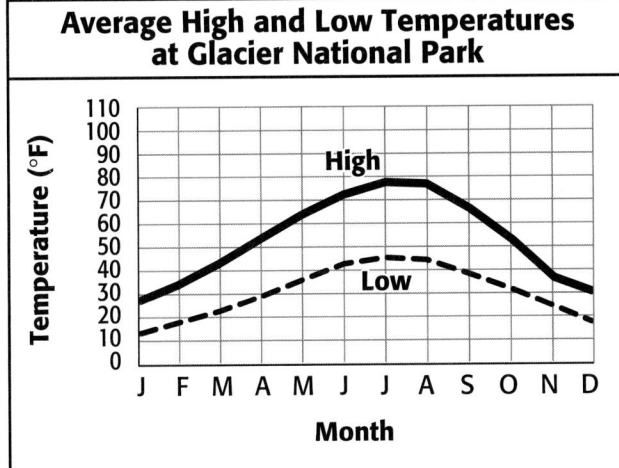

Average High and Low Temperatures at Glacier National Park

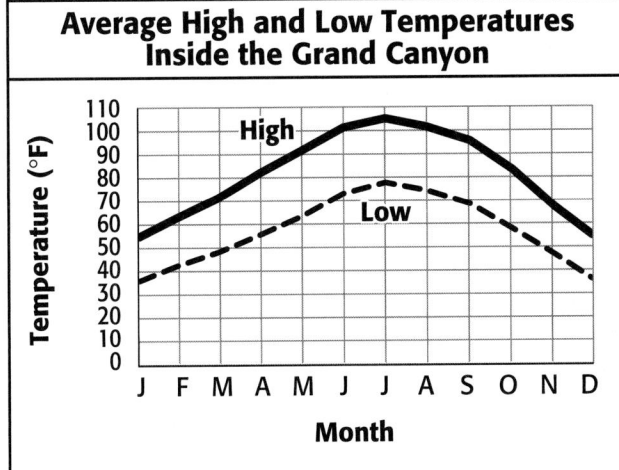

Average High and Low Temperatures Inside the Grand Canyon

1. What is the average high temperature for each location in July?

   A Glacier Park: 79°F; Grand Canyon: 106°F

   B Glacier Park: 47°F; Grand Canyon: 78°F

   C Glacier Park: 63°F; Grand Canyon: 92°F

   D Glacier Park: 70°F; Grand Canyon: 100°F

2. What is the average low temperature for each location in January?

   F Glacier Park: 15°F; Grand Canyon: 56°F

   G Glacier Park: 30°F; Grand Canyon: 36°F

   H Glacier Park: 15°F; Grand Canyon: 36°F

   I Glacier Park: 22°F; Grand Canyon: 46°F

3. In which location would animals be more likely to estivate? to hibernate?

   A Glacier Park; Grand Canyon

   B Glacier Park; Glacier Park

   C Grand Canyon; Grand Canyon

   D Grand Canyon; Glacier Park

4. During which three months would animals be most likely to estivate?

   F May, June, and July

   G June, July, and August

   H December, January, and February

   I January, February, and March

Read each question below, and choose the best answer.

1. Manuel wants to build a fence so that he can let his pet dog out in the backyard without worrying about it wandering away from home. If he builds the fence to be 3 m long and 4.5 m wide, what will the size of the fenced area be?

   A 7.5 m

   B 7.5 m²

   C 13.5 m²

   D 135 m²

2. A bird gathers insects for its three baby birds each day. If each baby eats three bugs per day, how do you express the number of bugs that the mother bird gathers for her babies over a period of 3 weeks in exponential notation?

   F $3^3 \times 7^3$

   G $3^3 + 7^1$

   H $3^3 \times 7^1$

   I $3^1 \times 7^3$

3. In which of the following lists are the numbers in order from smallest to largest?

   A 0.027, 0.072, 0.270, 0.720

   B 0.027, 0.072, 0.720, 0.270

   C 0.072, 0.027, 0.270, 0.720

   D 0.720, 0.270, 0.072, 0.027

Science in Action

Science, Technology, and Society

Kanzi

Did you know that some chimpanzees raised in captivity can learn to understand some parts of human language? These animals cannot vocally speak any human words. But researchers working with Kanzi, a bonobo chimp who has grown up in Georgia, have used technology to help him communicate. Kanzi uses a board that has more than 400 buttons with symbols on them that represent different words. Kanzi presses a button to communicate the word represented by that button. This board of buttons allows Kanzi to communicate with people.

Weird Science

Guide Horses

You've probably heard of trained dogs guiding visually impaired people. But have you heard of guide horses? Guide horses are miniature—about 2 ft tall! They can learn to follow orders that help them guide people through streets, crowds, and escalators.

Guide horses are trained to stay calm in tough situations. Trainers take the horses to busy streets or malls so that the horses can learn to follow the trainer's lead and to focus in spite of distractions. The horses even learn to disobey orders that could be dangerous. This ability allows the horses to help people avoid dangers they can't see.

Social Studies ACTiViTY

People around the world train animals to help people. For example, some people train camels to carry people. Research ways people in different cultures train animals, and present a poster to your class.

Language Arts ACTiViTY

WRITING SKILL What would you ask Kanzi if you could speak to him? Think of a question that you would like to ask an animal. Imagine its response. Write this response in a creative essay. Write in the first person.

George Archibald

Dancing with Cranes Imagine a man flapping his arms in a dance with a whooping crane. Does this sound funny? When Dr. George Archibald danced with a crane named Tex, he wasn't joking around. To help this endangered species survive, Archibald wanted cranes to mate in captivity so that he could release cranes into the wild. But the captive cranes wouldn't do their courtship dance. Archibald's cranes had imprinted on the humans that raised them. *Imprinting* is a process in which birds learn to recognize their species by looking at their parents. The birds saw humans as their own species, and could only reproduce if a human did the courtship dance. So, Archibald decided to dance. His plan worked! After some time, Tex hatched a baby crane.

After that, Archibald found a way to help the captive cranes imprint on other cranes. He and his staff now feed baby cranes with hand puppets that look like crane heads. They play recordings of real crane sounds for the young cranes. They even wear crane suits when they are near older birds. These cranes are happy to do their courtship dance with each other instead of with Archibald.

Math ACTIVITY

Suppose you want to drive a group of cranes from Madison, Wisconsin, to Orlando, Florida. Find and measure this distance on a map. If your truck goes 500 km per gas tank and a tank costs $30, how much would gas cost on your trip?

To learn more about these Science in Action topics, visit go.hrw.com and type in the keyword HL5ANMF.

Current Science

Check out Current Science® articles related to this chapter by visiting go.hrw.com. Just type in the keyword HL5CS14.

2 Invertebrates

About the PHOTO

No, this creature isn't an alien! It's a sea slug, a relative of garden slugs and snails. This sea slug lives in the cold Pacific Ocean, near the coast of California. Its bright coloring comes from the food that the slug eats. This animal doesn't breathe with lungs. Instead, it brings oxygen into its body through the orange clubs on its back. Like all invertebrates, sea slugs don't have a backbone.

PRE-READING ACTIVITY

FOLDNOTES **Tri-Fold** Before you read the chapter, create the FoldNote entitled "Tri-Fold" described in the **Study Skills** section of the Appendix. Write what you know about invertebrates in the column labeled "Know." Then, write what you want to know in the column labeled "Want." As you read the chapter, write what you learn about invertebrates in the column labeled "Learn."

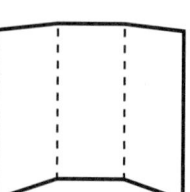

START-UP ACTIVITY

Classify It!

Animals are classified according to their different traits. In this activity, you will classify invertebrates.

Procedure

1. Look at the **pictures** that your teacher has provided. These animals do not have a backbone.

2. Which animals are the most alike? Organize them into groups according to their shared traits.

3. Decide which animals within each group are the most alike. Put these animals into smaller groups inside of their larger group.

4. Construct a table that organizes your classification groups.

Analysis

1. What features did you use to classify the animals into the larger groups? Explain why you think these features are the most important.

2. What features did you use to place the animals in smaller groups? Explain your reasoning.

3. Compare your table with those of your classmates. What similarities or differences do you find?

Simple Invertebrates

Humans and snakes have them, but octopuses and butterflies don't. What are they? Backbones!

Animals that don't have backbones are called **invertebrates** (in VUHR tuh brits). They make up about 96% of all animal species. So far, more than 1 million invertebrates have been named. Most biologists think that millions more have not been identified yet.

Invertebrate Characteristics

Invertebrates come in many different shapes and sizes. Grasshoppers, clams, earthworms, and jellyfish are examples of invertebrates. They are all very different from each other. Some invertebrates have heads, and others do not. Some invertebrates eat food through their mouths. Others absorb food particles through their tissues. But all invertebrates are similar because they do not have backbones.

Invertebrates have three basic body plans, or types of *symmetry*. Symmetry can be bilateral (bie LAT uhr uhl) or radial (RAY dee uhl). Some animals have no symmetry at all. Animals that don't have symmetry are *asymmetrical* (AY suh MEH tri kuhl). Most animals have bilateral symmetry. **Figure 1** shows examples of each kind of symmetry.

READING WARM-UP

Objectives
- Describe the body plans, nervous systems, and guts of invertebrates.
- Explain how sponges get food.
- Describe three cnidarian traits.
- Describe the three kinds of flatworms.
- Describe the body of a roundworm.

Terms to Learn

invertebrate   gut
ganglion   coelom

READING STRATEGY

Reading Organizer As you read this section, create an outline of the section. Use the headings from the section in your outline.

Figure 1 Animal Body Plans

Bilateral Symmetry

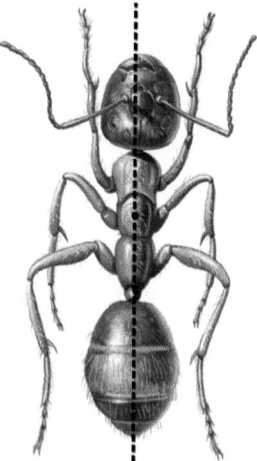

This ant has **bilateral symmetry.** The two sides of its body mirror each other. On each side of its body, the ant has one eye, one antenna, and three legs.

Radial Symmetry

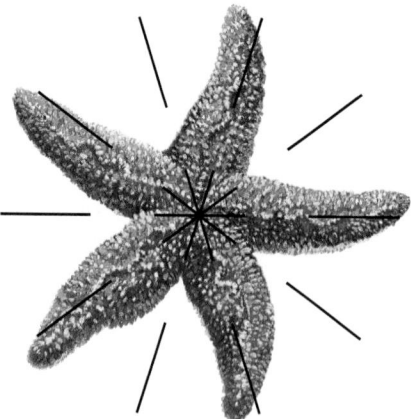

This sea star has **radial symmetry.** Its body is organized around the center, like spokes on a wheel.

Asymmetry

This sponge is **asymmetrical.** You cannot draw a straight line to divide its body into two or more equal parts. Its body is not organized around a center.

Neurons and Ganglia

All animals except sponges have special tissues that make fibers called *neurons*. Neurons allow animals to sense their environment. Neurons also carry messages around the body to control an animal's actions. Simple invertebrates have neurons arranged in networks or in nerve cords. *Nerve cords* are packs of neurons that carry messages along a single path.

In some invertebrates, many nerve cells come together as ganglia (singular, *ganglion*). A **ganglion** (GANG glee uhn) is a concentrated mass of nerve cells. Each ganglion controls different parts of the body. Ganglia are connected by nerve cords. In complex invertebrates, ganglia are controlled by a brain. The *brain* is an organ that controls nerves throughout the body.

Guts

Almost all animals digest food in a gut. A **gut** is a pouch lined with cells that release chemicals that break down food into small particles. The cells in the gut then absorb the food particles. In complex animals, the gut is inside a coelom (SEE luhm). A **coelom** is the body cavity that surrounds the gut. The coelom contains many organs, such as the heart and lungs. But these organs are separated from the gut. This arrangement keeps gut movement from disturbing other body processes. **Figure 2** shows an earthworm's coelom.

✓ **Reading Check** How is the coelom related to the gut? (*See the Appendix for answers to Reading Checks.*)

invertebrate an animal that does not have a backbone

ganglion a mass of nerve cells

gut the digestive tract

coelom a body cavity that contains the internal organs

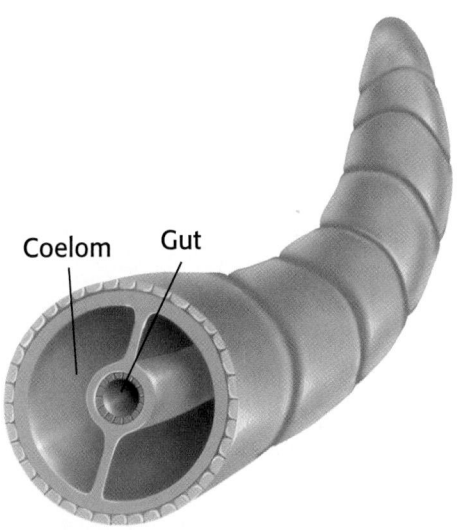

Coelom   Gut

Figure 2 *Earthworms have a fluid-filled coelom that contains the gut.*

Sponges

Sponges are the simplest invertebrates. They are asymmetrical and have no tissues, gut, or neurons. Adult sponges move only millimeters per day—if they move at all. In fact, sponges were once thought to be plants! But sponges can't make their own food. That's one reason they are classified as animals. **Figure 3** shows a sponge.

Figure 3 *Some sponges are brightly colored.*

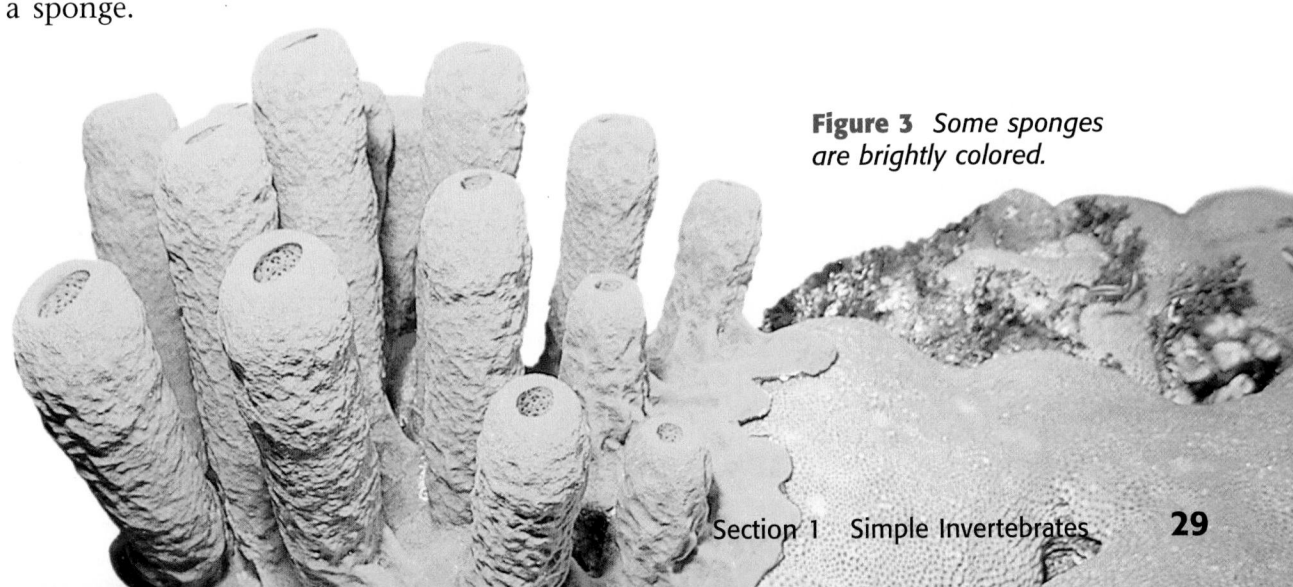

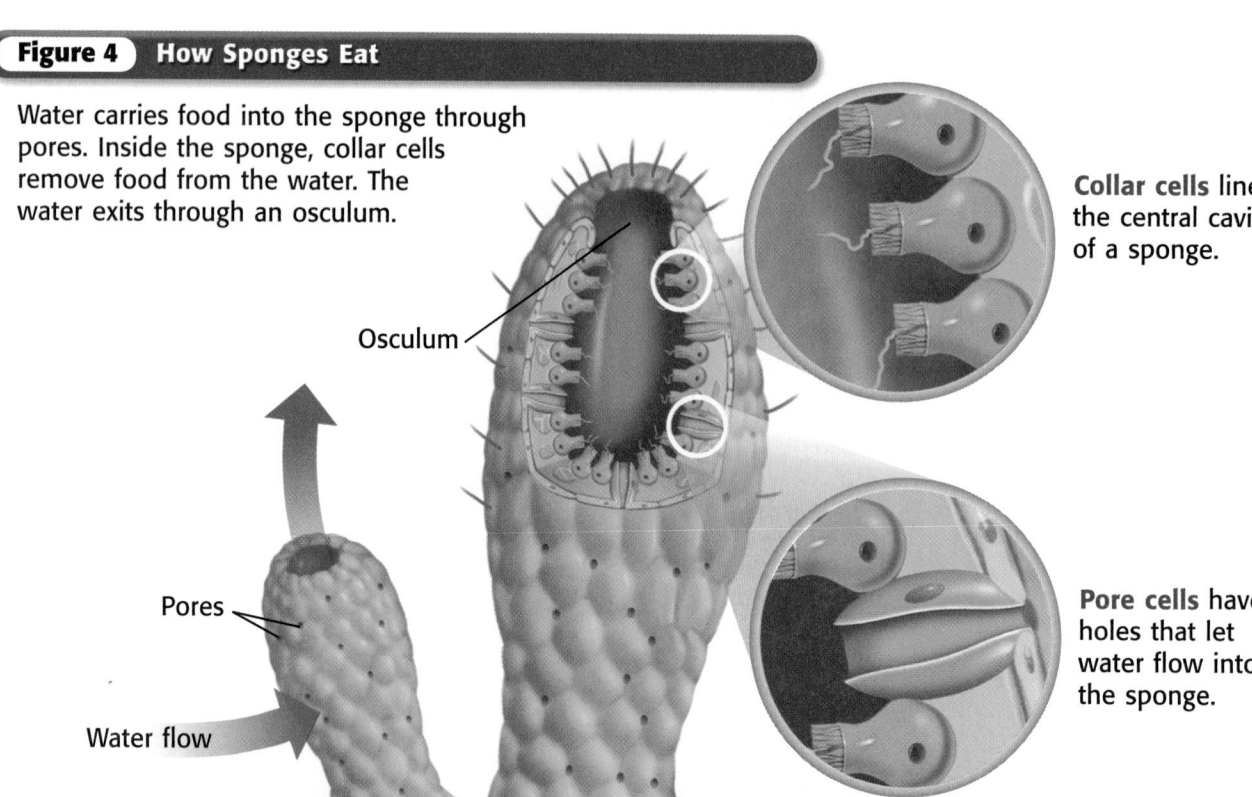

Figure 4 How Sponges Eat

Water carries food into the sponge through pores. Inside the sponge, collar cells remove food from the water. The water exits through an osculum.

Osculum

Pores

Water flow

Collar cells line the central cavity of a sponge.

Pore cells have holes that let water flow into the sponge.

Several Sponges

Suppose that a big sponge breaks into seven pieces. Each piece begins to grow into a new sponge. Then, each new sponge breaks into five smaller pieces, and each of these new pieces forms a new sponge. How many sponges would you have?

How Do Sponges Eat?

Sponges feed on tiny plants and animals. Because sponges cannot move in search of food and do not have a gut, they have a special way of getting food. A sponge sweeps water into its body through its pores. *Pores* are the holes on the outside of a sponge's body. Water flows into a cavity in the middle of the body, bringing oxygen and food. Special cells called *collar cells* line this cavity. Collar cells filter and digest food from the water that enters the body. Water leaves the body through a hole at the top of the sponge. This hole is called an *osculum* (AHS kyoo luhm). **Figure 4** shows this process.

✓ *Reading Check* How does water enter a sponge's body?

Body Part Abilities

Sponges have some unusual abilities. If you forced a sponge's body through a strainer, the separated cells could come back together and re-form into a new sponge. If part of a sponge is broken off, the missing part can *regenerate,* or grow back. And if a sponge is broken into pieces, or fragmented, new sponges may form from each fragment. Though sponges can use regeneration as a form of reproduction, they also use sexual reproduction.

Kinds of Sponges

All sponges live in water, and most live in the ocean. As shown in **Figure 5,** sponges come in many different shapes and sizes. Most sponges have a skeleton made of small, hard fibers called *spicules* (SPIK YOOLZ). Some spicules are straight, some are curved, and others have complex star shapes. A sponge's skeleton supports its body and helps protect it from predators. Sponges are divided into groups according to the kinds of skeletons they have.

Cnidarians

Do you know anyone who has been stung by a jellyfish? It is a very painful experience! Jellyfish are members of a group of invertebrates that have stinging cells. Animals in this group are called *cnidarians* (ni DER ee uhns).

Cnidarians are more complex than sponges. Cnidarians have complex tissues and a gut for digesting food. They also have a simple network of nerve cells. Most cnidarians can move more quickly than sponges can. But some cnidarians do share a special trait with sponges. If the body cells are separated, they can come back together to re-form the cnidarian.

Two Body Forms

A cnidarian body can have one of two forms—the *medusa* or the *polyp* form. These body forms are shown in **Figure 6.** Medusas swim through the water. Polyps usually attach to a surface. Some cnidarians change forms at different times in their lives. But many cnidarians are polyps for their whole lives.

Figure 5 *Sponges come in many shapes and sizes.*

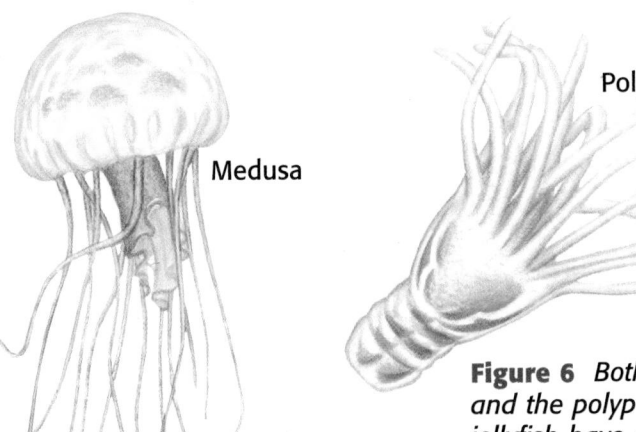

Polyp

Medusa

Figure 6 *Both the medusa and the polyp forms of a jellyfish have radial symmetry.*

CONNECTION TO Environmental Science

Threatened Reefs Coral reefs are home to many beautiful cnidarians. But living coral reefs are threatened by overfishing, pollution, mining, coral harvesting, coastal development, and damage from swimmers and boats. Scientists are looking for ways to protect coral reefs. One solution is to teach people not to touch or collect living corals. Make a poster about how people can protect coral reefs by leaving them alone.

ACTIVITY

Figure 7 *Each stinging cell contains a tiny spear.*

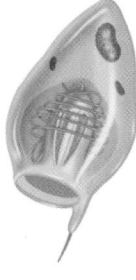

Before Firing
Coiled inside each stinging cell is a tiny, barbed spear.

After Firing
When the tiny spear is fired, the long, barbed strand ejects into the prey. Larger barbs also cover the base of the strand.

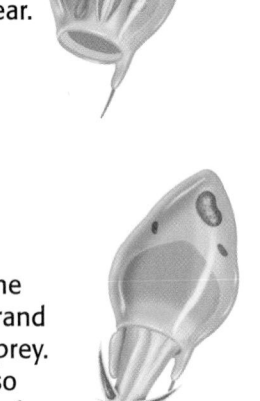

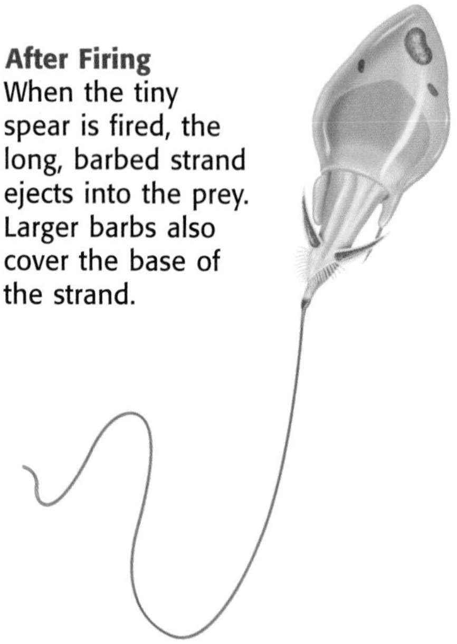

Stinging Cells

All cnidarians have tentacles covered with stinging cells. When an organism brushes against the tentacles, it activates hundreds of stinging cells. Each stinging cell uses water pressure to fire a tiny, barbed spear into the organism. **Figure 7** shows a stinging cell before and after firing. The tiny spears can release a painful—and sometimes paralyzing—poison into their targets. Cnidarians use their stinging cells to protect themselves and to catch food.

Kinds of Cnidarians

There are three major classes of cnidarians: hydrozoans (HIE dro ZOH uhn), jellyfish, and sea anemones and corals. **Figure 8** shows each kind of cnidarian. Hydrozoans are common cnidarians that live in both freshwater and marine environments. Most spend their entire lives as polyps. Jellyfish catch other invertebrates and fish in their tentacles. They spend most of their lives as medusas. Sea anemones and corals spend their lives as polyps. They are often brightly colored.

Most corals are small and live in colonies. The colonies build huge skeletons that are made of calcium carbonate. Each new generation of corals builds on top of the last generation. Over thousands of years, these tiny animals build massive underwater reefs. Coral reefs can be found in warm, tropical waters throughout the world.

Figure 8 **Kinds of Cnidarians**

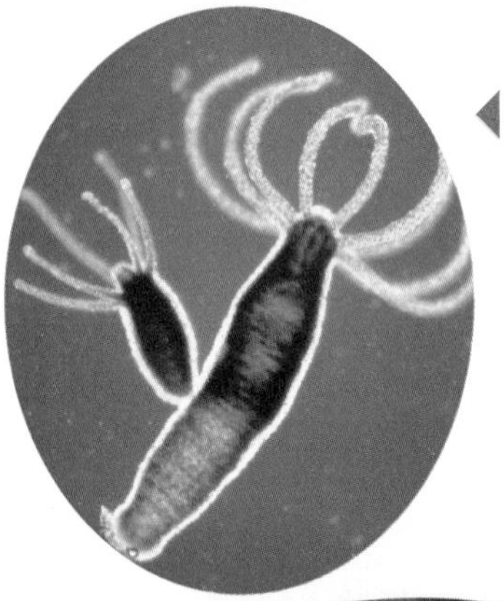

◄ Hydrozoan

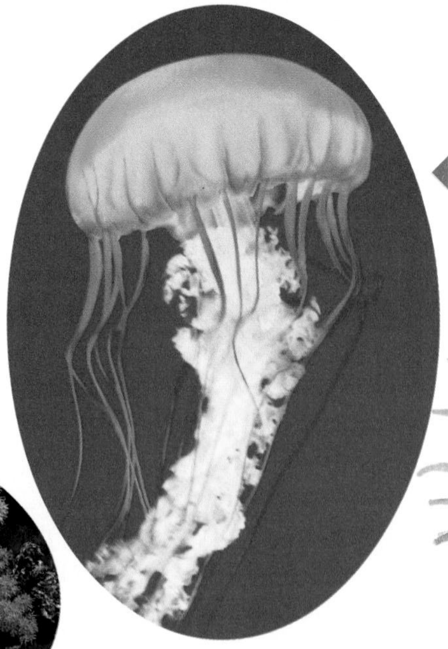

◄ Jellyfish

Sea anemone ▶

◄ Coral

Eyespot   Sensory lobe

Figure 9 *This planarian has a head with eyespots and sensory lobes. Planarians are often about 15 mm long.*

Flatworms

When you think of worms, you probably think of earthworms. But there are many other kinds of worms. Many of them are too tiny to see without a microscope. The simplest worms are the flatworms. Flatworms are divided into three major classes: planarians (pluh NER ee uhnz) and marine flatworms, flukes, and tapeworms.

All flatworms have bilateral symmetry. Many flatworms also have a clearly defined head and two large eyespots. Even though the eyespots cannot focus, a flatworm knows the direction that light is coming from. Some flatworms also have a bump on each side of their head. These bumps are *sensory lobes*. Sensory lobes are used for detecting food. You can see these traits in the planarian shown in **Figure 9.**

✓ Reading Check **What are the three major classes of flatworms?**

Planarians

Planarians live in freshwater lakes and streams or on land in damp places. Most planarians are predators. They eat other animals or parts of other animals and digest food in a gut. They find food by using their sensory lobes. The planarian's head, eyespots, and sensory lobes are clues that it has a well-developed nervous system. Planarians even have a brain for processing information about their surroundings.

Flukes

Flukes are parasites. A *parasite* is an organism that invades and feeds on the body of another living organism that is called a *host*. Most flukes live and reproduce inside the bodies of other animals. A fluke's fertilized eggs pass out of the other animal's body with waste products. If these fertilized eggs infect drinking water or food, animals may eat them. The fertilized eggs will develop into new flukes inside the animals.

Flukes have tiny heads without eyespots or sensory lobes. They have special suckers and hooks for attaching to animals. **Figure 10** shows a fluke.

Figure 10 *Flukes use suckers to attach to their host. Most flukes are just a few millimeters long.*

Figure 11 *Tapeworms can reach enormous sizes. Some can grow to be longer than a school bus!*

CONNECTION TO
Social Studies

Tapeworms People and animals can become infected by tapeworms when they swallow something that contains tapeworm eggs or larvae. These eggs or larvae can come from unclean food, water, or surfaces. Animals can even get tapeworms by swallowing infected fleas. In a group, research one of the following topics: What are some different kinds of tapeworms? What are the effects of tapeworm infection? How can tapeworm infection be prevented? Then, present your research to the rest of the class.

ACTIVITY

Tapeworms

Tapeworms are similar to flukes. Like flukes, they have a small head with no eyespots or sensory lobes. They live and reproduce in other animals. They also feed on these animals as parasites. But tapeworms have a unique body that is very specialized for their internal environment. Tapeworms do not have a gut. These organisms simply attach to the intestines of another animal and absorb nutrients. The nutrients move directly through the tapeworm's tissues. **Figure 11** shows a tapeworm that can infect humans.

Roundworms

Roundworms have bodies that are long, slim, and round, like spaghetti. Like other worms, they have bilateral symmetry. Roundworms have a simple nervous system. A ring of ganglia forms a simple brain. Parallel nerve cords connect the two ends of their body. **Figure 12** shows one kind of roundworm.

Most species of roundworms are very small. A single rotten apple could contain 100,000 roundworms! These tiny worms break down the dead tissues of plants and animals. This process helps make soil rich and healthy.

Not all roundworms eat dead tissues. Many roundworms are parasites. Some of these roundworms, including pinworms and hookworms, infect humans. *Trichinella spiralis* (TRIK i NEL uh spuh RAL is) is a parasitic roundworm that is passed to people from infected pork. This roundworm causes the disease trichinosis (TRIK i NOH sis). This illness causes fever, fatigue, and digestive problems. Cooking pork thoroughly will kill any roundworms living in the meat.

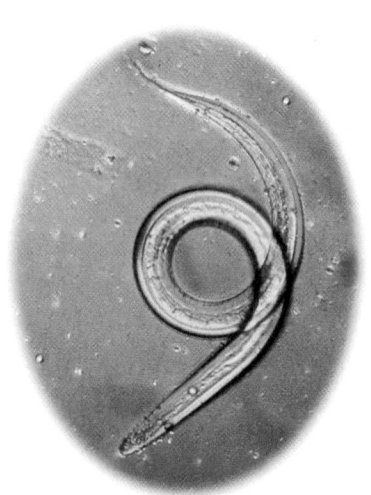

Figure 12 *This hookworm is a tiny larva. Even as an adult, it will be less than 15 mm long.*

✓ Reading Check Name three roundworms that are parasites and that can affect humans.

SECTION Review

Summary

- Invertebrates are animals that do not have a backbone. Most invertebrates have neurons and a gut. The gut is surrounded by the coelom.

- Almost all animals have radial or bilateral symmetry. But some animals, including sponges, are asymmetrical.

- Sponges filter food from water with collar cells. Collar cells also digest food. Sponges can regenerate body parts. They are classified by the kinds of skeletons they have.

- Cnidarians have stinging cells and have two body forms: the medusa and the polyp. Hydrozoans, jellyfish, and sea anemones and corals are cnidarians.

- Planarians, flukes, and tapeworms are three classes of flatworms. Planarians have eyespots and sensory lobes. Flukes and tapeworms are parasites.

- Roundworms are tiny worms that break down dead plant and animal tissue. Some roundworms are parasites.

Using Key Terms

Complete each of the following sentences by choosing the correct term from the word bank.

invertebrate	gut
ganglion	coelom

1. A(n) ___ is a mass of nerve cells that controls an animal's actions.

2. A(n) ___ does not have a backbone.

3. The ___ is a special space in an animal's body that surrounds the ___ and other organs.

Understanding Key Ideas

4. Which of the following is a trait shared by all invertebrates?
   a. having no backbone
   b. having radial symmetry
   c. having a brain
   d. having a gut

5. What do sponges use to digest food?
   a. an osculum
   b. pores
   c. collar cells
   d. a gut

6. Describe cnidarian body forms and stinging cells.

7. How is a roundworm similar to a piece of spaghetti?

Interpreting Graphics

All invertebrate nervous systems are made up of some or all of the same basic parts. The drawing below shows the nervous system of a segmented worm. Use this drawing to answer the questions that follow.

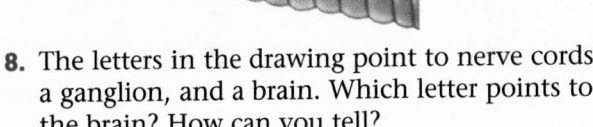

8. The letters in the drawing point to nerve cords, a ganglion, and a brain. Which letter points to the brain? How can you tell?

9. How is the brain connected to the ganglion?

Critical Thinking

10. **Making Inferences** Explain why it would be important for a parasite that its host survive.

Mollusks and Annelid Worms

Have you ever eaten clams or calamari? Have you ever seen earthworms on the sidewalk after it rains?

If you have, then you already know a thing or two about mollusks and annelid worms. These animals are more complex than sponges, cnidarians, flatworms, and roundworms. For example, mollusks and annelid worms have a circulatory system that carries materials throughout their bodies.

Mollusks

Snails, slugs, clams, oysters, squids, and octopuses are all mollusks. Most of these animals live in the ocean. But some live in fresh water, and some live on land.

Most mollusks fit into three classes. The *gastropods* (GAS troh PAHDZ) include slugs and snails. The *bivalves* include clams and other shellfish that have two shells. *Cephalopods* (SEF uh loh PAHDZ) include squids and octopuses.

How Do Mollusks Eat?

Each kind of mollusk has its own way of eating. Snails and slugs eat with a ribbonlike organ—a tongue covered with curved teeth. This organ is called a *radula* (RAJ u luh). **Figure 1** shows a close-up of a slug's radula. Slugs and snails use the radula to scrape algae from rocks, chunks of tissue from seaweed, or pieces of leaves from plants. Clams and oysters attach to one place and use gills to filter tiny plants, bacteria, and other particles from the water. Octopuses and squids use tentacles to grab their food and to place it in their powerful jaws.

Figure 1 *The rows of teeth on a slug's radula help scrape food from surfaces. The radula here has been magnified 2,000 times.*

Ganglia and Brains

All mollusks have complex ganglia. They have special ganglia to control breathing, movement, and digestion. But octopuses and squids have the most advanced nervous system of all invertebrates. Cephalopods, such as the octopus in **Figure 2,** have large brains that connect all of their ganglia. Cephalopods are thought to be the smartest invertebrates.

Pumping Blood

Unlike simple invertebrates, mollusks have a circulatory system. The circulatory system transports materials through the body in the blood. Most mollusks have an open circulatory system. In an **open circulatory system,** a simple heart pumps blood through blood vessels that empty into *sinuses,* or spaces in the animal's body. Squids and octopuses have a closed circulatory system. In a **closed circulatory system,** a heart pumps blood through a network of blood vessels that form a closed loop.

✓ Reading Check What is the difference between an open circulatory system and a closed circulatory system? (*See the Appendix for answers to Reading Checks.*)

Mollusk Bodies

A snail, a clam, and a squid look quite different from one another. Yet if you look closely, you will see that their bodies all have similar structures. The body parts of mollusks are described in **Figure 3.**

Figure 2 *Octopuses are very smart. If they are given stones, they can build a cave to hide in.*

open circulatory system a circulatory system in which the circulatory fluid is not contained entirely within vessels

closed circulatory system a circulatory system in which the heart circulates blood through a network of blood vessels that form a closed loop

---

Figure 3 **Body Parts of Mollusks**

Mollusks are known for their broad, muscular **foot.** The foot helps the animal move. In gastropods, the foot makes mucus that the animal slides along.

The gills, gut, and other organs form the **visceral mass** (VIS uhr uhl MAS). It lies in the center of a mollusk's body.

A layer of tissue called the **mantle** covers the visceral mass. The mantle protects the bodies of mollusks that do not have a shell.

In most mollusks, the outside of the mantle secretes a **shell.** The shell protects the mollusk from predators and keeps land mollusks from drying out.

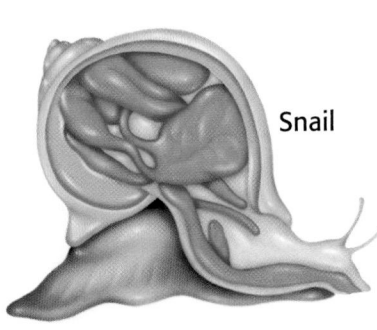

Snail

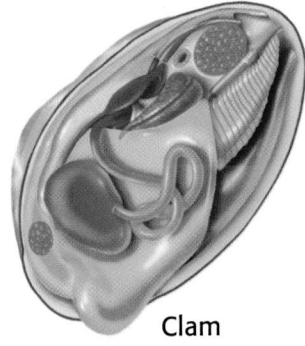

Clam

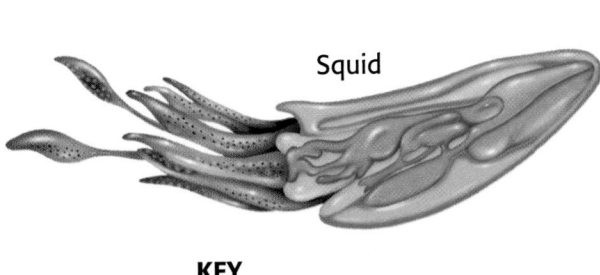

Squid

KEY

| Foot | Mantle |
| Visceral mass | Shell |

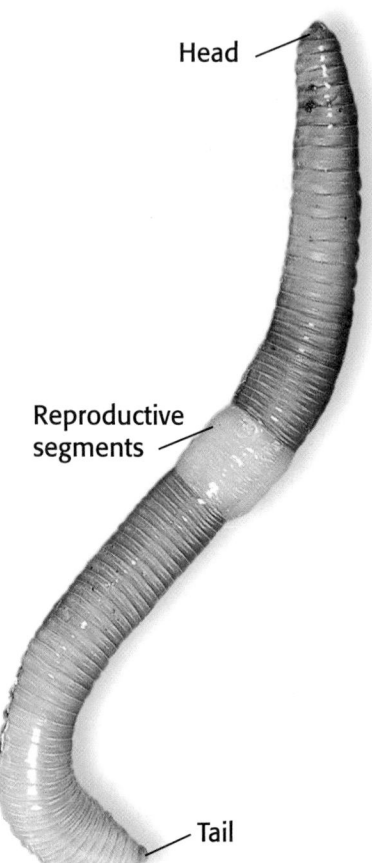

Head

Reproductive segments

Tail

Figure 4 *Except for the head, tail, and reproductive segments, all of the segments of this earthworm are identical.*

segment any part of a larger structure, such as the body of an organism, that is set off by natural or arbitrary boundaries

Annelid Worms

Annelid worms are often called segmented worms because their bodies have segments. A **segment** is an identical, or almost identical, repeating body part. You can see the segments of an earthworm in **Figure 4.**

Like roundworms and flatworms, annelid worms have bilateral symmetry. But annelid worms are more complex than other worms. Annelid worms have a closed circulatory system. They also have a complex nervous system with a brain. A nerve cord connects the brain to a ganglion in each segment.

Annelid worms live in salt water, in fresh water, or on land. They eat plant material or animals. Three major groups of annelid worms are earthworms, marine worms, and leeches.

Earthworms

Earthworms are the most familiar annelid worms. Each earthworm has 100 to 175 segments. Most of these segments are identical, but some look different from the others. These segments have special jobs, such as eating or reproducing.

Earthworms eat material in the soil. They break down plant and animal matter in the soil and leave behind wastes called *castings*. Castings help gardens by making the soil richer. Earthworms also improve garden soil by digging tunnels. The tunnels allow air and water to reach deep into the soil.

To move, earthworms use stiff hairs, or bristles, on the outside of their body. The bristles hold the back part of the worm in place while the front part pushes through the soil.

Marine Worms

If there were a beauty contest for worms, marine worms would win. These worms are called *polychaetes* (PAHL ih KEETS), which means "many bristles." They are covered in bristles and come in many colors. **Figure 5** shows a marine worm. Most of these worms live in the ocean. Some eat mollusks and other small animals. Others filter small pieces of food from the water.

Figure 5 *This marine worm is a predator that eats small animals. Can you see the segments of this worm?*

Leeches

Leeches are known as parasites that suck other animals' blood. This is true of some leeches. But other leeches are not parasites. Some leeches are scavengers that eat dead animals. Others are predators that eat insects, slugs, and snails.

Leeches that suck blood can be useful in medicine. After surgery, doctors sometimes use leeches to prevent dangerous swelling near a wound. **Figure 6** shows two leeches being used for this purpose. Leeches also make a chemical that keeps blood thin so that it does not form clots. The leech uses the chemical to keep blood flowing from its host. Doctors use this chemical to prevent blood clots in people with circulation problems. This chemical can also help break down blood clots that already exist.

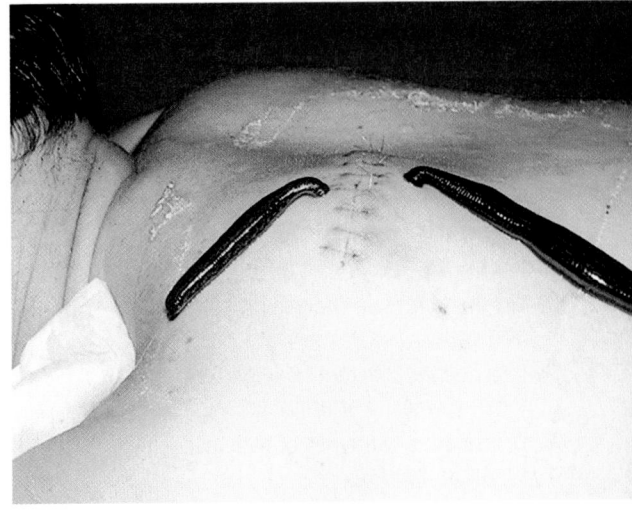

Figure 6 *Doctors sometimes use leeches to reduce swelling after surgery.*

✔ **Reading Check** What are two ways that doctors use leeches to help people?

SECTION Review

Summary

- Mollusks get food with gills, a radula, or tentacles and jaws.
- Mollusks have a complex nervous system.
- Mollusks have either an open circulatory system or a closed circulatory system.
- All mollusks have a foot, a visceral mass, and a mantle. Most mollusks also have a shell.
- The three major groups of annelid worms are earthworms, marine worms, and leeches.

Using Key Terms

1. Use the following terms in the same sentence: *open circulatory system* and *closed circulatory system*.

2. In your own words, write a definition for the term *segment*.

Understanding Key Ideas

3. Some mollusks use a radula to
   a. scrape algae off rocks.
   b. filter food from water.
   c. grab food from water.
   d. place food in their jaws.

4. What trait do all mollusk nervous systems share? What is unique about squids' and octopuses' nervous systems?

5. What are the four main body parts of most mollusks?

6. Describe three different kinds of annelid worms.

Math Skills

7. If a squid swims at 30 km/h, how far can it swim in 1 min?

Critical Thinking

8. **Predicting Consequences** Clams use gills to filter food from water. How could water pollution affect clams?

9. **Analyzing Ideas** Cephalopods do not have shells. What other traits do they have to help make up for this lack of protection?

For a variety of links related to this chapter, go to www.scilinks.org

Topic: Mollusks and Annelid Worms
SciLinks code: HSM0986

SECTION
3

Arthropods

Have you ever explored a park or field, looking for living things? How many animals do you think can live on one acre of land? If you could find all the arthropods in that area, you could count more than a million animals!

Arthropods have lived for hundreds of millions of years. They have adapted to nearly every environment. You are probably familiar with many of them, such as insects, spiders, crabs, and centipedes. Arthropods are the largest group of animals on Earth. At least 75% of all animal species are arthropods.

READING WARM-UP

Objectives

- List the four main characteristics of arthropods.
- Describe the different body parts of the four kinds of arthropods.
- Describe the two types of metamorphosis in insects.

Terms to Learn

exoskeleton   antenna
compound eye   metamorphosis

READING STRATEGY

Prediction Guide Before reading this section, write the title of each heading in this section. Next, under each heading, write what you think you will learn.

Characteristics of Arthropods

All arthropods share four characteristics: a segmented body with specialized parts, jointed limbs, an exoskeleton, and a well-developed nervous system.

Segmented and Specialized

Like annelid worms, arthropods are segmented. In some arthropods, such as centipedes, nearly every segment is identical. Only the segments that make up the head and tail are different from the rest. But most species of arthropods have segments that include specialized structures, such as wings, antennae, gills, pincers, and claws. During an arthropod's development, some segments grow together. This process forms three main body parts. These body parts are the *head,* the *thorax,* and the *abdomen.* You can see these three body parts in **Figure 1.**

Figure 1 *Like most arthropods, this dragonfly has a head, a thorax, and an abdomen.*

Jointed Limbs

Jointed limbs give arthropods their name. *Arthro* means "joint," and *pod* means "foot." Jointed limbs are legs or other body parts that bend at the joints. Having jointed limbs makes it easier for arthropods to move.

An External Skeleton

Arthropods have a hard outer covering. The hard, external structure that covers the outside of the body is an **exoskeleton.** You can see a crab's yellow and white exoskeleton in **Figure 2.** This structure is made of protein and a special substance called *chitin* (KIE tin). An exoskeleton does some of the same things that an internal skeleton does. Like your bones, it serves as a stiff frame that supports the body. It also allows the animal to move. An arthropod's muscles connect to different parts of the skeleton. When the muscles contract, they move the exoskeleton, which moves parts of the animal.

But the exoskeleton also does things that an internal skeleton doesn't do well. The exoskeleton acts like a suit of armor to protect organs inside the body. The exoskeleton also keeps water inside the animal's body. This feature allows arthropods to live on land without drying out.

✓ Reading Check How is an exoskeleton similar to an internal skeleton? (*See the Appendix for answers to Reading Checks.*)

Figure 2 *A ghost crab's exoskeleton protects its body from drying out on land.*

exoskeleton a hard, external, supporting structure

compound eye an eye composed of many light detectors

Sensing Surroundings

All arthropods have a head and a well-developed brain and nerve cord. The nervous system receives information from sense organs, including eyes and bristles. Some arthropods, such as the tarantula, use external bristles to sense their surroundings. The bristles detect motion, vibration, pressure, and chemicals.

Some arthropods have very simple eyes. These arthropods can detect light but cannot see images. But most arthropods have compound eyes. Arthropods that have compound eyes can see images. A **compound eye** is an eye that is made of many identical, light-sensitive units. The fruit fly in **Figure 3** has two compound eyes.

Figure 3 *Compound eyes are made of many identical, light-sensitive units that work together.*

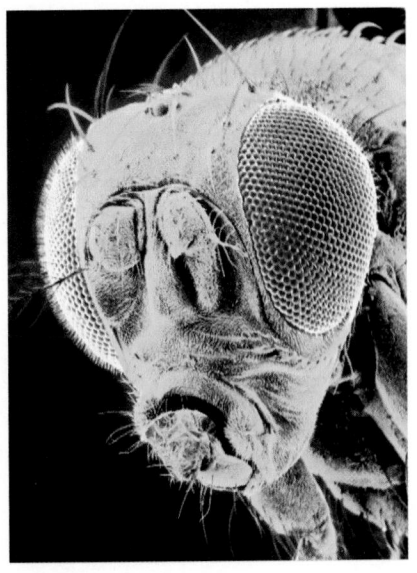

Centipede

Millipede

Figure 4 *Centipedes eat other animals. Millipedes eat plants.*

antenna a feeler that is on the head of an invertebrate, such as a crustacean or an insect, that senses touch, taste, or smell

Kinds of Arthropods

Arthropods are classified by the kinds of body parts they have. You can tell the difference between arthropods by looking at the number of legs, eyes, and antennae they have. An **antenna** is a feeler that senses touch, taste, or smell.

Centipedes and Millipedes

Centipedes and millipedes have one pair of antennae, a hard head, and one pair of mandibles. *Mandibles* are mouthparts that can pierce and chew food. One way to tell these animals apart is to count the number of legs on each segment. Centipedes have one pair of legs on each segment. They can have 30 to 354 legs. Millipedes have two pairs of legs on each segment. The record number of legs on a millipede is 752! **Figure 4** shows a centipede and a millipede. How many legs can you count on each?

Crustaceans

Shrimps, barnacles, crabs, and lobsters are crustaceans. Most crustaceans live in water. They have gills for breathing in the water, mandibles for eating, and two compound eyes. Each eye is located on the end of an eyestalk. Unlike all other arthropods, crustaceans have two pairs of antennae. The crustaceans in **Figure 5** show some of these traits. The lobster's gills are located under the exoskeleton.

Figure 5 *Water fleas and lobsters are two kinds of crustaceans.*

Antenna

Eyestalk

Antenna

Arachnids

Spiders, scorpions, mites, and ticks are arachnids (uh RAK nidz). **Figure 6** shows the two main body parts of an arachnid: the *cephalothorax* (SEF uh loh THAWR aks) and the abdomen. The cephalothorax is made of both a head and a thorax. Most arachnids have four pairs of legs. They have no antennae. Instead of mandibles, they have a pair of clawlike mouthparts called *chelicerae* (kuh LIS uhr EE). And instead of compound eyes, they have simple eyes. The number of eyes varies—some spiders have eight eyes!

Though some people fear spiders, these arachnids are more helpful than harmful. A few kinds of spider bites do need medical treatment. But the chelicerae of many spiders cannot even pierce human skin. And spiders usually use their chelicerae to catch small insects. Spiders kill more insect pests than any other animal does.

Ticks live in forests, brushy areas, and even grassy lawns. Their bodies can be just a few millimeters long. The segments of these small bodies are joined as one part. Ticks are parasites that use chelicerae to slice into a host's skin. These parasites attach onto the host and feed on the host's blood. A few ticks that bite humans can carry diseases, such as Lyme disease. But most people who are bitten by ticks do not get sick.

Reading Check How are spiders helpful to humans?

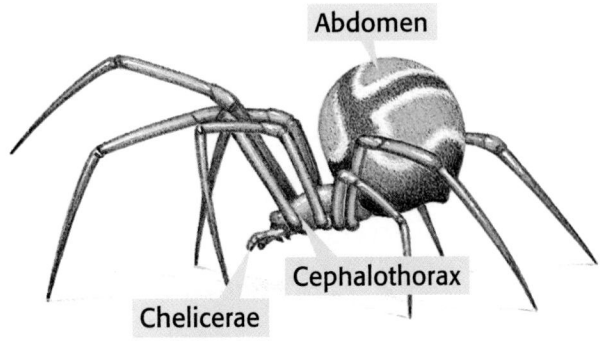

Figure 6 *Arachnids have two main body parts and special mouthparts called chelicerae.*

Abdomen

Cephalothorax

Chelicerae

Insects

Insects make up the largest group of arthropods. If you put all the insects in the world together, they would weigh more than all the other animals combined! **Figure 7** shows a few kinds of insects. Although they look different, they all have three main body parts, six legs, and two antennae.

Sticky Webs

1. Place a **piece of tape** on your desk, sticky side up. The tape represents a web. Your fingers will represent an insect's legs, and then they will represent a spider's legs.

2. Holding the tape in place by the edges, "walk" your fingers across the tape. What happens?

3. Dip your fingers in **cooking oil,** and "walk" them across the tape again. What happens this time?

4. Use the results to explain why spiders don't get stuck in webs.

▲ Bumblebee

◀ Praying mantis

▲ Dragonfly

Figure 7 *These are just a few of the many different insects. Can you see any traits that they have in common?*

Figure 8 *All insect bodies have these three main parts.*

The World of Insects

The only place on Earth where insects do not live is in ocean water. They live on land, in fresh water, and near the sea in beach areas. Many insects are helpful. Most flowering plants depend on insects to carry pollen between plants. Farmers depend on insects to pollinate fruit crops. But some insects are pests that destroy crops or spread disease. And others, such as fleas and mosquitoes, bite us and suck our blood.

Insect Bodies

As shown in **Figure 8,** an insect's body has three parts: the head, the thorax, and the abdomen. On the head, insects have one pair of antennae, one pair of compound eyes, and mandibles. The thorax is made of three segments, each of which has one pair of legs. Some insects have no wings. Others may have one or two pairs of wings on the thorax.

Complete Metamorphosis

metamorphosis a phase in the life cycle of many animals during which a rapid change from the immature form of an organism to the adult form takes place

As an insect develops, it changes form. This process is called **metamorphosis** (MET uh MAWR fuh sis). Most insects go through a complex change called complete metamorphosis. As shown in **Figure 9,** complete metamorphosis has four main stages: egg, larva, pupa (PYOO puh), and adult. Butterflies, beetles, flies, bees, wasps, and ants go through this change.

Figure 9 **The Stages of Complete Metamorphosis**

e The adult butterfly pumps blood-like fluid into its wings until they are full-sized. The butterfly is now ready to fly.

d Adult body parts replace the larval body parts. The **adult** splits its chrysalis.

c After its final molt, the caterpillar makes a chrysalis and becomes a **pupa.** The pupal stage may last a few days or several months. During this stage, the insect is inactive.

a An adult lays **eggs.** An embryo forms inside each egg.

b A **larva** hatches from the egg. Butterfly and moth larvae are called *caterpillars.* The caterpillar eats leaves and grows rapidly. As the caterpillar grows, it sheds its outer layer several times. This process is called *molting.*

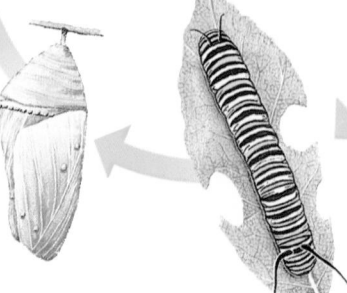

Incomplete Metamorphosis

Grasshoppers and cockroaches are some of the insects that go through incomplete metamorphosis. Incomplete metamorphosis is less complicated than complete metamorphosis. As shown in **Figure 10,** incomplete metamorphosis has three main stages: egg, nymph, and adult. Some nymphs shed their exoskeleton several times in a process called *molting.*

An insect in the nymph stage looks very much like an adult insect. But a nymph does not have wings and is very small. Through molting, it develops into an adult.

✓ Reading Check What are the three stages of incomplete metamorphosis?

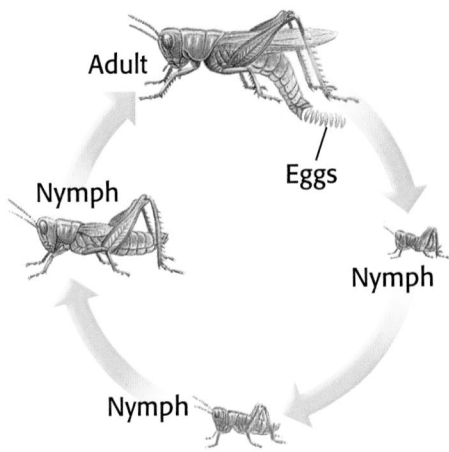

Figure 10 *The grasshopper nymphs look like smaller versions of the adult.*

SECTION Review

Summary

- At least 75% of all animal species are arthropods.
- The four main characteristics shared by arthropods are jointed limbs, a hard exoskeleton, body segments, and a well-developed nervous system.
- The four kinds of arthropods are centipedes and millipedes, crustaceans, arachnids, and insects. Insects are the largest group.
- Insects can go through complete or incomplete metamorphosis.

Using Key Terms

1. Use the following terms in the same sentence: *compound eye* and *antenna*.

2. In your own words, write a definition for each of the following terms: *exoskeleton* and *metamorphosis*.

Understanding Key Ideas

3. Which of the following is NOT a trait shared by all arthropods?
   a. exoskeleton
   b. body segments
   c. antennae
   d. jointed limbs

4. Which of the following arthropods is an arachnid?
   a. butterfly
   b. tick
   c. centipede
   d. lobster

5. What is the difference between complete metamorphosis and incomplete metamorphosis?

6. Name the four kinds of arthropods. How do their bodies differ?

7. Which arthropods have chelicerae? Which have mandibles?

Math Skills

8. How many segments does a millipede with 752 legs have? How many segments does a centipede with 354 legs have?

Critical Thinking

9. **Applying Concepts** Suppose that you find an arthropod in a swimming pool. The organism has compound eyes, antennae, and wings. Is it a crustacean? Why or why not?

10. **Forming Hypotheses** Suppose you have found several cocoons on a plant outside your school. Develop a hypothesis about what animal is inside the cocoon. How could you find out if your hypothesis is correct?

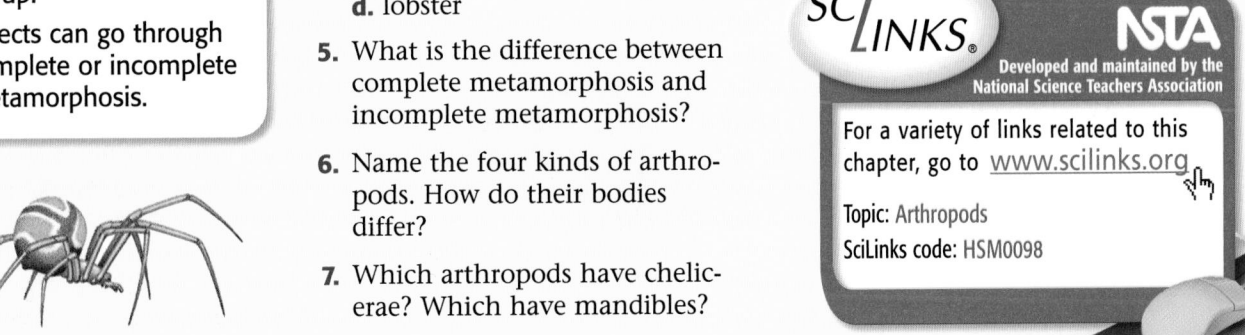

SCi LINKS® **NSTA**
Developed and maintained by the
National Science Teachers Association

For a variety of links related to this chapter, go to www.scilinks.org

Topic: Arthropods
SciLinks code: HSM0098

Echinoderms

Would you touch an object that was covered in sharp spines? Probably not—the spines could hurt you! Some invertebrates are covered in spines that protect them from predators. The predators avoid spines, just like you do.

These spiny invertebrates are called *echinoderms* (ee KIE noh DUHRMZ). Sea stars (starfish), sea urchins, and sand dollars are some familiar members of this group. All echinoderms are marine animals. That means they live in the ocean. Echinoderms live on the sea floor in all parts of the world's oceans. Some of them eat shellfish, some eat dead plants and animals, and others eat algae that they scrape off rocks.

Spiny Skinned

The name *echinoderm* means "spiny skinned." But the animal's skin is not the spiny part. The spines are on the animal's skeleton. An echinoderm's internal skeleton is called an **endoskeleton** (EN doh SKEL uh tuhn). Endoskeletons can be hard and bony or stiff and flexible. The spines covering these skeletons can be long and sharp. They can also be short and bumpy. The animal's skin covers the endoskeleton.

Bilateral or Radial?

Adult echinoderms have radial symmetry. But they develop from larvae that have bilateral symmetry. **Figure 1** shows a sea urchin larva and an adult sea urchin. Notice how the symmetry is different in the two forms.

Figure 1 *The sea urchin larva has bilateral symmetry. The adult sea urchin has radial symmetry.*

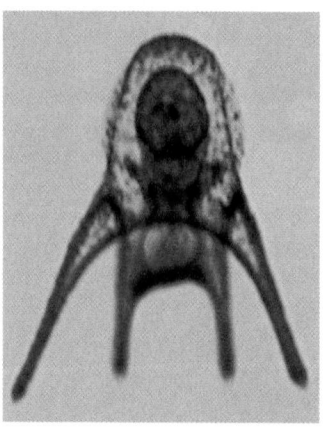

Larva

Adult

endoskeleton an internal skeleton made of bone or cartilage

The Nervous System

All echinoderms have a simple nervous system similar to that of a jellyfish. Around the mouth is a circle of nerve fibers called the *nerve ring*. In sea stars, a *radial nerve* runs from the nerve ring to the tip of each arm, as shown in **Figure 2.** The radial nerves control the movements of the sea star's arms.

At the tip of each arm is a simple eye that senses light. The rest of the body is covered with cells that sense touch and chemical signals in the water.

✓ Reading Check How are the movements of a sea star's arms controlled? (*See the Appendix for answers to Reading Checks.*)

Water Vascular System

One characteristic that is unique to echinoderms is the water vascular system. The **water vascular system** is a system of canals filled with fluid. It uses water pumps to help the animal move, eat, breathe, and sense its environment. **Figure 3** shows the water vascular system of a sea star. Notice how water pressure from the system is used for many functions.

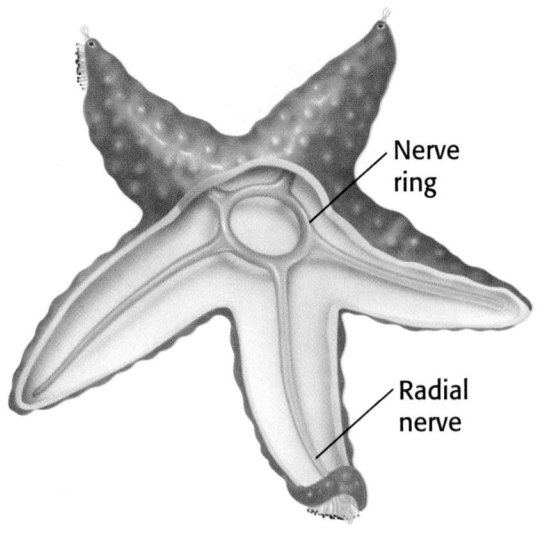

Figure 2 *Sea stars have a simple nervous system.*

Nerve ring

Radial nerve

water vascular system a system of canals filled with a watery fluid that circulates throughout the body of an echinoderm

Figure 3 The Water Vascular System

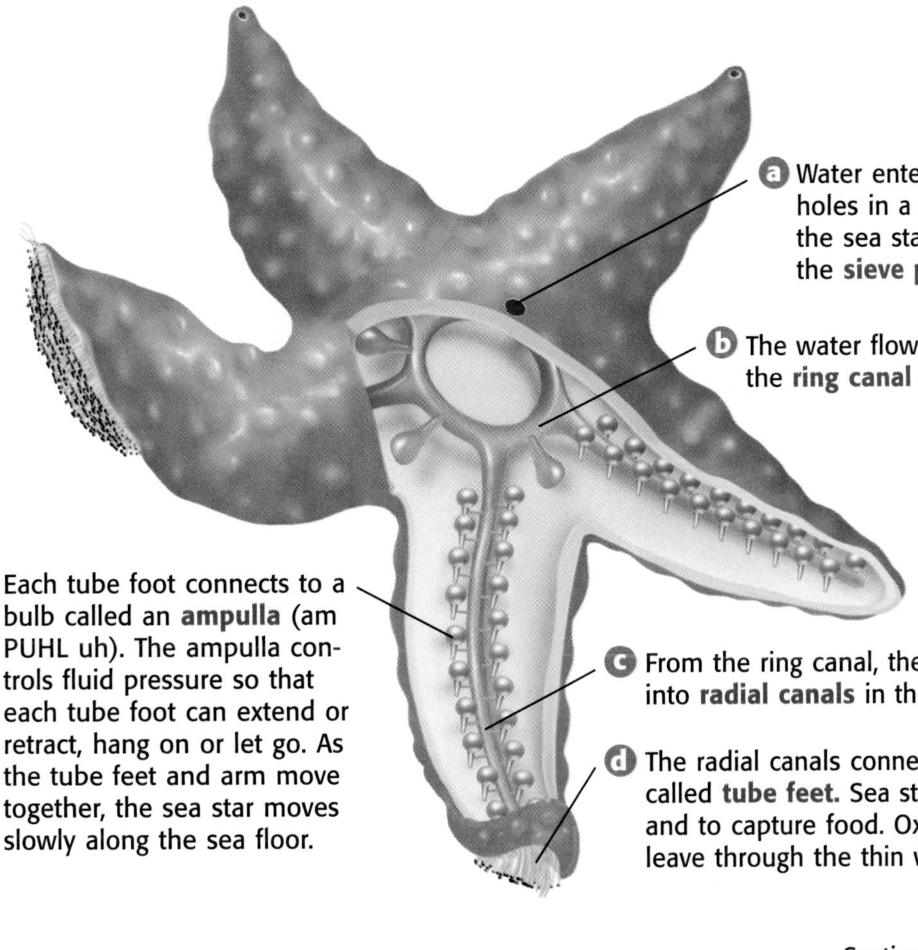

ⓐ Water enters the system through holes in a flat plate on top of the sea star. This plate is called the **sieve plate.**

ⓑ The water flows through a tube to the **ring canal** around the mouth.

ⓔ Each tube foot connects to a bulb called an **ampulla** (am PUHL uh). The ampulla controls fluid pressure so that each tube foot can extend or retract, hang on or let go. As the tube feet and arm move together, the sea star moves slowly along the sea floor.

ⓒ From the ring canal, the water flows into **radial canals** in the arms.

ⓓ The radial canals connect to dozens of tiny suckers called **tube feet.** Sea stars use tube feet to move and to capture food. Oxygen enters and wastes leave through the thin walls of the tube feet.

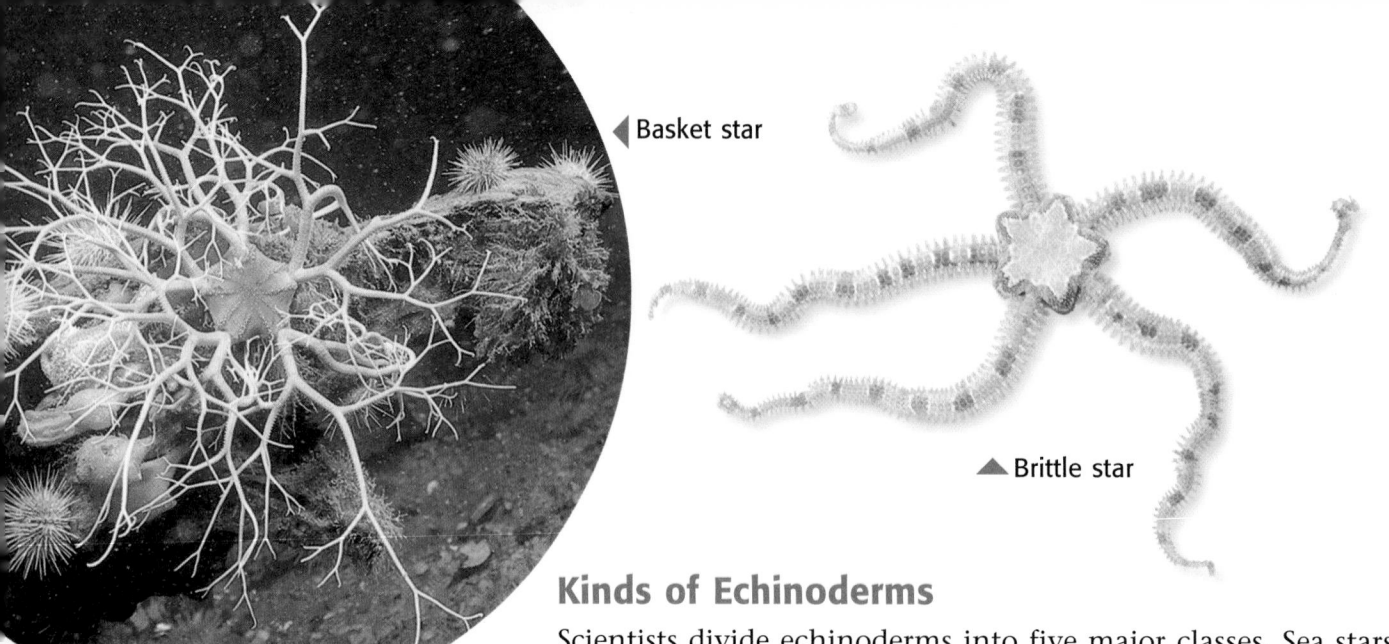

◀ Basket star

▲ Brittle star

Figure 4 *Brittle stars and basket stars move around more than other echinoderms do.*

Kinds of Echinoderms

Scientists divide echinoderms into five major classes. Sea stars are the most familiar echinoderms, and they make up one class. But there are other classes of echinoderms that may not be as familiar to you.

Brittle Stars and Basket Stars

Brittle stars and basket stars look like their close relatives, sea stars. But these echinoderms have long, slim arms and are often smaller than sea stars. Also, they don't have suckers on their tube feet. **Figure 4** shows a brittle star and a basket star.

Sea Urchins and Sand Dollars

Sea urchins and sand dollars are round. Their endoskeletons form a solid, shell-like structure. As shown in **Figure 5,** they have no arms. But they use their tube feet to move in the same way that sea stars move. Some sea urchins can also walk on their spines. Sea urchins feed on algae they scrape from rocks and other objects. They chew the algae with special teeth. Sand dollars burrow into soft sand or mud. They eat tiny particles of food they find there.

Figure 5 *Sea urchins and sand dollars use their spines for defense and for movement.*

Sea urchin

Sand dollars

Sea Lilies and Feather Stars

Sea lilies and feather stars may have 5 to 200 feathery arms. Their arms stretch away from their body and trap small pieces of food. A sea lily's cup-shaped body sits on top of a long stalk, which sticks to a rock. Feather stars, such as the one shown in **Figure 6,** do not have a stalk.

✓ Reading Check What is the difference between a feather star and a sea lily?

Sea Cucumbers

Like sea urchins and sand dollars, sea cucumbers have no arms. A sea cucumber has a soft, leathery body. Unlike other echinoderms, sea cucumbers are long and have a wormlike shape. **Figure 7** shows a sea cucumber.

Figure 7 *Like other echinoderms, sea cucumbers move with tube feet.*

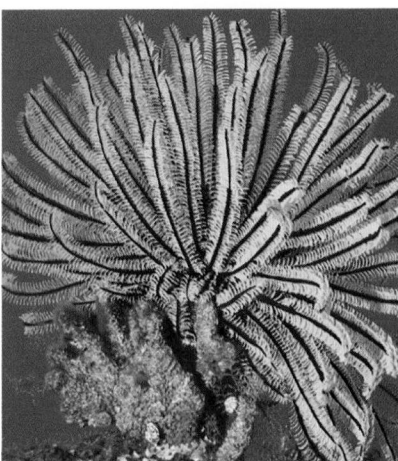

Figure 6 *Like sea stars, brittle stars, and basket stars, feather stars can regrow lost arms.*

SECTION Review

Summary

- Echinoderms are marine animals that have an endoskeleton, a water vascular system, and a nerve ring with radial nerves.
- Echinoderms start life with bilateral symmetry and then develop radial symmetry.
- The different classes of echinoderms include sea stars, sea urchins and sand dollars, brittle stars and basket stars, feather stars and sea lilies, and sea cucumbers.

Using Key Terms

1. Use each of the following terms in a separate sentence: *endoskeleton* and *water vascular system*.

Understanding Key Ideas

2. Which of the following is NOT a trait found in echinoderms?
   a. an endoskeleton
   b. spiny skin
   c. a water vascular system
   d. a nerve ring

3. What is the path taken by water as it flows through the parts of the water vascular system?

4. How are sea cucumbers different from other echinoderms?

5. How does an echinoderm's body symmetry change with age?

6. Name five different classes of echinoderms. List at least one trait for each group.

Math Skills

7. A sea lily lost 12 of its 178 arms in a hurricane. What percentage of its arms were NOT damaged?

Critical Thinking

8. **Making Comparisons** How are echinoderms different from and similar to other invertebrates?

9. **Making Inferences** Suppose you found a sea star with four long arms and one short arm. What might explain the difference?

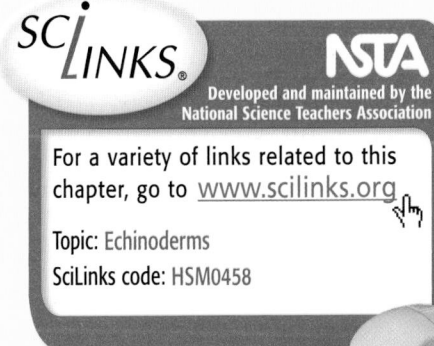

Skills Practice Lab

OBJECTIVES

Observe the structure of a sponge.

Determine how the size of a sponge's holes affect the amount of water the sponge can absorb.

MATERIALS

- beaker
- bowl (large enough for sponge and water)
- calculator (optional)
- kitchen sponge
- natural sponge
- paper towel
- water

SAFETY

Soaking Sponges

Early biologists thought sponges were plants because sponges are like plants in some ways. In many species, the adults attach to a surface and stay there. They cannot chase their food. Instead, sponges absorb and filter a lot of water to get food. In this activity, you will observe the structure of a sponge. You will also consider how the size of the sponge's holes affects the amount of water the sponge can absorb.

Ask a Question

1. Look at the natural sponge. Identify the pores on the outside of the sponge. See if you can find the sponge's central cavities and oscula.

2. Notice the size and shape of the sponge's holes. Look at the holes in the kitchen sponge and the paper towel. Think of a question about how the holes in each item affect its ability to absorb water.

Form a Hypothesis

3. Formulate a testable hypothesis to answer your question. Record your hypothesis.

Test the Hypothesis

④ Read steps 5–9. Design and draw a data table for the data that you will collect. Remember, you will collect data for the natural sponge, the kitchen sponge, and the paper towel.

⑤ Use a balance to measure the mass of the natural sponge. Record the mass.

⑥ Place the natural sponge in the bowl. Use the graduated cylinder to add water to the sponge, 10 mL at a time, until the sponge is completely soaked. Record the amount of water added.

⑦ Gently remove the sponge from the bowl. Measure the amount of water left in the bowl. How much water did the sponge absorb? Record your data.

⑧ Calculate how many milliliters of water your sponge holds per gram of dry sponge. For example, if your sponge's dry mass is 12 g and it holds 59.1 mL of water, then your sponge holds 4.9 mL of water per gram (59.1 mL ÷ 12 g = 4.9 mL/g).

⑨ Repeat steps 5–8 with the kitchen sponge and the paper towel.

Analyze the Results

① **Analyzing Results** Compare your results from steps 5–9. Which item held the most water per gram of dry mass?

Draw Conclusions

② **Evaluating Data** Did your results support your hypothesis? Explain your answer.

③ **Evaluating Results** Do you see a connection between the size of an item's holes and its ability to hold water?

④ **Analyzing Results** What can you conclude about how the size and shape of a sponge's holes affect its feeding ability?

Applying Your Data

WRITING SKILL Use the Internet to see if scientists have done research that backs up your ideas about how the size and shape of a sponge affect its feeding abilities. Write your findings in a report to present to the class.

Chapter Review

USING KEY TERMS

1 In your own words, write a definition for each of the following terms: *ganglion, water vascular system,* and *coelom.*

2 Use the following terms in the same sentence: *open circulatory system* and *invertebrate.*

Complete each of the following sentences by choosing the correct term from the word bank.

antennae	exoskeleton
coelom	gut
compound eyes	metamorphosis
endoskeleton	segments

3 Almost all invertebrates digest food in a(n) ___.

4 Repeating ___ make up the bodies of annelid worms and arthropods.

5 A crab's ___ keeps it from losing water.

6 Arthropods use ___ to see images.

7 Echinoderms have spines on their ___.

8 Arthropods use ___ to touch, taste, and smell.

9 Insects change form during ___.

UNDERSTANDING KEY IDEAS

Multiple Choice

10 No invertebrates have

  a. a brain.
  b. a gut.
  c. ganglia.
  d. a backbone.

11 Which animals have a nerve ring?

  a. sponges
  b. echinoderms
  c. crustaceans
  d. flatworms

12 Which of the following is NOT a flatworm?

  a. a tapeworm
  b. an earthworm
  c. a planarian
  d. a fluke

13 Which body part is NOT present in all mollusks?

  a. foot
  b. visceral mass
  c. mantle
  d. shell

Short Answer

14 Describe how a sponge eats.

15 What are the four main characteristics of arthropods?

16 Describe the body of a roundworm.

17 What are three ways that different mollusks eat?

18 Which insects go through complete metamorphosis? go through incomplete metamorphosis?

19 How is an adult echinoderm different from an echinoderm larva?

20 How are cephalopod nervous systems unique among mollusks?

CRITICAL THINKING

21 Concept Mapping Use the following terms to create a concept map: *segments, invertebrates, endoskeleton, antennae, exoskeleton, water vascular system, metamorphosis,* and *compound eyes.*

22 Applying Concepts You have discovered a new animal that has radial symmetry and tentacles with stinging cells. Can this animal be classified as a cnidarian? Explain.

23 Making Inferences Unlike other mollusks, cephalopods can move quickly. Based on what you know about the structure and function of mollusks, why do you think that cephalopods have this ability?

24 Making Comparisons Why don't roundworms, flatworms, and annelid worms belong to the same group of invertebrates?

25 Analyzing Processes Butterflies mate as adults and spend time eating and growing in their other stages. They have no wings during the larval or pupal stage of metamorphosis. Can you think of a reason that they would need wings in their adult form more than in the other stages of development? Explain your answer.

26 Predicting Consequences How do earthworms affect gardens? What do you think would happen to a garden if the gardener removed all the earthworms from it?

INTERPRETING GRAPHICS

The picture below shows an arthropod. Use the picture to answer the questions that follow.

27 Name the body segments labeled a, b, and c.

28 How many legs does this arthropod have?

29 To which segment are the arthropod's legs attached?

30 What kind of arthropod is this?

Standardized Test Preparation

Read each of the passages below. Then, answer the questions that follow each passage.

Passage 1 Giant squids are very similar to their smaller relatives. They have a torpedo-shaped body, two tentacles, eight arms, a mantle, and a beak. All of their body parts are much larger, though. A giant squid's eye may be as large as a volleyball! Given the size of giant squids, it's hard to imagine that they have any enemies in the ocean, but they do.

Toothed sperm whales eat giant squids. How do we know this? Thousands of squid beaks have been found in the stomach of a single sperm whale. The hard beaks of giant squids are <u>indigestible</u>. Also, many whales bear ring marks on their forehead and fins that match the size of the suckers found on giant squids.

1. Based on the passage, what do you think the word *indigestible* describes?

 A something that cannot be digested

 B something that causes indigestion

 C something that one cannot dig out

 D something that one cannot guess

2. What can you infer from this passage?

 F Giant squids only imagine that they have enemies.

 G A toothed sperm whale can eat 10,000 giant squids in one meal.

 H Giant squids defend themselves against toothed sperm whales.

 I Giant squids and sperm whales compete with each other for food.

3. How are giant squids different from other kinds of squids?

 A Giant squids have a torpedo-shaped body, a mantle, and a beak.

 B Giant squids have enemies in the ocean.

 C Giant squids have larger body parts.

 D Giant squids are the size of a volleyball.

Passage 2 Water bears are microscopic invertebrates that are closely related to arthropods. Most water bears live on wet mosses and lichens. Some of them eat roundworms and other tiny animals, but most feed on mosses. What makes water bears unique is their ability to shut down their body processes. They do this when their environment becomes too hot, too cold, or too dry. Shutting down body processes means that the organism doesn't eat, move, or breathe. But it doesn't die, either. It just dries out. When conditions improve, the water bear returns to normal life. Scientists think that the water bear's cells become coated with sugar when its body shuts down. This sugar may keep the cells from breaking down while they are inactive.

1. How do scientists think sugar helps water bears survive while their body processes are shut down?

 A Sugar coats their cells, keeping the cells from breaking down.

 B Sugar coats their cells, trapping moisture inside the cells.

 C Sugar coats their cells, keeping moisture from entering the cells.

 D Sugar provides water bears with nutrients.

2. What do water bears eat?

 F sugar

 G mosses

 H lichens

 I arthropods

3. Which is a unique characteristic of water bears?

 A They are related to arthropods.

 B They often live on mosses or lichens.

 C They can live at the bottom of the ocean.

 D They can shut down their body processes without dying.

The bar graph below shows the number of monarchs in a population from 1990 to 1994. Use the graph to answer the questions that follow.

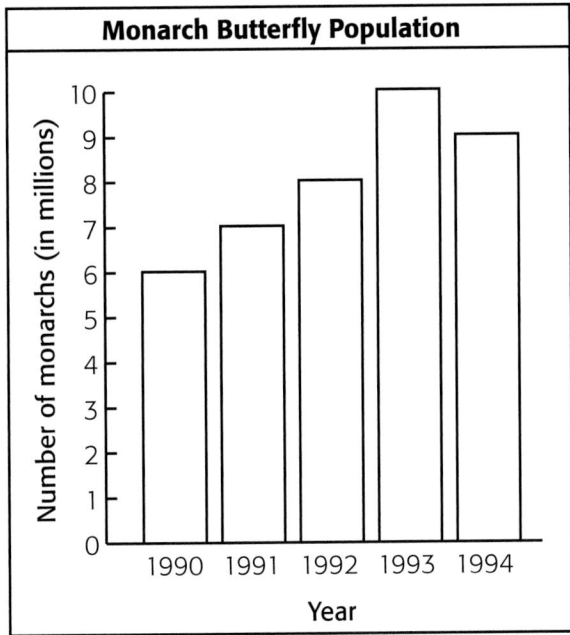

1. Compare the number of butterflies in the population during 1990, 1991, 1992, and 1993. Identify the statement that best describes how the population changed during those years.

  A The population increased.

  B The population remained the same.

  C The population decreased.

  D The population doubled yearly.

2. Why might butterfly scientists be surprised about the 1994 monarch population?

  F The 1994 population was the first population of 9 million ever recorded.

  G The 1994 population was the first decreased population recorded in 4 years.

  H The 1994 population was the first increased population recorded in 4 years.

  I The 1994 population was the first decreased population ever recorded.

3. What can you infer from the graph about how the monarch's environmental conditions changed between 1993 and 1994?

  A Conditions were worse in 1994.

  B Conditions did not change between 1993 and 1994.

  C Conditions were better in 1994.

  D This graph does not contain enough information to determine how conditions changed between 1993 and 1994.

4. What was the average population of monarchs during these 5 years?

  F 7 million

  G 8 million

  H 9 million

  I 40 million

Read each question below, and choose the best answer.

1. Raymond wanted to arrange his shell collection in order of size. Which group of shell lengths is listed in order from smallest to largest?

  A 1.6 cm, 0.25 dm, 0.017 m, 5.0 cm

  B 0.017 m, 0.25 dm, 1.6 cm, 5.0 cm

  C 1.6 cm, 5.0 cm, 0.25 dm, 0.017 m

  D 1.6 cm, 0.017 m, 0.25 dm, 5.0 cm

2. Raquelle wants to buy some earthworms to put in her garden. The earthworms are sold in containers that each hold 8 worms. How many containers will Raquelle need to buy if she wants 75 earthworms?

  F 9 containers

  G 10 containers

  H 15 containers

  I 83 containers

3. Maxwell found a huge basket star while he was scuba diving. The basket star had five arms, and each arm branched into three pieces. Each of these pieces branched into two more tips. How many tips did the basket star have?

  A 2 tips

  B 5 tips

  C 15 tips

  D 30 tips

Science in Action

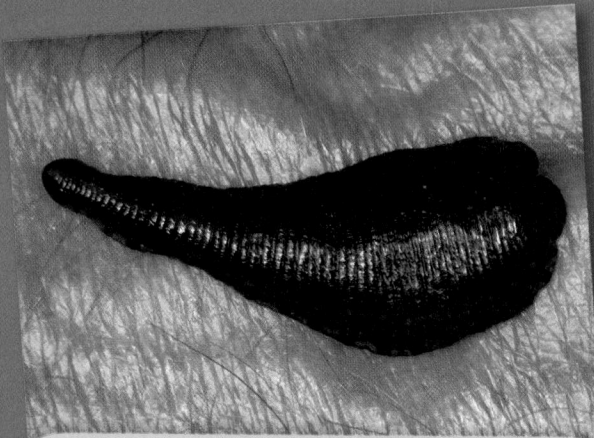

Weird Science

A Powerful Punch

The mantis shrimp packs a powerful punch! This animal is nick-named "killer shrimp" and "thumb-splitter." These crustaceans can be divided into two groups: the *smashers* and the *spearers*. The smashers have large front limbs that they use to club their prey with great speed and power. They can easily smash through the shells of clams, snails, and crabs. Larger species have been known to break double-walled aquarium glass! The spearers have sharp spines on their front limbs, and lash out with incredible speed—at about 1,000 cm/sec. That is one of the fastest animal movements known!

Science, Technology, and Society

Leeches to the Rescue

Bloodsucking leeches may sound scary, but they could save your toes! Leeches are used in operations to reattach lost limbs, fingers, or toes. During these operations, doctors can reconnect arteries, but not small veins, which are more delicate. As a result, blood flow in the limb, finger, or toe is impaired. The tissues may become full of loose blood. If this happens, the tissues of the reattached parts die. But if leeches suck the extra blood from the reattached part, the tissues can remain healthy until the veins grow back.

Language Arts ACTiViTY

The words *crustacean* and *crust* both come from the same Latin root—*crusta*. Think of how crustaceans are similar to crusts, and then guess the meaning of the Latin root.

Math ACTiViTY

Measure the widest and narrowest parts of the leech in the photo. Calculate how many times wider the wide part is than the narrow part. Which end of the leech do you think is the head? Why do you think so?

George Matsumoto

Marine Biologist Dr. George Matsumoto is a marine biologist at the Monterey Bay Aquarium in California. A seventh-grade snorkeling class first sparked his interest in ocean research. Since then, he's studied the deep seas by snorkeling, scuba diving, and using research vessels, remotely operated vehicles (ROVs), and deep-sea submersibles. On the Johnson Sea Link submersible, he traveled down to 1,000 m (3,281 ft) below sea level!

Marine biology is a field full of strange and wonderful creatures. Matsumoto focuses on marine invertebrates, particularly the delicate animals called comb jellies. These invertebrates are beautiful animals that have not been studied very much. Comb jellies are also called *ctenophores* (TEN uh FAWRZ), which means "comb-bearers." They have eight rows of cilia that look like the rows of a comb. These cilia help ctenophores move through the water. By studying ctenophores and similar marine invertebrates, Matsumoto and other marine scientists can learn about the ecology of ocean communities.

Social Studies ACTIVITY

WRITING SKILL One ctenophore from the United States took over both the Black Sea and the Sea of Azov by eating small fish and other food. This crowded out bigger fish, changing the ecosystem and ruining the fisheries. Write a paragraph about how Matsumoto's work as a marine biologist could help solve problems like this one.

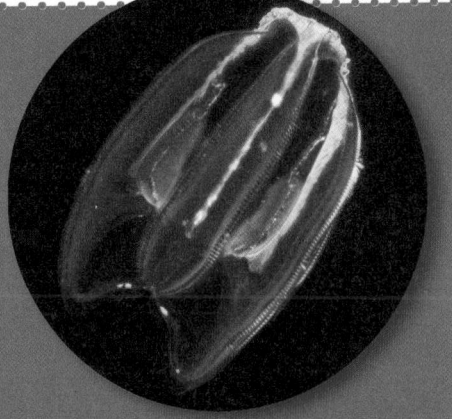

To learn more about these Science in Action topics, visit go.hrw.com and type in the keyword HL5INVF.

Current Science

Check out Current Science® articles related to this chapter by visiting go.hrw.com. Just type in the keyword HL5CS15.

3

Fishes, Amphibians, and Reptiles

About the PHOTO

This unlucky caiman must have been quite a match for the snake. But somehow the snake's body strength overcame the caiman's muscular jaws. Each of these animals has a unique trait that makes the animal a strong predator. But as reptiles, these animals have many traits in common. For example, both animals are covered in thick skin, and both use lungs to breathe.

PRE-READING ACTIVITY

Graphic Organizer

Comparison Table Before you read the chapter, create the graphic organizer entitled "Comparison Table" described in the **Study Skills** section of the Appendix. Label the columns with "Fishes," "Amphibians," and "Reptiles." Label the rows with "Characteristics" and "Kinds." As you read the chapter, fill in the table with details about the characteristics and kinds of each animal.

START-UP ACTIVITY

Oil and Water

A shark stores a lot of oil in its liver. In this activity, you will build a model of an oily liver to see how an oily liver can help keep a shark from sinking.

Procedure

1. Use **two beakers** to measure equal amounts of **water** and **cooking oil.**

2. Use a **funnel** to fill **one balloon** with the water that you measured.

3. Using the funnel, fill a **second balloon** with the cooking oil.

4. Tie the balloons so that no air remains inside. Be careful not to squeeze the oil or water out of the balloons while tying them.

5. Put each balloon in a **fish tank** that is full of **water.** Observe what happens to each of the balloons.

Analysis

1. Compare where the two balloons come to rest in the tank of water.

2. A shark's oily liver helps keep the shark from sinking. How does the structure of the shark's oily liver help achieve this result?

3. Why do you think it was important to remove the air from the balloons before putting them in the water? What might have happened if you did not remove the air from the balloons?

Fishes: The First Vertebrates

You may have seen a dinosaur skeleton at a museum. And you've probably seen a lot of fish. Have you ever thought about what you might have in common with these animals or what they might have in common with each other?

The skeletons of humans and fish have many bones that are similar to dinosaur bones. Dinosaur bones are just bigger. For example, all of these skeletons have a backbone. Animals that have a backbone are called **vertebrates** (VUHR tuh brits).

Chordates

Vertebrates belong to the phylum Chordata. Members of this phylum are called *chordates* (KAWR DAYTS). Vertebrates make up the largest group of chordates. But there are two other groups of chordates—lancelets (LANS lits) and tunicates (TOO ni kits). These chordates are much simpler than vertebrates. They do not have a backbone or a well-developed head. **Figure 1** shows an example of each group of chordates.

The three groups of chordates share certain characteristics. All chordates have each of four particular body parts at some point in their life. These parts are shown in the lancelet in **Figure 2** on the next page.

vertebrate an animal that has a backbone

Figure 1 *Tunicates (right), lancelets (lower right), and vertebrates, such as the fish (lower left), are chordates.*

Figure 2 **Chordate Body Parts**

Tail
Chordates have a tail that begins behind the anus. Some chordates have a tail only in the embryo stage.

Notochord
A stiff but flexible rod called a notochord (NOHT uh KAWRD) gives the body support. In most vertebrates, the embryo's notochord is replaced by a backbone.

Hollow Nerve Cord
A hollow nerve cord runs along the back and is full of fluid. In vertebrates, this nerve cord is called the *spinal cord.*

Pharyngeal Pouches
All chordate embryos have pharyngeal (fuh RIN jee uhl) pouches. These pouches develop into gills or other body parts as the embryo matures.

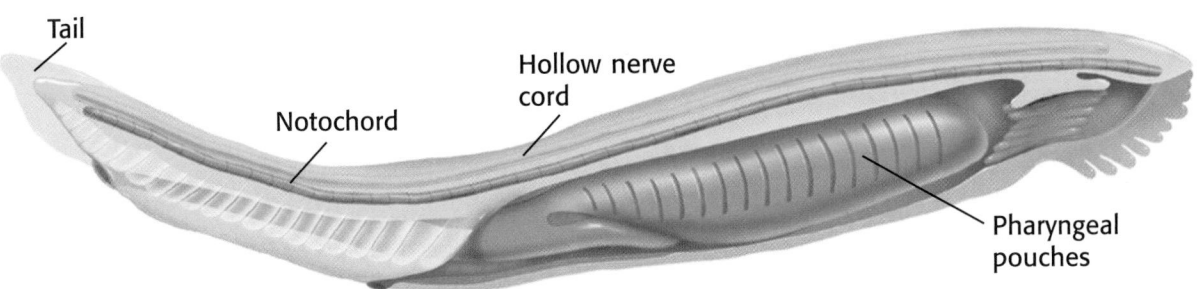

Tail
Notochord
Hollow nerve cord
Pharyngeal pouches

Vertebrate Characteristics

Fishes, amphibians, reptiles, birds, and mammals are vertebrates. Many things set vertebrates apart from lancelets and tunicates. One major difference is that only vertebrates have a backbone. The backbone is a strong but flexible column of bones that are called *vertebrae* (VUHR tuh BRAY). **Figure 3** shows the vertebrae of a human. The vertebrae surround and protect the spinal cord. They also help support the rest of the body.

Another difference between vertebrates and other chordates is the head. Vertebrates have a well-developed head protected by a skull. The skull is made of either cartilage or bone. *Cartilage* is the tough material that the flexible parts of our ears and nose are made of. The skeletons of all vertebrate embryos are made of cartilage. But as most vertebrates grow, the cartilage is replaced by bone. Bone is much harder than cartilage.

Because bone is so hard, it can be easily fossilized. Scientists have discovered many fossils of vertebrates. These fossils give scientists valuable clues about how organisms are related to each other. For example, fossil evidence indicates that fish appeared about 500 million years ago. These fossils show that fish were the first vertebrates on Earth.

✓ Reading Check What material makes up the skeleton of a human embryo? (*See the Appendix for answers to Reading Checks.*)

Figure 3 *The vertebrae interlock to form the backbone.*

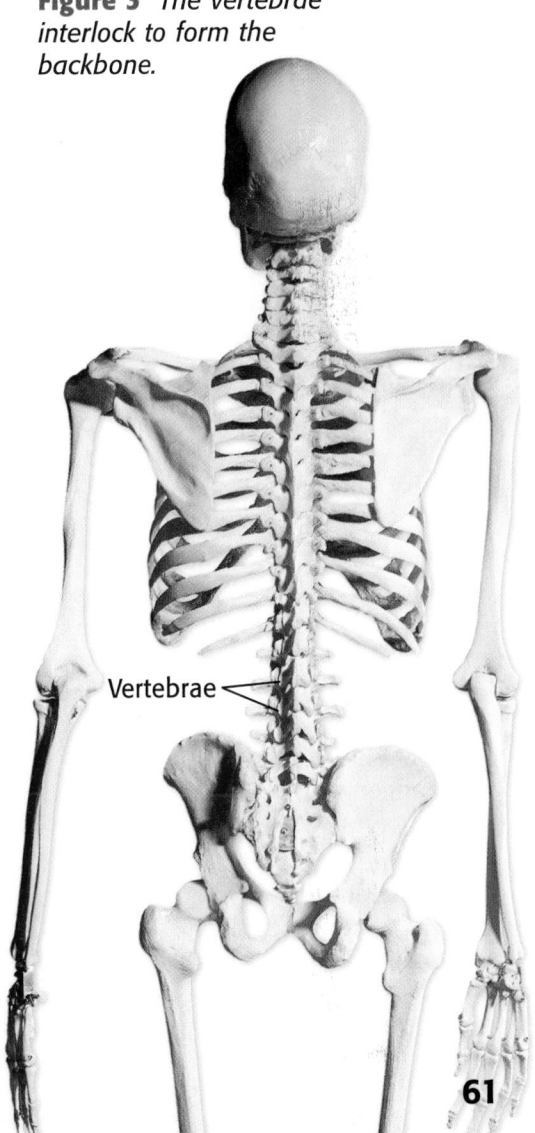

Vertebrae

Figure 4 *Most fishes, including this leafy sea dragon, are ectotherms.*

endotherm an animal that can use body heat from chemical reactions in the body's cells to maintain a constant body temperature

ectotherm an organism that needs sources of heat outside of itself

Body Temperature

1. Use a **thermometer** to take your temperature every hour for 6 h.

2. Make a graph of your body temperature. Place the time of day on the *x*-axis and your temperature on the *y*-axis.

3. Does your temperature change throughout the day? How much does it change?

4. Do you think exercise changes your body temperature?

5. How do you think your results would be different if you were an ectotherm?

Are Vertebrates Warm or Cold?

All vertebrates need to live at the proper temperature. An animal's cells work properly only at certain temperatures. If an animal's body temperature is too high or too low, its body cannot function well. Some animals heat their own bodies. Others depend on the environment to control their temperature.

Staying Warm

The body temperature of birds and mammals does not change much as the temperature of the environment changes. Birds and mammals use energy released by the chemical reactions in their cells to warm their bodies. Animals that have a stable body temperature are called **endotherms** (EN doh THUHRMZ). They are sometimes called *warmblooded animals*. Because of their stable temperature, endotherms can stay warm in cold weather.

Cold Blood?

Some animals depend on their surroundings to stay warm. Their body temperature changes as the temperature of the environment changes. Animals that do not control body temperature through activity in their cells are called **ectotherms** (EK toh THUHRMZ). They are sometimes called *coldblooded animals*. Nearly all amphibians and reptiles are ectotherms. Most fishes, such as the one in **Figure 4,** are also ectotherms. Being an ectotherm is one of many traits that most fishes share.

✓ Reading Check How would the body temperature of most fishes change if the temperature of the environment increased?

Fish Characteristics

Fishes come in many shapes, sizes, and colors. There are more than 25,000 species of fishes, and many look very different from each other. But all fishes share several characteristics. Some traits help fishes live in the water. Other traits, such as a strong body and a brain, help fishes catch or find food.

Born to Swim

Fishes have many body parts that help them swim. Strong muscles attached to the backbone allow many fishes to swim quickly after their prey. To steer, stop, and balance, fishes use *fins,* which are fan-shaped structures that help fishes move. And many fishes have bodies covered by bony structures called *scales.* Scales protect the body and lower friction as fishes swim through the water. **Figure 5** shows some body parts of a fish.

Making Sense of the World

Fishes have a brain that keeps track of information coming in from the senses. All fishes have the senses of vision, hearing, and smell. Most fishes also have a lateral line system. The **lateral line** is a row or rows of tiny sense organs that detect water vibrations, such as those caused by another fish swimming by. These organs are found along each side of the body and usually extend onto the head.

Underwater Breathing

Fishes use their gills to breathe. A **gill** is an organ that removes oxygen from the water. Oxygen in the water passes through the thin membrane of the gills to the blood. The blood then carries oxygen through the body. Gills are also used to remove carbon dioxide from the blood.

Making More Fish

Most fishes reproduce by *external fertilization.* The female lays unfertilized eggs in the water, and the male drops sperm on them. But some species of fish use *internal fertilization.* In this case, the male deposits sperm inside the female. Usually, the female then lays fertilized eggs that have embryos inside. But in some species, the embryos develop inside the female.

CONNECTION TO Physics

How Fish See the World You have to move a magnifying lens back and forth to bring an object into focus. Fish eyes focus on objects in the same way. Fish use muscles to change the position of the lenses in their eyes. By moving the eye lenses, fish can bring objects into focus. To understand how fish see the world, use a magnifying lens to look at objects in your classroom.

ACTiViTY

lateral line a faint line visible on both sides of a fish's body that runs the length of the body and marks the location of sense organs that detect vibrations in water

gill a respiratory organ in which oxygen from the water is exchanged with carbon dioxide from the blood

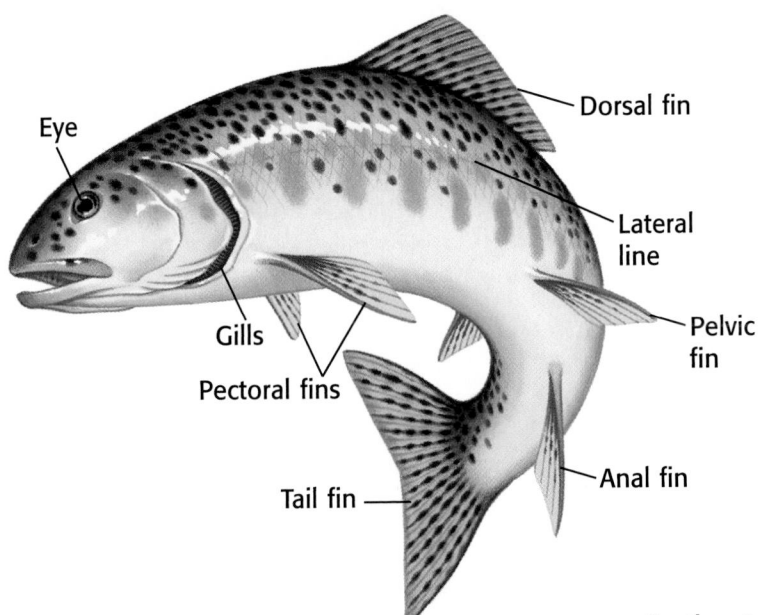

Eye
Dorsal fin
Lateral line
Pelvic fin
Gills
Pectoral fins
Anal fin
Tail fin

Figure 5 *Fishes have many shapes and sizes, but all fishes have gills, fins, and a tail.*

Kinds of Fishes

There are five very different classes of fishes. Two classes are now extinct. But scientists have been able to study the fossils of the extinct fishes. The three classes of fishes living today are *jawless fishes, cartilaginous* (KART'l AJ uh nuhs) *fishes,* and *bony fishes.*

Jawless Fishes

The first fishes did not have jaws. You might think that having no jaws would make eating difficult and would lead to extinction. But the jawless fishes have thrived for half a billion years.

The two kinds of modern jawless fishes are hagfish and lampreys, as shown in **Figure 6.** These fishes are eel-like. They have smooth, slimy skin and a round, jawless mouth. Their skeleton is made of cartilage, and they have a notochord but no backbone. These fishes have a skull, a brain, and eyes.

Jawless fishes do not need jaws to eat. Hagfish eat dead fishes on the ocean floor. For this reason, they are sometimes called *vultures of the sea.* Lampreys suck other animals' blood and flesh. They have a suction cup–like mouth that has teeth. They don't need jaws because they don't bite or chew.

✓ **Reading Check** Describe how jawless fishes eat.

INTERNET ACTIVITY

For another activity related to this chapter, go to **go.hrw.com** and type in the keyword **HL5VR1W.**

Figure 6 **Jawless Fishes**

▼ **Hagfish** can tie their flexible bodies into knots. They slide the knot from their tail end to their head to remove slime from their skin or to escape from predators.

▼ **Lampreys** can live in salt water or fresh water, but they must reproduce in fresh water.

Figure 7 Cartilaginous Fishes

▲ Unlike rays, **skates** have a small dorsal fin.

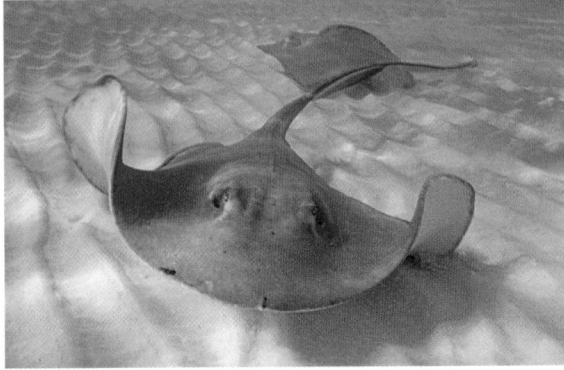

▲ Rays, such as this **stingray,** feed on shellfish and worms on the sea floor. A ray swims by moving its fins up and down.

◄ Sharks, such as this **hammerhead shark,** rarely prey on humans. They usually eat other fish.

Cartilaginous Fishes

Did you know that a shark is a fish? Sharks belong to a class of fishes called cartilaginous fishes. In most vertebrates, soft cartilage in the embryo is slowly replaced by bone. But in sharks, skates, and rays, the skeleton never changes to bone. So, they are called *cartilaginous fishes.*

Cartilaginous fishes have fully functional jaws. These fishes are strong swimmers and expert predators. Many have excellent senses of sight and smell, and they have a lateral line system. **Figure 7** shows some cartilaginous fishes.

To stay afloat, cartilaginous fishes store a lot of oil in their liver. The oil helps the fishes be more buoyant because the oil is less dense than water. But even with oily livers, these fishes are denser than water. They have to keep moving to stay afloat. When they stop swimming, they slowly sink.

Some cartilaginous fishes also swim to keep water moving over their gills. If these fishes stop swimming, they will suffocate. Other cartilaginous fishes do not have to swim. They can lie on the ocean floor and pump water across their gills.

swim bladder a gas-filled sac that is used to control buoyancy; also known as a *gas bladder*

Bony Fishes

When you hear the word *fish,* you probably think of a bony fish. Goldfish, tuna, trout, catfish, and cod are bony fishes. This class of fishes is the largest. Ninety-five percent of all fishes are bony fishes. They range in size from about 1 cm to 8.6 m long. Some bony fishes are shown in **Figure 8.**

Bony fishes are very different from other fishes. As their name suggests, bony fishes have a skeleton made of bone. Also, their bodies are covered by bony scales. Unlike other fishes, bony fishes can rest in one place without swimming. They have a swim bladder that keeps them from sinking. The **swim bladder** is a balloonlike organ that is filled with oxygen and other gases. These gases are lighter than water, so they help the fish be more buoyant. The swim bladder is sometimes called a *gas bladder.*

There are two main groups of bony fishes. Almost all bony fishes are *ray-finned fishes.* Ray-finned fishes have paired fins supported by thin rays of bone. Ray-finned fishes include many familiar fishes, such as eels, herrings, trout, minnows, and perch.

Lobe-finned fishes make up the second group of bony fishes. Lobe-finned fishes have fins that are muscular and thick. There are seven living species of lobe-finned fishes. Six of these species are lungfishes. Lungfishes have air sacs. Because air sacs can gulp air, they are like lungs. Scientists think that ancient fishes from this group were the ancestors of amphibians.

Reading Check How do bony fishes differ from cartilaginous fishes?

Figure 8 **Bony Fishes**

▼ **Lungfishes** live in shallow waters that often dry up in the summer.

▼ **Masked butterfly fish** live in warm waters around coral reefs.

▼ **Pikes** are fast predators that move in quick bursts of speed to catch fish and invertebrates.

SECTION
Review

Summary

- Chordates include lancelets, tunicates, and vertebrates. At some point during their development, chordates have a notochord, a hollow nerve cord, pharyngeal pouches, and a tail.

- Most chordates are vertebrates. Vertebrates differ from other chordates in that they have a backbone composed of vertebrae.

- Endotherms control body temperature through the chemical reactions of their cells. Ectotherms do not.

- Fishes share many characteristics. Most have fins and scales to help them swim. Many have a lateral line system to sense water movement. Fishes breathe with gills.

- There are three groups of living fishes: jawless fishes, cartilaginous fishes, and bony fishes. Jawless fishes do not have a backbone. Cartilaginous fishes have an oily liver. Bony fishes have a swim bladder.

- The oily liver and the swim bladder both help fishes keep from sinking.

Using Key Terms

1. Use each of the following terms in a separate sentence: *vertebrate, lateral line system, gill,* and *swim bladder.*

2. In your own words, write a definition for each of the following terms: *endotherm* and *ectotherm.*

Understanding Key Ideas

3. At some point in its life, every chordate has each of the following EXCEPT

   a. a tail.

   b. a notochord.

   c. a hollow nerve cord.

   d. a backbone.

4. Which vertebrates are ectotherms?

5. What are four characteristics shared by most fishes?

6. What are the three classes of living fish? Give an example of each.

7. Most bony fishes reproduce by external fertilization. What does this mean?

Critical Thinking

8. **Analyzing Relationships** Describe the ways that cartilaginous fishes and bony fishes maintain buoyancy. Why do you think that jawless fishes do not use one of these methods?

9. **Applying Concepts** How could moving a fishbowl from a cold window sill to a warmer part of the house affect a pet fish?

Interpreting Graphics

Use the bar graph below to answer the questions that follow.

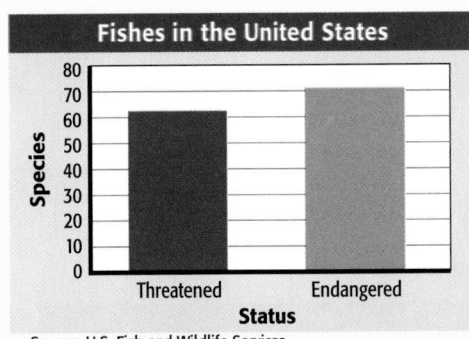

Fishes in the United States

Species / Status (Threatened, Endangered)

Source: U.S. Fish and Wildlife Services

10. How many fish species in the United States are threatened? How many are endangered?

11. What is the total number of threatened and endangered fish species in the United States?

Amphibians

Did you know that some animals are able to breathe through their skin? Do these animals live on land or in the water? Actually, they live both on land and in the water.

About 350 million years ago, fishes lived wherever there was water. But no vertebrates lived on land. The land had many resources for vertebrates. It had plants and insects for vertebrates to eat, and there were few predators. But to live on land, vertebrates needed lungs for breathing and legs for walking.

Moving to Land

Amphibians (am FIB ee uhnz) are animals that can live in water and have lungs and legs. Scientists think that amphibians evolved from the ancestors of lungfish-like fishes. These ancient fishes developed lungs that got oxygen from the air. A **lung** is a saclike organ that takes oxygen from the air and delivers oxygen to the blood. These fishes also had strong fins that could have evolved into legs.

Most of today's amphibians are frogs or salamanders, such as those in **Figure 1.** But early amphibians looked different. Fossils show that the first amphibians looked like a cross between a fish and a salamander. Many were very large—up to 10 m long. Early amphibians could stay on dry land longer than today's amphibians can. But they still had to return to the water to keep from drying out or overheating. They also returned to the water to mate and to lay eggs.

✓ Reading Check How do amphibians get oxygen from the air? (*See the Appendix for answers to Reading Checks.*)

Figure 1 *Frogs and salamanders are two kinds of the amphibians on Earth today.*

Characteristics of Amphibians

Amphibian means "double life." Most amphibians live part of their lives in water and part of their lives on land. Amphibian eggs do not have a shell or a membrane that prevents water loss. For this reason, embryos must develop in a wet environment. Most amphibians live in the water after hatching and then later develop into adults that can live on land.

But even adult amphibians are only partly adapted to life on land. Amphibians are ectotherms. So, their body temperature depends on the temperature of their environment. Water helps amphibians keep their bodies at a stable temperature. Also, water helps adults keep from losing too much moisture through their skin.

Thin Skin

Amphibian skin is thin, smooth, and moist. The skin is so thin that amphibians absorb water through it instead of drinking. But they can also lose water through their skin and easily become dehydrated. Their thin skin is one reason that most amphibians live in water or in damp habitats.

Amphibians can breathe by gulping air into their lungs. But many also absorb oxygen through their skin, which is full of blood vessels. In fact, a few amphibians, such as the salamander in **Figure 2,** breathe only through their skin.

Many amphibians also have brightly colored skin. The colors often warn predators that the skin contains poison glands. These poisons may simply be irritating, or they may be deadly. The skin of the poison arrow frog, shown in **Figure 3,** has one of the most deadly toxins known.

lung a respiratory organ in which oxygen from the air is exchanged with carbon dioxide from the blood

Figure 2 *The four-toed salamander has no lungs. It gets all of its oxygen through its skin.*

Figure 3 *The skin of this poison arrow frog is full of poison glands. Hunters in South America rub the tips of their arrows in the deadly toxin.*

CONNECTION TO Social Studies

WRITING SKILL **Troublesome Toads** In the 1930s, cane toads were shipped from Hawaii to Australia to eat cane grubs that were destroying sugar cane crops. But the toad populations grew out of control, and the toads did not eat the grubs. Native species that ate the toads were killed by the toads' poison glands. Research another animal that has caused disastrous effects in a new environment. In your **science journal,** write three paragraphs about this animal.

Figure 4 Amphibian Metamorphosis

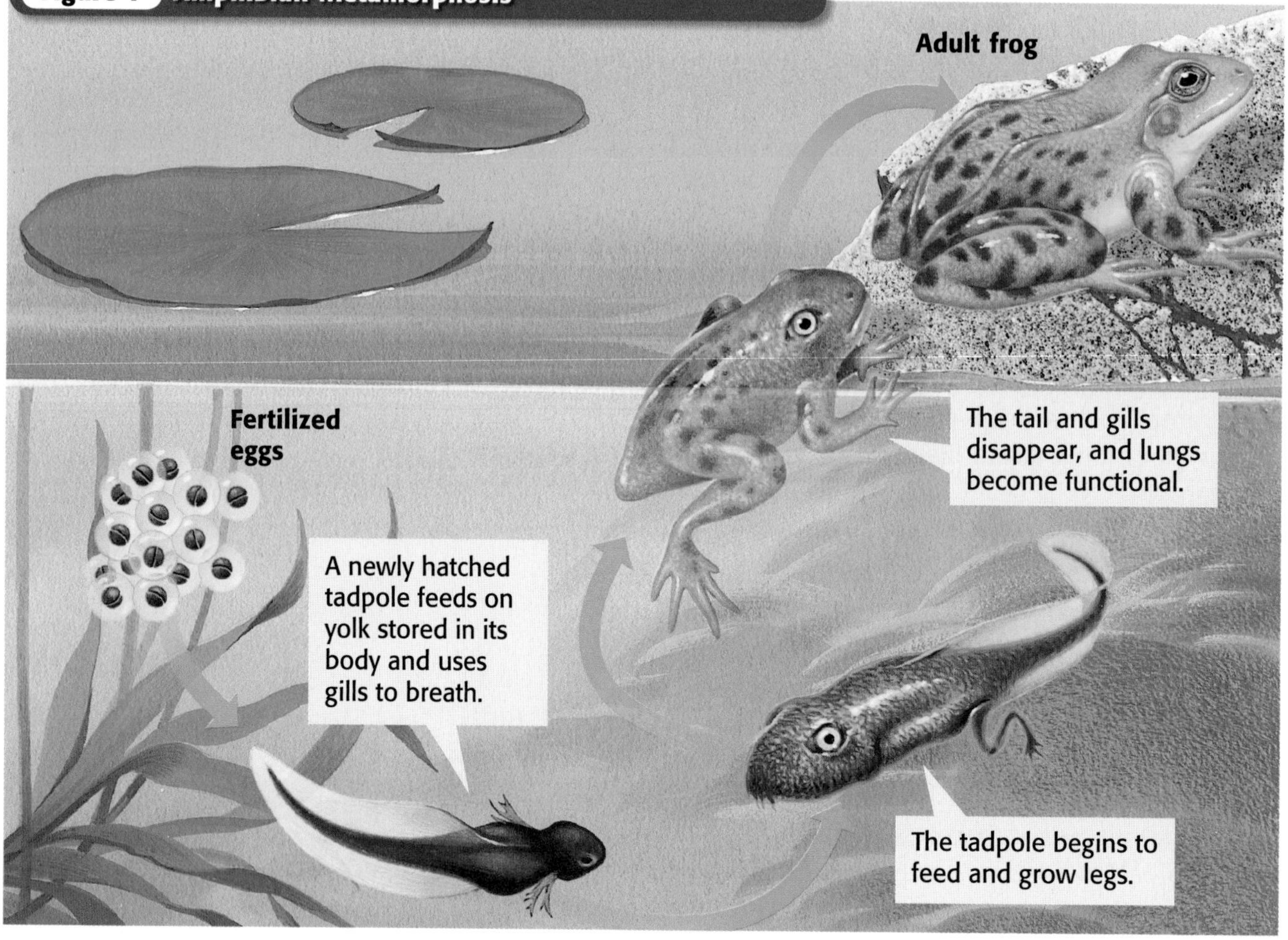

Adult frog

Fertilized eggs

The tail and gills disappear, and lungs become functional.

A newly hatched tadpole feeds on yolk stored in its body and uses gills to breath.

The tadpole begins to feed and grow legs.

tadpole the aquatic, fish-shaped larva of a frog or toad

metamorphosis a phase in the life cycle of many animals during which a rapid change from the immature form of an organism to the adult form takes place

Figure 5 *Darwin's frogs live in Chile and Argentina. A male frog may carry 5 to 15 embryos in its vocal sacs.*

Leading a Double Life

Most amphibians don't just get bigger as they grow into adults. They change form as they grow. After hatching, a frog or toad embryo becomes a tadpole. A **tadpole** is an immature frog or toad that must live in the water. It gets oxygen through gills and uses its long tail to swim. Later, the tadpole loses its gills and develops structures such as lungs and limbs that allow it to live on land. This change from an immature form to an adult form is called **metamorphosis** (MET uh MAWR fuh sis) and is shown in **Figure 4.** Most adult amphibians can live on land. However, they still need to keep their skin moist.

A few amphibians develop in other ways. Some do not go through full metamorphosis. They hatch as tiny versions of adults, but they have gills. Some develop on land in wet places. For example, Darwin's frogs lay eggs on moist ground. When an embryo begins to move, an adult male Darwin's frog takes it into his mouth and protects it inside his vocal sacs. When the embryo has finished developing, the adult opens his mouth and a tiny frog jumps out. **Figure 5** shows a Darwin's frog.

Kinds of Amphibians

More than 5,400 species of amphibians are alive today. They belong to three groups: caecilians (see SIL ee uhnz), salamanders, and frogs and toads.

Caecilians

Most people are not familiar with caecilians. However, scientists have discovered more than 160 species of caecilians. These amphibians live in tropical areas of Asia, Africa, and South America. They look like earthworms or snakes, but they have the thin, moist skin of amphibians. Several traits distinguish caecilians from other amphibians. For example, caecilians do not have legs, as shown in **Figure 6.** And unlike other amphibians, some caecilians have bony scales in their skin.

Figure 6 *Caecilians do not have legs. They live in damp soil in the Tropics and eat small invertebrates in the soil.*

Salamanders

There are about 500 known species of salamanders. As adults, most salamanders live under stones and logs in the woods of North America. Two salamanders are shown in **Figure 7.** Of modern amphibians, salamanders are the most like prehistoric amphibians in overall form. Although salamanders are much smaller than their ancestors, they have a similar body shape, a long tail, and four strong legs. They range in size from a few centimeters long to 1.5 m long.

Salamanders do not develop as tadpoles. But most of them do lose gills and grow lungs during their development. A few species, such as the axolotl (AK suh LAHT'l), never lose their gills. These species live their entire life in the water.

✓ Reading Check How does a salamander's body change during development?

Figure 7 Salamanders

▼ The **marbled salamander** lives in damp places, such as under rocks or logs or among leaves.

▼ This **axolotl** is an unusual salamander. It keeps its gills and never leaves the water.

Figure 8 Frogs and Toads

▼ Frogs, such as this **bull frog,** have smooth, moist skin.

▼ Toads, such as this **Fowler's toad,** spend less time in water than frogs do. Their skin is drier and bumpier.

Frogs and Toads

About 90% of all amphibians are frogs or toads. Frogs and toads are very similar. In fact, toads are a type of frog. You can see a frog and a toad in **Figure 8.**

Frogs and toads live all over the world, except for very cold places. They are found in deserts and rain forests. They are highly adapted for life on land. Adults have strong leg muscles for jumping. They have well-developed ears for hearing and vocal cords for calling. They also have a long, sticky tongue. The tongue is attached to the front of the mouth so that it can be flipped out quickly to catch insects.

Singing Frogs

Frogs are well known for their nighttime choruses, but many frogs sing in the daytime, too. Like humans, they force air from their lungs across vocal cords in the throat to make sounds. But frogs have something we lack. A thin-walled sac of skin called the *vocal sac* surrounds their vocal cords. When frogs sing, the sac inflates with vibrating air. The frog in **Figure 9** has an inflated vocal sac. The sac increases the volume of the song so that the song can be heard over long distances.

Frogs sing to communicate messages that help in attracting mates and marking territories. Usually, frogs sing songs that they know without having to learn the songs. But some frogs can change the notes they sing. For example, to make its voice louder, one frog uses a tree's acoustics. It sits in a hole in a tree trunk and tries many notes until it finds the loudest one. Then, it sings this note repeatedly to be as loud as possible.

Figure 9 *Most frogs that sing are males. Their songs communicate messages to other frogs.*

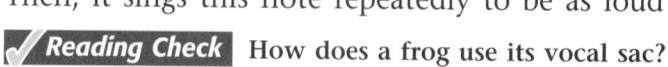 **Reading Check** How does a frog use its vocal sac?

Amphibians as Ecological Indicators

Amphibians are often called *ecological indicators*. In other words, unhealthy amphibians can be an early sign of changes in an ecosystem. When large numbers of amphibians begin to die or show deformities, a problem with the environment may exist. For example, the disappearance of the golden toad, shown in **Figure 10,** caused concern about the toad's environment.

Amphibians are ecological indicators because they are very sensitive to changes in their environment. Their thin skin absorbs any chemicals in the water or air. And their lungs take in chemicals from the air. Climate change is another factor that may affect amphibians. As ectotherms, their body temperature depends on the temperature of their environment.

Figure 10 *Golden toads were seen regularly in Costa Rica until 1989. After that year, they disappeared.*

SECTION Review

Summary

- Amphibians were the first vertebrates to live on land.
- Amphibians breathe by gulping air into the lungs and by absorbing oxygen through the skin.
- Amphibians start life in water, where they use gills to breathe. During metamorphosis, they lose their gills and grow legs that allow them to live on land as adults.
- The three groups of amphibians are caecilians, salamanders, and frogs and toads.
- Because amphibians are very sensitive to environmental changes, they are sometimes called *ecological indicators*.

Using Vocabulary

1. Use each of the following terms in a separate sentence: *lung, tadpole,* and *metamorphosis.*

Understanding Key Ideas

2. The first vertebrates to live on land were
   a. fish.
   b. dinosaurs.
   c. amphibians.
   d. reptiles.

3. Many adult amphibians breathe by using
   a. only their gills.
   b. only their lungs.
   c. only their skin.
   d. their lungs and skin.

4. Describe metamorphosis in amphibians.

5. Why do adult amphibians have to live near water or in a very wet habitat?

6. Why are amphibians sometimes called *ecological indicators*?

7. Name the three types of amphibians. How are they similar? How are they different?

8. How are frogs and toads similar? How are they different?

Math Skills

9. A certain toad species spends 2 months of its life as a tadpole and 3 years of its life as an adult. What percentage of its life is spent in the water? What percentage is spent on land?

Critical Thinking

10. **Analyzing Relationships** Describe the relationship between lungfishes and amphibians. How are these animals alike? How are they different?

11. **Evaluating Conclusions** Scientists think that climate change may have caused the golden toad to become extinct. What other causes are possible, and how could scientists test these ideas?

SCiLINKS®

NSTA
Developed and maintained by the National Science Teachers Association

For a variety of links related to this chapter, go to www.scilinks.org

Topic: Amphibians
SciLinks code: HSM0058

Reptiles

How are reptiles different from amphibians? Amphibians need to spend part of their lives in or near the water. But most reptiles can spend their whole lives on land.

Living on Land

About 35 million years after amphibians moved onto land, some of them began to change. They grew thick, dry skin that reduced water loss. Their legs changed and grew stronger, so they could walk easily. They also laid eggs that did not dry out on dry land. They had become reptiles, the first animals to live out of the water.

Many reptiles are now extinct. Dinosaurs that lived on land are the most well known prehistoric reptiles. But there were many other ancient reptiles. Some could swim, others could fly, and many were similar to reptiles that are alive today. A few living reptiles are shown in **Figure 1.**

▲ Crocodile

▼ South American emerald boa

Figure 1 *These animals are just a few of the many kinds of reptiles on Earth today.*

▲ Giant tortoise

Characteristics of Reptiles

Reptiles are well adapted for life on land. For example, all reptiles—even reptiles that live in water—have lungs to breathe air. Reptiles also have thick skin, use their surroundings to control their temperature, and have a special kind of egg that is laid on land.

Thick Skin

Thick, dry skin is a very important adaptation for life on land. This skin forms a watertight layer that keeps cells from losing water by evaporation. Unlike amphibians, most reptiles cannot breathe through their skin. Most reptiles, such as the snake in **Figure 2,** depend on only their lungs for oxygen.

Body Temperature

Nearly all reptiles are ectotherms. They cannot keep their bodies at a stable temperature. They are active when it is warm outside, and they slow down when it is cool. A few reptiles can get some heat from their own body cells. But most reptiles live in mild climates. They cannot handle the cold polar regions, where mammals and birds can thrive.

The Amazing Amniotic Egg

The most important adaptation to life on land is the amniotic (AM nee AHT ik) egg. An **amniotic egg** is an egg that holds fluid that protects the embryo. Reptiles, birds, and mammals have amniotic eggs. Reptiles' amniotic eggs have a shell, as shown in **Figure 3.** The amniotic eggs of birds and egg-laying mammals also have a shell. The shell protects the embryo and keeps the egg from drying out. A reptile's amniotic egg can be laid under rocks, in the ground, or even in the desert.

✔️ **Reading Check** Why don't reptile eggs dry out on land? (*See the Appendix for answers to Reading Checks.*)

Figure 2 *Many people think snakes are slimy, but the skin of snakes and other reptiles is scaly and dry.*

amniotic egg a type of egg that is surrounded by a membrane, the amnion, and that in reptiles, birds, and egg-laying mammals contains a large amount of yolk and is surrounded by a shell

Figure 3 *Compare these amphibian and reptile eggs. The reptile eggs are amniotic, but the amphibian eggs are not.*

Figure 4 An Amniotic Egg

The amniotic egg of a bird shares important features with reptilian amniotic eggs.

The **shell** protects the egg from damage and keeps the egg from drying out. The shell has small pores that allow oxygen to pass through to the growing embryo and allow carbon dioxide to be removed.

The **albumen** (al BYOO min) provides water and protein to the embryo.

The **amniotic sac** is filled with fluid. The amniotic fluid surrounds and protects the embryo.

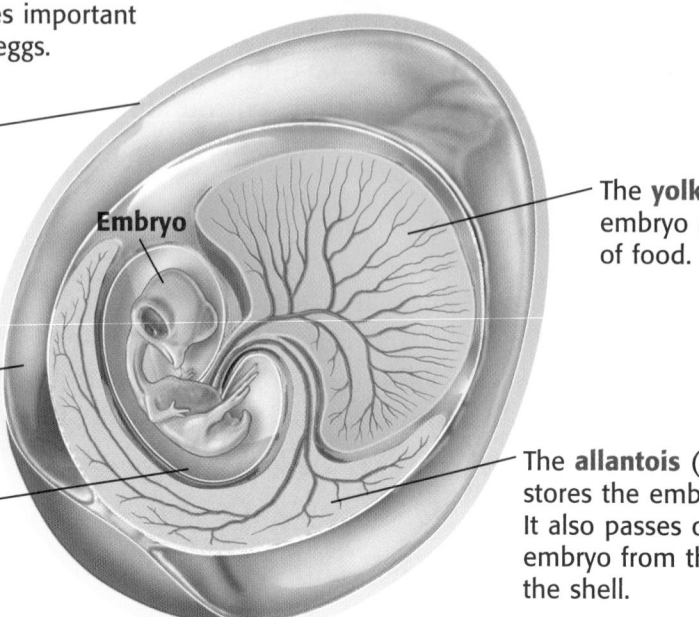

Embryo

The **yolk** gives the embryo a rich supply of food.

The **allantois** (uh LAN toh is) stores the embryo's wastes. It also passes oxygen to the embryo from the pores in the shell.

Parts of the Amniotic Egg

The shell is just one important part of the amniotic egg of a reptile, bird, or egg-laying mammal. All of the parts of the amniotic egg are described in **Figure 4.** Together, these parts protect the embryo from predators, infections, and water loss.

Reptile Reproduction

Reptiles usually reproduce by internal fertilization. After the egg is fertilized inside the female, a shell forms around the egg. Then, the female lays the egg. Most reptiles lay their eggs in soil or sand. But a few reptiles do not lay their eggs. Instead, the embryos develop inside the mother, and the young are born live. In either case, the embryo develops into a tiny young reptile that looks like a small adult. Reptiles do not go through metamorphosis.

Kinds of Reptiles

The Age of Dinosaurs lasted from 300 million years ago until about 65 million years ago. During this time, most land vertebrates were reptiles. But today, about 8,000 species of living reptiles are known to exist. This number is much smaller than the number of reptile species that lived in the past. Turtles and tortoises, crocodiles and alligators, lizards and snakes, and tuataras are the four groups of reptiles that still live today. **Figure 5** shows one example of a modern reptile.

Reading Check What are the four groups of living reptiles?

Figure 5 *This panther chameleon is a modern lizard.*

Figure 6 Turtles and Tortoises

▼ This **green sea turtle** has a streamlined shell that helps the turtle swim and turn rapidly.

▼ The **Texas tortoise** is one of four living species of tortoises native to North America.

Turtles and Tortoises

Turtles and tortoises are distantly related to other living reptiles. Generally, tortoises live on land, and turtles spend all or much of their lives in the water. However, even sea turtles come on land to lay their eggs. **Figure 6** shows a turtle and a tortoise.

The trait that makes turtles and tortoises so unique is their shell. The shell makes them slow and inflexible, so outrunning predators is unlikely. But many turtles can draw their head and limbs into the armorlike shell to protect themselves.

Crocodiles and Alligators

Crocodiles and alligators spend most of their time in the water. Their eyes and nostrils are on the top of their flat head. So, they can watch their surroundings while most of their body is hidden underwater. Hiding in this way gives them a great advantage over their prey. Crocodiles and alligators are meat eaters. They eat invertebrates, fish, turtles, birds, and mammals. **Figure 7** shows how to tell the difference between an alligator and a crocodile.

Figure 7 Crocodiles and Alligators

▼ A crocodile, such as this **American crocodile,** has a narrow head and a pointed snout.

▼ An alligator, such as this **American alligator,** has a broad head and a rounded snout.

Figure 8 Snakes

▼ **Cape cobras** are famous for their deadly venom. These aggressive snakes live in very dry areas.

▲ **Sinaloan milk snakes** are not poisonous, but they look a lot like poisonous coral snakes.

Snakes and Lizards

Today, the most common reptiles are snakes and lizards. Snakes are carnivores. They have special organs in the mouth that help them smell prey. When a snake flicks its tongue out, tiny molecules in the air stick to its tongue. The snake then touches its tongue to the organs in its mouth. The molecules on the tongue tell the snake what prey is nearby. Some snakes kill their prey by squeezing it until it suffocates. Other snakes have fangs for injecting venom. But no matter how snakes kill their prey, they eat it in the same way. Snakes can open their mouths very wide. So, snakes can eat animals and eggs by swallowing them whole. **Figure 8** shows two kinds of snakes.

Most lizards eat small insects and worms, but some lizards eat plants. One giant lizard—the Komodo dragon—eats deer, pigs, and goats! Lizards have a loosely connected lower jaw, but they do not swallow large prey whole. Lizards do have other eye-catching abilities, though. For example, many lizards can break their tails off to escape predators and then grow new tails. **Figure 9** shows two kinds of lizards.

Figure 9 Lizards

The **frilled lizard** ▶ puffs out its frills to look threatening.

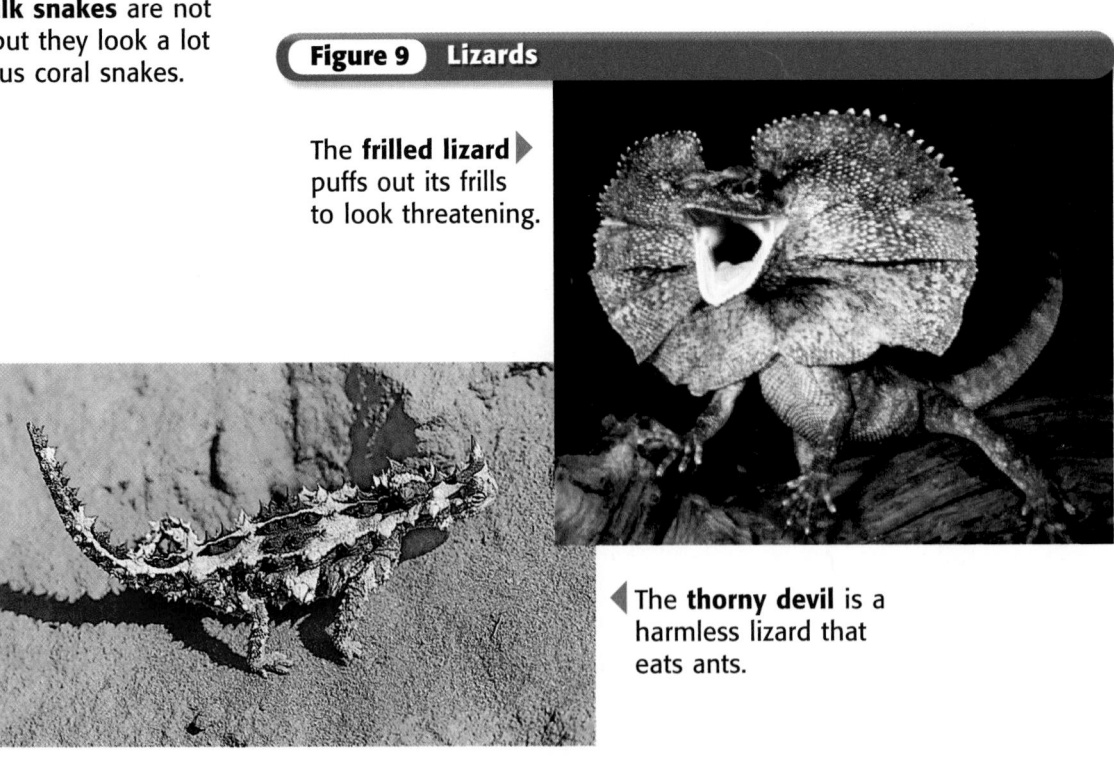

◀ The **thorny devil** is a harmless lizard that eats ants.

Tuataras

Tuataras (TOO uh TAH ruhs) live on only a few islands off the coast of New Zealand. **Figure 10** shows a tuatara in the wild. Tuataras look similar to lizards and can grow to be about 60 cm long.

Although tuataras look like lizards, the two reptiles are classified in different groups. Unlike many lizards, tuataras do not have visible ear openings on the outside of the body. Also, unlike many reptiles, tuataras are most active when the temperature is low. During the day, tuataras rest and absorb sunlight. At night, they search for food.

✓ **Reading Check** Name two unique traits of tuataras.

Figure 10 *Tuataras have survived without changing for about 150 million years.*

SECTION Review

Summary

● Reptiles have thick, scaly skin that protects them from drying out. They also have lungs, and they depend on their surroundings to control their body temperature.

● A tough shell keeps the amniotic egg of a reptile from drying out and protects the embryo.

● Reptiles reproduce by internal fertilization.

● There are four groups of modern reptiles. The groups are: turtles and tortoises, crocodiles and alligators, lizards and snakes, and tuataras.

Using Vocabulary

1. In your own words, write a definition for the term *amniotic egg*.

Understanding Key Ideas

2. Reptiles are well adapted to living on land because they
   a. have thick, scaly skin.
   b. have lungs.
   c. lay amniotic eggs.
   d. All of the above

3. A reptile can lay its egg on land because
   a. the egg's shell prevents fertilization.
   b. the egg's shell keeps moisture inside the egg.
   c. the egg's shell keeps carbon dioxide inside the egg.
   d. the egg's shell allows water to leave the egg.

4. Name three ways that an amniotic egg protects reptile embryos.

5. Explain how most reptiles reproduce.

6. Name the four groups of modern reptiles, and give an example of each kind.

7. What special adaptations do snakes have for eating?

Math Skills

8. Suppose that a sea turtle lays 104 eggs. If 50% of the hatchlings reach the ocean alive and 25% of those survivors reach adulthood, how many adults result from the eggs?

Critical Thinking

9. **Applying Concepts** Mammals give birth to live young. The embryo develops inside the female's body. Which parts of a reptilian amniotic egg could a mammal do without? Explain.

10. **Analyzing Ideas** Rattlesnakes can't see well, but they can detect temperature changes of three-thousandths of a degree Celsius. How could this ability be useful to the snakes?

SCiLINKS.®

NSTA
Developed and maintained by the National Science Teachers Association

For a variety of links related to this chapter, go to www.scilinks.org

Topic: Reptiles
SciLinks code: HSM1299

OBJECTIVES

Make a model of a fish that has a swim bladder.

Describe how swim bladders help fish maintain buoyancy.

MATERIALS

- balloon, slender
- container for water at least 15 cm deep
- cork, small
- PVC pipe, 12 cm in length, 3/4 in. diameter
- rubber band
- water

SAFETY

Floating a Pipe Fish

Bony fishes control how deep or shallow they swim by using a special structure called a *swim bladder*. As gases are absorbed and released by the swim bladder, the fish's body rises or sinks in the water. In this activity, you will make a model of a fish that has a swim bladder. Your challenge will be to make the fish rest in one place, without rising or sinking, halfway between the top of the water and the bottom of the container. You will probably need to do several trials and a lot of observing and analyzing.

Ask a Question

1. Think of a question about the amount of gases needed to keep a pipe fish model resting halfway between the top of the water and the bottom of the container.

Form a Hypothesis

2. Formulate a testable hypothesis that answers your question. Estimate how much air you will need in the balloon so that your pipe fish will come to rest halfway between the top of the water and the bottom of the container. Will you need to inflate the balloon halfway, a small amount, or all the way?

Test the Hypothesis

3 Inflate your balloon. Hold the neck of the balloon so that no air escapes, and push the cork into the end of the balloon. If the cork is properly placed, no air should leak out when the balloon is held underwater.

4 Place your swim bladder inside the pipe, and place a rubber band along the pipe as shown. The rubber band will keep the swim bladder from coming out of either end of the pipe.

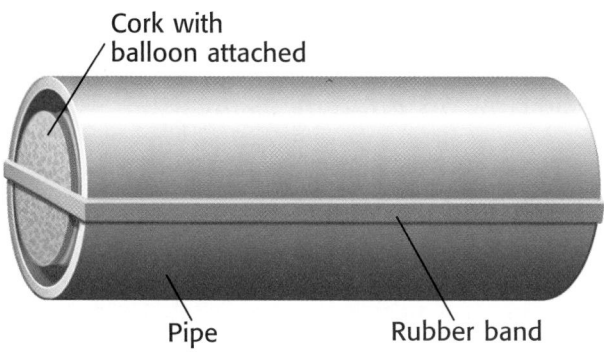

Cork with balloon attached

Pipe   Rubber band

5 Place your pipe fish in the water, and note where the fish rests without sinking or rising. Record your observations.

6 If the pipe fish does not rest at the halfway point, take it out of the water, adjust the amount of air in the balloon, and try again.

7 You can release small amounts of air from the bladder by carefully lifting the neck of the balloon away from the cork. You can add more air by removing the cork and blowing more air into the balloon. Keep adjusting and testing until your fish rests, without sinking or rising, halfway between the bottom of the container and the top of the water.

Analyze the Results

1 **Analyzing Results** Was the estimate you made in your hypothesis the correct amount of air your balloon needed to rest at the halfway point? Explain your answer.

2 **Examining Data** Consider the length and volume of the entire pipe fish. How much air was needed to make the fish rest at the correct place? State your answer as a proportion or percentage. (Remember that the volume of a cylinder is equal to the height or length of the cylinder multiplied by the area of its base.)

3 **Evaluating Data** Analyze the information you gathered in this activity to explain how the structure of a fish's swim bladder complements its function. What are some limitations to your model?

Draw Conclusions

4 **Interpreting Information** Some fast-swimming fishes, such as sharks, and marine mammals, such as whales and dolphins, do not have a swim bladder. Do research at a library or on the Internet to find out how these animals keep from sinking to the bottom of the ocean. Can you find any reasons why a swim bladder would be helpful to them? How could a swim bladder cause problems for these animals?

Chapter Review

USING KEY TERMS

1 In your own words, write a definition for each of the following terms: *metamorphosis, amniotic egg,* and *vertebrate.*

2 Use the following terms in the same sentence: *lung, gills,* and *tadpole.*

For each pair of terms, explain how the meanings of the terms differ.

3 *endotherm* and *ectotherm*

4 *swim bladder* and *lateral line*

UNDERSTANDING KEY IDEAS

Multiple Choice

5 Which of the following structures is not present in some chordates?

 a. a tail

 b. a backbone

 c. a notochord

 d. a hollow nerve cord

6 Which fishes do not have jaws?

 a. sharks, skates, and rays

 b. hagfish and lampreys

 c. bony fishes

 d. None of the above

7 Both amphibians and reptiles

 a. have lungs.

 b. have gills.

 c. breathe only through their skin.

 d. have amniotic eggs.

8 Metamorphosis occurs in

 a. fishes and amphibians.

 b. amphibians.

 c. fishes, amphibians, and reptiles.

 d. amphibians and reptiles.

9 Both bony fishes and cartilaginous fishes have

 a. fins.

 b. an oily liver.

 c. a swim bladder.

 d. skeletons made of bone.

Short Answer

10 How do amphibians breathe?

11 What characteristics allow fishes to live in the water?

12 What characteristics allow reptiles to live on land?

13 How does a reptile embryo in an amniotic egg get oxygen?

14 Describe the stages of metamorphosis in a frog.

15 What two things are present in all vertebrates but not in some chordates?

16 Describe the three kinds of amphibians.

17 Explain why amphibians can be effective ecological indicators.

18 Concept Mapping Use the following terms to create a concept map: *dinosaur, turtle, reptiles, amphibians, fishes, shark, salamander,* and *vertebrates.*

19 Applying Concepts If the air temperature outside is 43°C and the ideal body temperature of a lizard is 38°C, would you most likely find that lizard in the sun or in the shade? Explain your answer.

20 Identifying Relationships Describe three characteristics of amphibian skin. How do amphibians use their skin? How does the structure of amphibian skin relate to its function?

21 Making Inferences Suppose that you have found an animal that has a backbone and gills, but the animal does not seem to have a notochord. Is the animal a chordate? How can you be sure of your answer?

22 Analyzing Processes If you found a shark that lacks the muscles needed to pump water over its gills, what would that information tell you about how the shark lives?

23 Forming Hypotheses If you found a reptile that you did not recognize, what questions would you need to ask to determine which of the four reptile groups the reptile belongs to? Explain how you could form a hypothesis about the reptile's group based on the answers to these questions.

INTERPRETING GRAPHICS

The graph below shows body temperatures of two organisms and the ground temperature of their environment. Use the graph to answer the questions that follow.

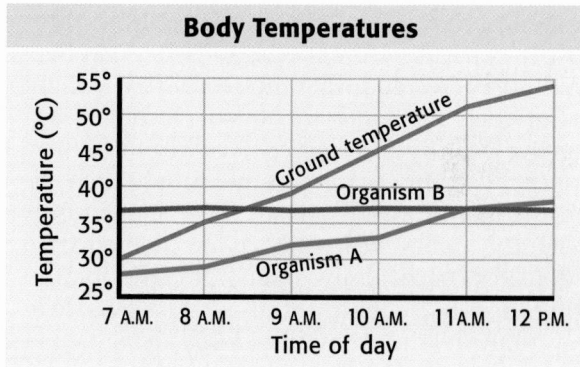

Body Temperatures

24 How do the body temperatures of organism A and organism B change as the ground temperature changes?

25 Which of these organisms is most likely an ectotherm? Explain your answer.

26 Which of these organisms is most likely an endotherm? Explain your answer.

Standardized Test Preparation

Read each of the passages below. Then, answer the questions that follow each passage.

Passage 1 Only a few kinds of fishes are endotherms. These fishes depend on their environment for most of their body heat but can heat parts of their bodies by internal cell activity. Because they can produce heat within their bodies, endothermic fishes can hunt for prey in extremely chilly water. As a result, they face limited competition with other fishes because few species of fishes can live in cold areas. Yet endothermic fishes pay a high price for their ability to <u>inhabit</u> very cold areas. Producing heat by internal cell activity uses a lot of energy. For this reason, some fishes, such as swordfish, marlin, and sailfish, have adaptations that let the fishes heat only a few body parts. These fishes warm only their eyes and brain. Heating just these parts of the body uses less energy than heating the entire body does.

1. In this passage, what does *inhabit* mean?
   A to use energy in
   B to live in
   C to heat up
   D to eat in

2. Which of the following statements is a fact according to the passage?
   F Tuna always live in very cold areas.
   G Most prey live in extremely chilly water.
   H Some fishes that heat parts of their body can hunt for prey in cold water.
   I The eyes and the brain are the most important parts of a fish's body.

3. Which fishes can heat certain parts of their bodies and hunt in extremely cold waters?
   A most fishes
   B swordfish, marlin, and sailfish
   C no fishes
   D tropical fishes

Passage 2 Fishes are quicker and much more <u>maneuverable</u> than most ships and submarines. So, why aren't ships and submarines built more like fishes—with tails that flap back and forth? This question caught the attention of some scientists at MIT, and they decided to build a robot model of a bluefin tuna. This robot fish is 124 cm long. It contains six motors and has a skeleton made of aluminum ribs and hinges. These scientists think that if ships were designed more like the bodies of fishes, the ships would use much less energy than they currently use. If the new design does require less energy—and thus less fuel—the ships will save money.

1. According to the passage, what is one reason that scientists are designing a robot model of a fish?
   A Designing ships to work more like fishes' bodies might save energy.
   B Fishes' bodies do not use much energy.
   C Bluefin tuna have tails that move back and forth.
   D Designing ships to work more like fishes' bodies could reduce ocean pollution levels.

2. What does *maneuverable* probably mean?
   F able to move easily
   G able to move like a robot
   H made of aluminum
   I fuel efficient

3. Which of the following statements is a fact according to the passage?
   A Fueling ships is very expensive.
   B Some MIT scientists built a robot fish.
   C Designing a ship that moves like a fish will save money.
   D Fishes are 124 cm long.

The chart below shows the kinds of amphibians that are threatened or endangered in the United States. Use the chart below to answer the questions that follow.

Threatened and Endangered Amphibian Species in the United States

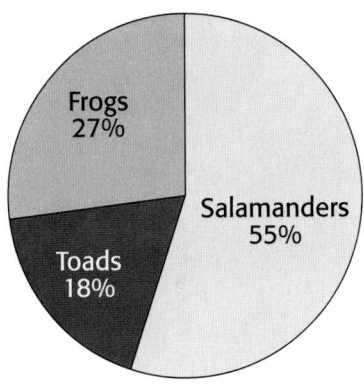

Source: U.S. Fish and Wildlife Service.

1. Which amphibian group has the most threatened and endangered species in the United States?

   A frogs

   B salamanders

   C toads

   D caecilians

2. If the total number of threatened and endangered amphibian species in the United States is 22, how many species of salamanders are threatened or endangered?

   F 4

   G 6

   H 12

   I 22

3. If the total number of threatened and endangered amphibian species in the United States is 22, how many more species of salamanders are threatened or endangered than species of frogs and toads?

   A 12

   B 10

   C 6

   D 2

4. Which of the following statements about the pie chart is true?

   F The chart does not have any information about amphibians outside of the United States.

   G The chart shows that amphibians outside of the United States are also endangered and threatened.

   H The chart shows that frogs are more sensitive to environmental pollution than toads are.

   I The chart shows that amphibians are ecological indicators.

Read each question below, and choose the best answer.

1. Suppose that a snake eats a mouse that has one-third more mass than the snake does. If the snake has a mass of 4.2 kg, what is the mass of the mouse?

   A 1.4 kg

   B 2.8 kg

   C 4.2 kg

   D 5.6 kg

2. One year, there were 2,000 salamanders in a state park. If the population decreased by 8% each year for 3 years, what would the salamander population be after the 3-year period?

   F 1,520 salamanders

   G 1,557 salamanders

   H 1,840 salamanders

   I 1,898 salamanders

3. What is the volume of a rectangular fish tank that is 1 m wide, 2 m long, and 1.5 m tall?

   A 3 m²

   B 3 m³

   C 4.5 m

   D 4.5 m³

Science in Action

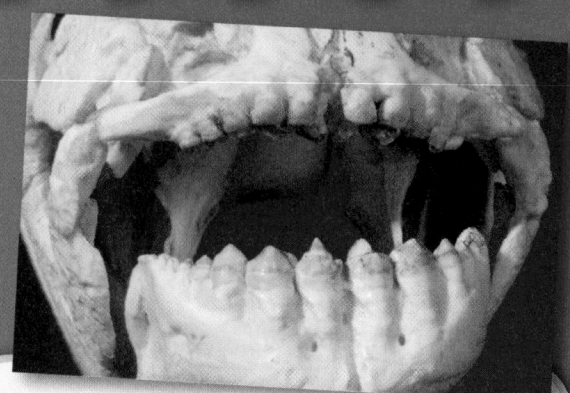

Weird Science

Fish That Eat Fruit

Have you ever thought about fish teeth? You probably know what shark teeth look like. So, you shouldn't be surprised that fish teeth are usually very different from your own teeth. But take a look at the fish shown above. This fish is *frugivorous* (froo JIV uh ruhs), which means that it eats fruit. Some frugivorous fishes live in the Amazon River in Brazil. Parts of the Amazon River basin flood for much of the year, which causes the water level to rise and spread under fruit trees. Fruit falls from the trees into the water, so these fishes have evolved to eat fruit. Eating fruit requires teeth that can bite and chew, just like human teeth. So, these fishes' teeth have evolved into a form that is similar to human teeth!

Math ACTIVITY

Suppose the water level in a river rose 8 m when it was flooded. At this time, 4 meters of a certain tree are above water. This tree is 16 m tall. What was the original depth of the river before it was flooded?

Scientific Discoveries

Giant Crocodiles

Have you ever watched a crocodile at a zoo or on TV? Even when crocodiles are resting and not moving, we instinctively know to be wary of them. Most crocodiles today are about 3.5 m long. But Paul Sereno recently discovered a fossil in the Sahara that shows how big crocodiles used to be. The fossil crocodile that Sereno found is 12 m—about the length of seven adult humans lying head to toe! This crocodile lived 110 million years ago. Sereno's find answered many questions raised by other crocodile fossils that had been found before. Now scientists can estimate the animal's huge size with accuracy.

Language Arts ACTIVITY

WRITING SKILL Imagine that you discovered an animal living today that was 4 times the size of an average organism of that species. For example, imagine discovering a rattlesnake that was 4 times the size of an average rattlesnake. Write a story about your discovery, and include your ideas about how size affected the life of the organism.

Dagmar Werner

Raising Iguanas At the Carara Biological Preserve in Costa Rica, thousands of iguana eggs sit just below the surface of the Earth in sun-heated incubators. Why would anyone bother to incubate thousands of iguana eggs? Dr. Dagmar Werner leads this project in an attempt to restore an iguana population that has been severely reduced in the past several decades. The lizards have suffered from the effects of hunting, pollution, and habitat destruction by people who clear the rain forest for farming.

Dr. Werner combined her captive-breeding program at the preserve with an education program that shows farmers that there is more than one way to make a profit from the rain forest. She encourages local farmers to raise iguanas, which can be released into the wild or sold for food, instead of raising cattle (and cutting down the rain forest to do so). Known as the "chicken of the trees," the iguana has been a favored source of meat among native rain-forest inhabitants for thousands of years. Farmers not only profit from the sale of iguana meat but also produce iguana leather and other handicrafts.

According to Dr. Werner, "Many locals have never thought of wild animals as creatures that must be protected in order to survive. That's why so many go extinct." To get her message across, Dr. Werner has established an organization that sponsors festivals and education seminars in local communities. These activities promote the traditional appeal of the iguana, increase civic pride in the animal, and heighten awareness about the iguana's economic importance.

Social Studies ACTIVITY

WRITING SKILL Dr. Werner's project helps the iguanas because it takes hunting pressure off the iguana population. But it also helps farmers by increasing their income and preventing habitat destruction. Can you think of a project that could help both the people and the environment in your own community? Write a three-paragraph description of an environmental project that could work for your community.

go.hrw.com

To learn more about these Science in Action topics, visit go.hrw.com and type in the keyword **HL5VR1F**.

Current Science

Check out Current Science® articles related to this chapter by visiting go.hrw.com. Just type in the keyword **HL5CS16**.

Birds and Mammals

About the PHOTO

Why would an animal covered in stiff plates of armor jump up to 1.2 m (4 ft) high—straight up in the air? Armadillos jump when they are frightened. Jumping sometimes surprises and scares off predators, giving the armadillo a chance to run away. Armadillos are mammals.

PRE-READING ACTIVITY

FOLDNOTES **Table Fold** Before you read the chapter, create the FoldNote entitled "Table Fold" described in the **Study Skills** section of the Appendix. Label the columns of the table fold with "Characteristics" and "Kinds." Label the rows with "Birds," "Placental mammals," and "Monotremes and marsupials." As you read the chapter, write examples of each topic under the appropriate column.

START-UP ACTIVITY

Let's Fly!

How do birds fly? This activity will give you a few hints.

Procedure

1. Carefully fold a **piece of paper** to make a paper airplane. Make the folds even and the creases sharp.

2. Throw the plane through the air very gently. What happened?

3. Take the same plane, and throw it more forcefully. Did anything change?

4. Reduce the size of the wings by folding them inward toward the center crease. Make sure the two wings are the same size and shape.

5. Throw the airplane two more times. Throw it gently at first, and then throw it with more force. What happened each time?

Analysis

1. Analyze what effect the force of your throw has on the paper airplane's flight. Do you think forces of different strengths affect bird flight in a similar way? Explain your answer.

2. What happened when the wings were made smaller? Why do you think this happened? Do you think wing size affects the way a bird flies? Explain your answer.

3. Based on your results, how would you design and throw the perfect paper airplane?

Characteristics of Birds

What do a powerful eagle, a lumbering penguin, and a dainty finch have in common? They all have feathers, wings, and a beak, which means they are all birds.

Birds share many characteristics with reptiles. Like reptiles, birds are vertebrates. Birds' feet and legs are covered by thick scales like those that cover reptiles' bodies. Also, bird eggs have an amniotic sac and a shell, just as reptile eggs do.

Birds also have many unique characteristics. For example, bird eggs have harder shells than reptile eggs do. And as shown in **Figure 1,** birds have feathers and wings. They also have a horny beak instead of jaws with teeth. Also, birds can use heat from activity in their cells to maintain a constant body temperature.

Feathers

One familiar characteristic of birds is their feathers. Feathers help birds stay dry and warm, attract mates, and fly.

Preening and Molting

Birds take good care of their feathers. They use their beaks to spread oil on their feathers in a process called **preening.** The oil is made by a gland near the bird's tail. The oil helps water-proof the feathers and keeps them clean. When feathers wear out, birds replace them by molting. **Molting** is the process of shedding old feathers and growing new ones. Most birds shed their feathers at least once a year.

READING WARM-UP

Objectives

● Describe two kinds of feathers.

● Describe how a bird's diet, breathing, muscles, and skeleton help it fly.

● Explain how lift works.

● Describe how birds raise their young.

Terms to Learn

preening   contour feather
molting   lift
down feather   brooding

READING STRATEGY

Prediction Guide Before reading this section, write the title of each heading in this section. Next, under each heading, write what you think you will learn.

preening in birds, the act of grooming and maintaining their feathers

molting the shedding of an exoskeleton, skin, feathers, or hair to be replaced by new parts

▼Hummingbird

▲ Great blue heron

▼ Toucan

Figure 1 *There are about 10,000 known species of birds on Earth today.*

Two Kinds of Feathers

Birds have two main kinds of feathers—down feathers and contour feathers. **Down feathers** are fluffy feathers that lie next to a bird's body. These feathers help birds stay warm. When a bird fluffs its down feathers, air is trapped close to the body. Trapping air keeps body heat near the body. **Contour feathers** are stiff feathers that cover a bird's body and wings. Their colors and shapes help some birds attract mates. Contour feathers have a stiff central shaft with many side branches, called *barbs*. The barbs link together to form a smooth surface, as shown in **Figure 2.** This streamlined surface helps birds fly.

✓ Reading Check What is the function of a bird's down feathers? (*See the Appendix for answers to Reading Checks.*)

High-Energy Animals

Birds need a lot of energy to fly. To get this energy, their bodies break down food quickly. This process generates a lot of body heat. In fact, the average body temperature of a bird is 40°C—three degrees warmer than yours. Birds cannot sweat to cool off if they get too hot. Instead, they lay their feathers flat and pant like dogs do.

Fast Digestion

Because birds need a lot of energy, they eat a lot. Hummingbirds need to eat almost constantly to get the energy they need! Most birds eat insects, nuts, seeds, or meat. These foods are high in protein and fat. A few birds, such as geese, eat grass, leaves, and other plants. Birds have a unique digestive system to help them get energy quickly. **Figure 3** shows this system. Modern birds don't have teeth, so they can't chew. Instead, food goes from the mouth to the crop. The *crop* stores food until it moves to the gizzard. Many *gizzards* have small stones inside. These stones grind up the food so that it can be easily digested in the intestine. This grinding action is similar to what happens when we chew our food.

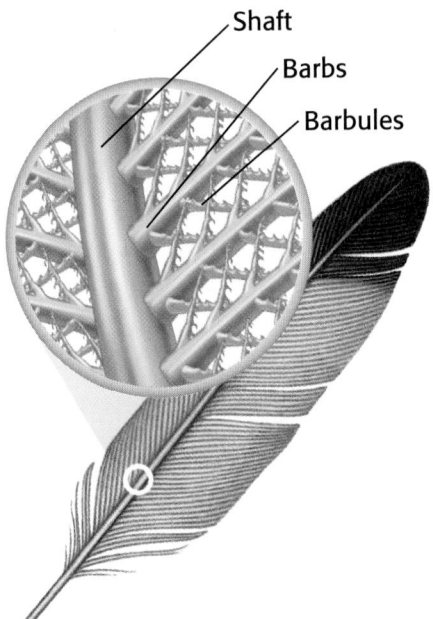

Figure 2 *The barbs of a contour feather have cross branches called* barbules. *Barbs and barbules give the feather strength and shape.*

Shaft
Barbs
Barbules

down feather a soft feather that covers the body of young birds and provides insulation to adult birds

contour feather one of the most external feathers that cover a bird and that help determine its shape

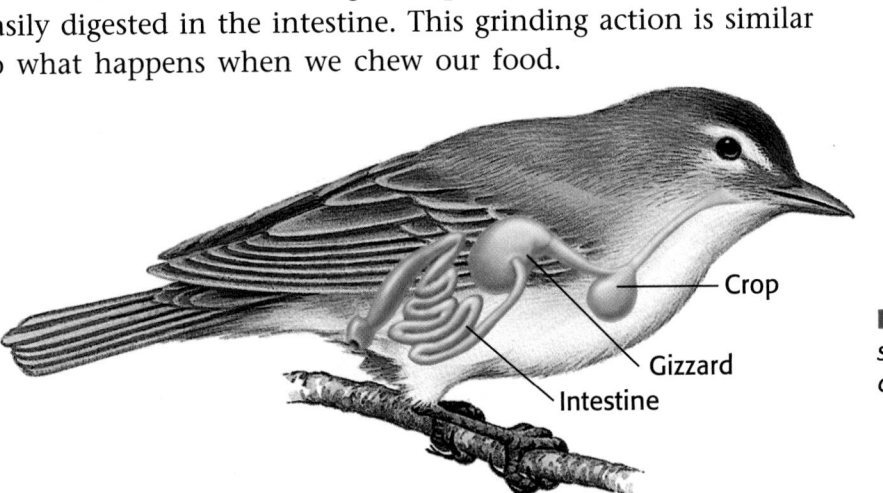

Crop
Gizzard
Intestine

Figure 3 *A bird's digestive system helps the bird rapidly change food into usable energy.*

Flying

Most birds can fly. Even flightless birds, such as ostriches, have ancestors that could fly. So, it is not surprising that birds have many adaptations for flight. The most obvious characteristic related to flight is the wings. But birds also have lightweight bodies. And they have powerful flight muscles and a rapidly beating heart. The fast heart rate helps birds get plenty of oxygen-rich blood to the flight muscles. **Figure 4** describes many bird characteristics that are important for flight.

Reading Check How does a bird's heart help the bird fly?

Figure 4 **Flight Adaptations of Birds**

Most birds have **large eyes** and excellent eyesight. Large eyes allow birds to see objects and food from a distance. Some birds, such as hawks and eagles, can see 8 times better than humans can see!

Lung

Air sacs

Birds have special organs called **air sacs** attached to their lungs. The air sacs store air. Because of the stored air, a bird's lungs have a continuous supply of air—whether the bird is inhaling or exhaling.

Birds have a **rapidly beating heart.** The heart pumps a fast, steady stream of oxygen-rich blood to the flight muscles. In small birds, the heart beats almost 1,000 times a minute! (Your heart beats about 70 times a minute.)

Wing shape is related to how a bird flies. Short, rounded wings allow a bird to quickly turn, drop, and pull up, much like the way a fighter plane moves. Long, narrow wings are best for soaring, just as a glider does.

Bird skeletons are compact and strong. Some of the vertebrae, ribs, and hipbones are fused together. For this reason, bird skeletons are more rigid than those of other vertebrates. A **rigid skeleton** allows a bird to move its wings powerfully and efficiently.

MATH PRACTICE

Flying Far

A certain bird flies 970 km (600 mi) when it goes south for the winter. It flies north each summer. If this bird lives for 8 years, how many total kilometers will it fly during migrations in its lifetime?

Keel

Birds that fly have **powerful flight muscles** that move the wings. These muscles are attached to a large breastbone called a **keel.** The keel anchors the flight muscles. It allows the bird to flap its wings with force and speed.

Cross supports

Birds have **hollow bones.** So, birds have much lighter skeletons than other vertebrates do. The bones have thin cross supports that give strength, much like the cross supports of many bridges.

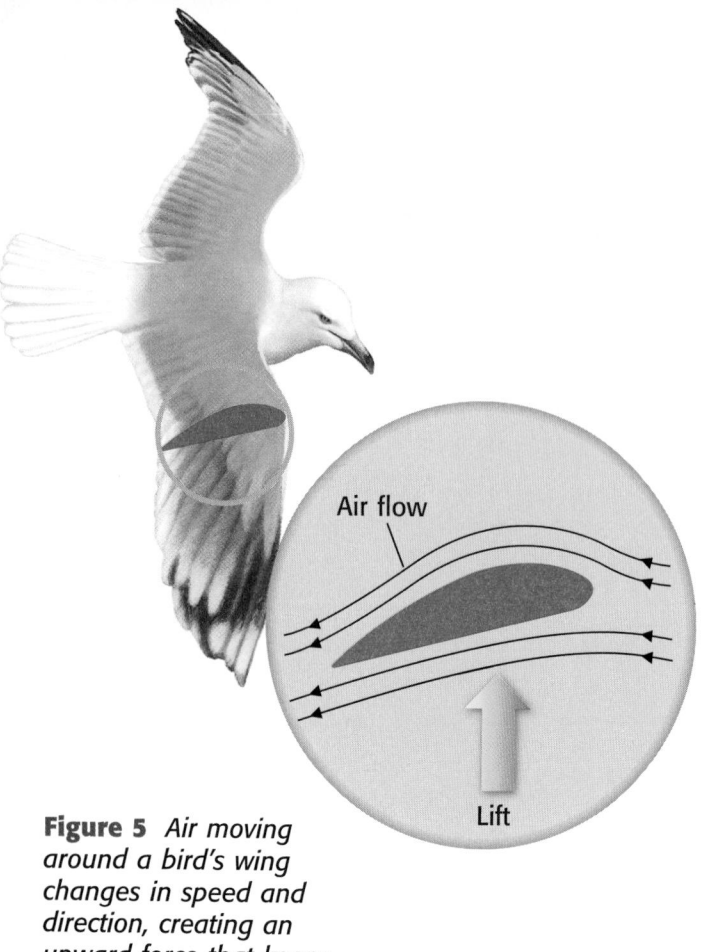

Getting off the Ground

How do birds overcome gravity to fly? Birds flap their wings to get into the air. They keep flapping to push themselves through the air. They are able to stay in the air because their wings cause lift. **Lift** is an upward force on a bird's wings.

As a bird flies through the air, some of the air is forced over the top of its wings. Some air is forced underneath the wings. **Figure 5** shows this airflow. A bird's wings are curved on top. The shape of the wings affects the air around them. As air flows over and under a bird's wings, the air's speed and direction change. These changes in the air's speed and direction affect the wings in a way that creates lift, the upward force that acts on the wings.

Lift is affected by flying speed and by wing shape. The faster a bird flies, the greater the lift. Also, the larger the wing is, the greater the lift. Birds with large wings can glide for long distances.

Figure 5 *Air moving around a bird's wing changes in speed and direction, creating an upward force that keeps a bird in the air.*

lift an upward force on an object that moves in a fluid

brooding to sit on and cover eggs to keep them warm until they hatch; to incubate

Raising Baby Birds

The way that birds reproduce is similar to the way that reptiles reproduce. Like reptiles, birds reproduce sexually by internal fertilization. Both birds and reptiles lay amniotic eggs in which there is a growing embryo. But unlike most reptiles, birds must keep their eggs warm for the embryos to live and grow.

Nests

Most birds build nests in which they lay their eggs. **Figure 6** shows a bird's nest with eggs in it. Birds keep their eggs warm by brooding. **Brooding** is the act of sitting on eggs and using body heat to keep them warm. Birds sit on their eggs until the eggs hatch. For some birds, such as gulls, the job of brooding is shared by both males and females. In many species of songbirds, the female broods the eggs, and the male brings food to the brooding female. In a few species, the male broods the eggs.

Reading Check How does the process of brooding keep a bird's eggs warm?

Figure 6 *This robin's nest is only one example of a bird's nest. Birds build nests of many different shapes and sizes.*

Precocial and Altricial

Some birds, such as chickens and ducks, are active soon after they hatch. These active chicks are *precocial* (pree KOH shuhl). Precocial chicks are covered with downy feathers. As soon as they can stand up, the chicks follow their parents around. These chicks depend on a mother for warmth and protection, but they can walk, swim, and feed themselves.

Some birds, such as hawks and songbirds, are weak and helpless for a while after hatching. These weak chicks are *altricial* (al TRISH uhl). When they hatch, they have no feathers and their eyes are closed. They cannot walk or fly. Their parents must keep them warm and feed them for several weeks. **Figure 7** shows a parent feeding its altricial chicks.

Figure 7 *Parents of altricial chicks bring food to the nest.*

SECTION Review

Summary

- Birds have feathers, a beak, wings, and a constant body temperature.
- Down feathers keep birds warm. Contour feathers help birds fly and attract mates.
- Birds must eat a high-energy diet to get energy for flying.
- Lightweight bodies and strong muscles help birds fly. Air sacs help them get enough oxygen to fly.
- Wings create lift as they cut through the air. Lift pushes the wings up to keep a bird in the air.
- Birds keep their eggs warm in a nest by brooding. When the chicks hatch, they are precocial or altricial.

Using Key Terms

1. Use each of the following terms in a separate sentence: *lift* and *brooding*.

For each pair of terms, explain how the meanings of the terms differ.

2. *down feather* and *contour feather*

3. *preening* and *molting*

Understanding Key Ideas

4. Which of the following is NOT a flight adaptation in birds?
   a. hollow bones
   b. air sacs
   c. down feathers
   d. rapidly beating heart

5. What do birds eat? Describe the path taken by a bird's food as it moves through the bird's digestive system.

6. How does the air around a bird's wings cause lift?

7. Explain the difference between precocial chicks and altricial chicks.

8. Name two ways that birds use their contour feathers. Name one way that birds use their down feathers.

Math Skills

9. Suppose that a bird that weighs 325 g loses 40% of its body weight during migration. What is the bird's weight when it reaches its destination?

Critical Thinking

10. **Analyzing Ideas** Why can't people fly without the help of technology? Name at least four human body characteristics that are poorly adapted for flight.

11. **Applying Concepts** Some people use the phrase "eats like a bird" to describe someone who does not eat very much. Does using the phrase in this way show an accurate understanding of a bird's eating habits? Why or why not?

SCILINKS®

NSTA

Developed and maintained by the National Science Teachers Association

For a variety of links related to this chapter, go to www.scilinks.org

Topic: Bird Characteristics
SciLinks code: HSM0167

Kinds of Birds

There are about 10,000 species of birds on Earth. Birds vary in color, shape, and size. They range in mass from the 1.6 g bee hummingbird to the 125 kg North African ostrich. The ostrich is almost 80,000 times more massive than the hummingbird!

Scientists group living bird species into 28 different orders. Songbirds, such as robins or bluebirds, make up the largest order. This order includes about 60% of all bird species. But birds are often grouped into four nonscientific categories: flightless birds, water birds, perching birds, and birds of prey. These categories don't include all birds. But they do show how different birds can be.

Flightless Birds

Not all birds fly. Most flightless birds do not have the large keel that anchors birds' flight muscles. Instead of flying, some flightless birds run quickly to move around. Others are skilled swimmers. **Figure 1** shows three kinds of flightless birds.

Figure 1 Flightless Birds

▼ Unlike other flightless birds, **penguins** have a large keel and very strong flight muscles. Their wings have changed over time to become flippers. They flap these wings to "fly" underwater.

◀ The **ostrich** is the largest living bird. It can reach a height of 2.5 m and a mass of 125 kg. An ostrich's two-toed feet look almost like hoofs. These birds can run up to about 60 km/h.

The **kiwi** is a small, chicken-sized bird from New Zealand. Kiwis sleep during the day. At night, they hunt for worms, caterpillars, and berries. ▶

Figure 2 Water Birds

The **blue-footed booby** is a tropical water bird. These birds have an elaborate courtship dance that includes raising their feet one at a time.

Male **wood ducks** have beautiful plumage to attract females. Like all ducks, they are strong swimmers and flyers.

The **common loon** can make very deep dives and remain underwater for several minutes while searching for fish.

Water Birds

Many flying birds are also comfortable in the water. These water birds include cranes, ducks, geese, swans, pelicans, and loons. These birds usually have webbed feet for swimming or long legs for wading. **Figure 2** above shows three different water birds.

Water birds find food both in the water and on land. Many of these birds eat plants, invertebrates, or fish. Some water birds have a rounded, flat beak for eating plants or small invertebrates. Others have a long, sharp beak for catching fish.

✔️ **Reading Check** What are the two kinds of beaks that are common in water birds? (*See the Appendix for answers to Reading Checks.*)

For another activity related to this chapter, go to **go.hrw.com** and type in the keyword **HL5VR2W**.

Perching Birds

Perching birds have special adaptations for resting on branches. Songbirds, such as robins, warblers, and sparrows, make up a large part of this group of birds. When a perching bird lands in a tree, its feet automatically close around a branch. If the bird falls asleep while it is perching, its feet will stay closed. The sleeping bird will not fall off the branch. **Figure 3** shows three kinds of perching birds.

✓ **Reading Check** What happens to a perching bird that falls asleep while it is perching on a branch?

Figure 3 Perching Birds

▼ **Parrots** have special feet for perching and climbing. They open seeds and slice fruit with their strong, hooked beak.

▲ **Chickadees** are lively, little birds that often visit garden feeders. They can dangle underneath a branch while hunting for insects, seeds, or fruits.

Most tanagers are tropical birds, but the **scarlet tanager** spends the summer in North America. The male is red, but the female is a yellow green color that blends into the trees. ▶

Birds of Prey

Birds of prey hunt and eat other vertebrates. These birds may eat insects or other invertebrates in addition to mammals, fish, reptiles, and birds. Take a look at the birds in **Figure 4.** Birds of prey have sharp claws on their feet and a sharp, curved beak. These traits help the birds catch and eat their prey. Birds of prey also have very good vision. Most of them hunt during the day, as the osprey does. But most owls hunt at night.

Figure 4 Birds of Prey

◀ Owls, such as this **northern spotted owl,** are the only birds of prey that hunt at night. They have a strong sense of hearing to help them find their prey in the dark.

◀ **Ospreys** eat fish. They fly over the water and catch fish with their clawed feet.

SECTION Review

Summary

● Some flightless birds do not have a large keel as other birds do. Many flightless birds are fast runners or swimmers.

● Many water birds have webbed feet for swimming or long legs for wading.

● Perching birds have feet that automatically close around a branch.

● Birds of prey have a sharp beak and claws for catching and eating their prey.

Understanding Key Ideas

1. Which of the following groups of birds includes birds that do NOT have a large keel?
   a. flightless birds
   b. water birds
   c. perching birds
   d. birds of prey

2. Why do some water birds have long legs?
   a. for swimming
   b. for wading
   c. for running
   d. for flying

3. Most birds of prey have very good eyesight. Why do you think good vision is important for these birds?

4. To which group of birds do songbirds belong? Name three examples of songbirds.

Math Skills

5. How quickly could an ostrich, running at a speed of 60 km/h, run a 400 m track event?

Critical Thinking

6. **Predicting Consequences** Would it be helpful for a duck to have the feet of a perching bird? Explain why or why not.

7. **Making Inferences** How could being able to run 60 km/h be helpful for an ostrich?

Characteristics of Mammals

What do you have in common with a bat, a donkey, a giraffe, and a whale? You're all mammals!

Mammals live in the coldest oceans, the hottest deserts, and almost every place in between. The tiniest bats weigh less than a cracker, and the blue whale can weigh more than twenty school buses. Though mammals vary in many ways, all of the approximately 5,000 modern species share certain characteristics. **Figure 1** shows a few of the many types of mammals.

The First Mammals

Fossil evidence indicates that about 280 million years ago, reptiles called *therapsids* (thuh RAP sihdz) existed. These animals had characteristics of both reptiles and mammals. True mammals appeared soon after. Mammals appeared in the fossil record more than 225 million years ago. They were about the size of mice. These animals were endotherms, so they were able to keep their body temperature constant. They did not depend on their surroundings to keep warm. This trait allowed them to look for food at night and to avoid being eaten by dinosaurs during the day.

When the dinosaurs died out, more land and food were available for the mammals. These resources allowed mammals to spread out and live in many different environments.

Figure 1 *Even though they look very different, all of these animals are mammals.*

▲ Mandrill baboon

▲ Rhinoceros

▼ Beluga whale

Figure 2 *Like all mammals, this calf drinks its mother's milk for its first meals.*

Common Characteristics

Dolphins, monkeys, and elephants have hair and specialized teeth, just as you do! Mammals share these and many other characteristics that make them unlike other animals.

Making Milk

All mammals have mammary glands. No other animal has these glands. **Mammary glands** are structures that make milk. However, only mature females produce milk in their mammary glands. All female mammals feed their young with this milk. **Figure 2** shows a cow nursing her calf.

All milk is made of water, proteins, fats, and sugars. But the amount of each nutrient is different in different milk. For example, human milk has half the fat and twice the sugar of cow's milk.

Reading Check What is milk made of? (*See the Appendix for answers to Reading Checks.*)

Breathing Air

All animals need oxygen to get energy from their food. Like birds and reptiles, mammals use lungs to get oxygen from the air. But mammals have a muscle that helps them get air. The **diaphragm** (DIE uh FRAM) is a large muscle that helps bring air into the lungs. It lies at the bottom of the rib cage.

Endothermic

As oxygen helps to break down a mammal's food, energy is released. This energy keeps mammals warm. Has a dog or cat ever sat in your lap? If so, then you have felt how warm a mammal's body is. Like birds, mammals are endotherms. Their internal chemical changes keep their body temperature constant. The ability to stay warm helps them survive in cold areas and stay active when the weather is cool.

mammary gland in a female mammal, a gland that secretes milk

diaphragm a dome-shaped muscle that is attached to the lower ribs and that functions as the main muscle in respiration

Diaphragm Demo

1. Place your hand under your rib cage to feel your abdominal muscles (which are indirectly connected to your diaphragm). Breathe in and out.
2. Write down what your hand feels as you breathe.
3. Place your hand under your rib cage again. Contract your abdominal muscles, and try breathing. Then, relax your abdominal muscles, and breathe.
4. Write down what happens.
5. Explain your observations. Then, draw a picture of how the diaphragm moves.

Hair

Mammals have a few characteristics that keep them from losing their body heat. One way they stay warm is by having hair. Mammals are the only animals that have hair. All mammals—even whales—have hair. Mammals that live in cold climates, such as the fox in **Figure 3,** usually have thick coats of hair. These thick coats are called *fur.* Large mammals that live in warm climates, such as elephants, do not need warm fur. Humans have hair all over their bodies, as apes do. But human body hair is shorter and more fine than ape hair.

Most mammals also have a layer of fat under their skin to keep them warm. This fat helps trap heat in the body. Whales and other mammals that live in cold oceans have an especially thick layer of fat. This thick layer of fat is called *blubber.*

Figure 3 *The thick fur of this arctic fox helps its body stay warm in the coldest winters.*

Specialized Teeth

Another unique mammal characteristic is specialized teeth. Modern birds don't have teeth. Fish and reptiles have teeth, but usually all of their teeth are identical. Mammals have teeth with different shapes and sizes for different jobs. Also, mammals replace their original baby teeth with a permanent set.

Your own mouth has three kinds of teeth. You have cutting teeth, called *incisors,* in the front of your mouth. Most people have four incisors on top and four on the bottom. Next to them are stabbing teeth, called *canines.* These help you grab and hold on to food. Your flat, grinding back teeth are *molars.*

Each kind of tooth helps mammals eat a certain kind of food. Meat-eating mammals have large canines to help them eat prey. Plant-eating mammals have larger incisors and molars to help them bite and grind plants. **Figure 4** shows the teeth of a meat-eating mammal and a plant-eating mammal.

Figure 4 *Mountain lions have sharp canine teeth for grabbing their prey. Horses have sharp incisors in front for cutting plants and flat molars in the back for grinding plants.*

Sexual Reproduction

All mammals reproduce sexually. Sperm fertilize eggs inside the female's body. Though there are a few exceptions, most mammals give birth to live young. Newborn mammals stay with at least one parent until they are grown. Mammal parents care for and protect their young during this time. **Figure 5** shows a brown bear with her young.

Reading Check How long does a young mammal stay with at least one parent?

Large Brains

A mammal's brain is much larger than that of most other animals that are the same size. This large brain allows mammals to learn and think quickly. It also allows mammals to respond quickly to events around them.

Mammals use vision, hearing, smell, touch, and taste to find out about the world around them. The importance of each sense often depends on a mammal's surroundings. For example, mammals that are active at night depend on their hearing more than on their vision.

Figure 5 *A mother bear will attack anything that threatens her cubs.*

SECTION Review

Summary

- Early mammals were small. Being endothermic helped them survive.
- Mammals have mammary glands, a diaphragm, and hair.
- All mammals are endotherms. Most have a layer of fat under their skin for extra warmth.
- Mammals have specialized teeth.
- Mammals reproduce sexually and raise young.
- Mammals have large brains and learn quickly.

Using Key Terms

1. Use each of the following terms in a separate sentence: *mammary gland* and *diaphragm.*

Understanding Key Ideas

2. Large brains help mammals survive by allowing them
   a. to think and learn quickly.
   b. to maintain their body temperature.
   c. to have hair all over their body.
   d. to depend on all of the senses equally.

3. What does a diaphragm do?

4. Name three characteristics that are unique to mammals.

5. Describe three characteristics that help mammals stay warm.

6. How are mammal teeth different from reptile and fish teeth?

7. How do mammals reproduce?

Math Skills

8. What is the mass of a 90,000 kg whale in grams? in milligrams?

Critical Thinking

9. **Making Inferences** Early endothermic mammals could be active at night. If this protected them from certain dinosaurs, were the dinosaurs endothermic? Explain.

10. **Applying Concepts** How could the teeth of a skull give you clues about a mammal's diet?

Developed and maintained by the National Science Teachers Association

For a variety of links related to this chapter, go to www.scilinks.org

Topic: Characteristics of Mammals
SciLinks code: HSM0259

103

Placental Mammals

Both elephants and mice begin life by developing inside a mother. Elephants need up to 23 months to develop inside the mother. But mice need only a few weeks!

Mammals are divided into groups based on how they develop. The groups are placental mammals, monotremes, and marsupials. Most mammals are placental mammals. A **placental mammal** is a mammal whose embryos develop inside the mother's body. The embryos grow in an organ called the *uterus*. An organ called the *placenta* attaches the embryos to the uterus. The placenta carries food and oxygen from the mother's blood to the embryo and carries wastes away from the embryo.

The time in which an embryo develops within the mother is called a **gestation period** (jes TAY shuhn PIR ee uhd). This period lasts a different amount of time for each kind of placental mammal. In humans, this period lasts about 9 months.

Living placental mammals are divided into 18 orders. The most common orders are described on the following pages.

Anteaters, Armadillos, and Sloths

A few mammals have unique backbones that have special connections between the vertebrae. This group includes anteaters, armadillos, and sloths. These mammals are sometimes called "toothless mammals," but only anteaters have no teeth. The others have small teeth. Most mammals in this group eat insects they catch with their long, sticky tongues. **Figure 1** shows two mammals from this group.

Figure 1 **Anteaters, Armadillos, and Sloths**

▼ **Giant anteaters** never destroy the nests of the insects they eat. They open a nest and eat a few insects. Then, they move on to another nest.

▲ **Armadillos** eat insects, frogs, mushrooms, and roots. Threatened armadillos roll up into a ball, or they may jump to scare a predator. They are protected by their tough plates.

Figure 2 Insectivores

The **star-nosed mole** has sensitive feelers on its nose. These help the mole find earthworms to eat. Moles have poor vision.

Hedgehogs live throughout Europe, Asia, and Africa. Their spines keep them safe from most predators.

Insectivores

Insectivores make up another group of mammals that eat insects. This group includes moles, shrews, and hedgehogs. Most insectivores are small and have long, pointed noses that help them smell their food. They have small brains and simple teeth. Some eat worms, fish, frogs, lizards, and small mammals in addition to insects. **Figure 2** shows two insectivores.

Rodents

More than one-third of mammal species are rodents. Rodents live on every continent except Antarctica. They include squirrels, mice, rats, guinea pigs, porcupines, and chinchillas. Most rodents have sensitive whiskers. They all have one set of incisors in the upper jaw. Rodents gnaw and chew so much that these teeth wear down. But that doesn't stop their chewing—their incisors grow continuously! **Figure 3** shows two rodents.

placental mammal a mammal that nourishes its unborn offspring through a placenta inside its uterus

gestation period in mammals, the length of time between fertilization and birth

Reading Check What do rodents do with their sharp incisors? *(See the Appendix for answers to Reading Checks.)*

Figure 3 Rodents

Like all rodents, **porcupines** have gnawing teeth.

The **capybara** (KAP i BAH ruh) of South America is the largest rodent in the world. Females have a mass of up to 70 kg—as much as a grown man.

Figure 4 Rabbits, Hares, and Pikas

Pikas are small animals that live high in the mountains. Pikas gather plants and pile them into "haystacks" to dry. In the winter, pikas use the dry plants for food and insulation.

▲ The large ears of this **black-tailed jack rabbit** help it hear well and keep cool. They also work with a sensitive nose and large eyes to detect predators.

Rabbits, Hares, and Pikas

Rodents are similar to a group of mammals that includes rabbits, hares, and pikas (PIE kuhz). **Figure 4** shows two members of this group. Like rodents, they have sharp gnawing teeth. But unlike rodents, they have two sets of incisors in their upper jaw. Also, their tails are shorter than rodents' tails.

✓ **Reading Check** How are rabbits different from rodents?

Flying Mammals

Bats are the only mammals that fly. **Figure 5** shows two kinds of bats. Bats are active at night. They sleep in protected areas during the day. Most bats eat insects or other small animals. But some bats eat fruit or plant nectar. A few bats, called *vampire bats,* drink the blood of birds or mammals.

Most bats use echoes to find their food and their way. Using echoes to find things is called *echolocation*. Bats make clicking noises as they fly. The clicks echo off trees, rocks, and insects. Bats know what is around them by hearing these echoes.

Figure 5 Flying Mammals

◀ **Fruit bats,** also called *flying foxes,* live in tropical regions. They pollinate plants as they go from one plant to another, eating fruit.

▲ The **spotted bat** is found in parts of the American Southwest. Like most bats, it eats flying insects. It uses its large ears during echolocation.

Figure 6 Carnivores

▼ **Coyotes** are members of the dog family. They live throughout North America and in parts of Central America.

▼ **Walruses,** like all pinnipeds, eat in the ocean but sleep and mate on land. They use their huge canines in courtship displays, for defense, and to climb onto ice.

Carnivores

Mammals that have large canine teeth and special molar teeth for slicing meat are called *carnivores*. Many mammals in this group eat only meat. But some mammals in this group are omnivores or herbivores that eat plants. For example, black bears eat grass, nuts, and berries and rarely eat meat. The carnivore group includes cats, dogs, otters, bears, raccoons, and hyenas. *Pinnipeds*, a group of fish-eating ocean mammals, are also carnivores. Seals, sea lions, and walruses are pinnipeds. **Figure 6** shows two carnivores.

Trunk-Nosed Mammals

Elephants are the only living mammals that have a trunk. The trunk is a combination of an upper lip and a nose. An elephant uses its trunk in the same ways we use our hands, lips, and nose. An elephants uses its trunk to put food in its mouth. It also uses its trunk to spray water on its back to cool off. **Figure 7** shows two species of elephants.

Figure 7 Trunk-Nosed Mammals

◀ Elephants are social. The females live in herds of mothers, daughters, and sisters. These elephants are **African elephants.**

These **Indian elephants** have smaller ears and tusks than African elephants do. ▶

Hoofed Mammals

Horses, pigs, deer, and rhinoceroses are some of the many mammals that have thick hoofs. A *hoof* is a thick, hard pad that covers a mammal's toe. The hoof is similar to a toenail or a claw, but it covers the entire toe. Most hoofed mammals are fast runners. They also have large, flat molars. These teeth help hoofed mammals grind the plants that they eat.

Hoofed mammals include two orders—odd-toed and even-toed. Odd-toed hoofed mammals have one or three toes on each foot. Horses and zebras have one large, hoofed toe. Rhinoceroses have three toes. Even-toed hoofed mammals have two or four toes on each foot. Pigs, cattle, camels, deer, and giraffes are even-toed. **Figure 8** shows some hoofed mammals.

Figure 8   Hoofed Mammals

Tapirs are large, odd-toed mammals. They live in forests in Central America, South America, and Southeast Asia. Tapirs are active mostly at night.

Giraffes are the tallest living mammals. They have long necks and long legs and are even-toed. They eat leaves from tall trees.

Camels are even-toed mammals. The hump of a camel is a large lump of fat that provides energy for the camel when food is scarce. Camels can live without drinking water for a long time, so they can live in very dry places.

Figure 9 Cetaceans

▼ **Spinner dolphins** spin like a football when they leap from the water. Like all dolphins, they are intelligent and highly social.

Cetaceans

Cetaceans (suh TAY shuhnz) are a group of mammals made up of whales, dolphins, and porpoises. All cetaceans live in the water. **Figure 9** shows two kinds of cetaceans. At first glance, they may look more like fish than like mammals. But unlike fish, cetaceans have lungs and nurse their young.

Most of the largest whales are toothless. They strain tiny, shrimplike animals from sea water. However, dolphins, porpoises, sperm whales, and killer whales all have teeth to help them eat. Like bats, these animals use echolocation to find fish and other animals.

Manatees and Dugongs

The smallest group of mammals that live in the water are manatees (MAN uh TEEZ) and dugongs (DOO gawngz). This group includes three species of manatees and the dugong. Manatees and dugongs use their front flippers and a tail to swim slowly through the water. **Figure 10** shows a manatee.

Manatees and dugongs live along ocean coasts and in rivers. They are large animals that eat mostly seaweed and water plants. These animals spend all of their time in the water, but they lift their noses from the water to breathe air.

✓ Reading Check How much of their time do dugongs and manatees spend in the water?

▼ **Humpback whales** are toothless. Like all toothless whales, they strain sea water through special plates in their mouth. These plates are made of a substance called *baleen*. The baleen traps tiny sea life for the whale to eat.

Figure 10 *Manatees are also called* sea cows.

Section 4 Placental Mammals **109**

Primates

Scientists classify prosimians, monkeys, apes, and humans as *primates*. These animals have five fingers on each hand and five toes on each foot. Most have flat fingernails instead of claws. Primates have a larger brain than most other mammals the same size have. They are considered highly intelligent mammals. Primates also have unique arrangements of body parts that help them do complicated things. For example, all primates have forward-facing eyes that can focus on a single point. And primates have opposable thumbs, which allow them to hold objects.

Many primates live in trees. They climb with their grasping hands and feet. Flexible shoulder joints allow them to swing between branches. They eat leaves and fruits, and some primates even hunt animals. **Figure 11** shows some primates.

✓ **Reading Check** What traits help many primates live in trees?

CONNECTION TO
Language Arts

WRITING SKILL **Funky Monkey** In many parts of the world, cities have taken over natural, nonhuman primate habitat. Some nonhuman primates have moved into the city and adopted new lifestyles. Macaques have been known to steal ice-cream cones from children or hop on a bus for a short ride! Write a story in your **science journal** about people living with monkeys in a city.

Figure 11 Primates

Orangutans and other apes often walk upright. Apes usually have larger brains and bodies than monkeys do.

Spider monkeys, like many monkeys, have grasping tails. Their long arms, legs, and tails help them move among the trees.

▲ The **proboscis monkey** has an enormous nose! The males have larger noses than the females do. That difference makes some scientists wonder if the male's nose is used to attract females.

Summary

- Placental mammals develop inside the mother during a gestation period. Placental mothers nurse their young after birth.
- Anteaters, armadillos, and sloths have unique backbones.
- Moles, shrews, and hedgehogs eat insects.
- Squirrels, rats, and porcupines are rodents.
- Rabbits, hares, and pikas are similar to rodents but have an extra pair of incisors.
- Bats are flying mammals.

- Cats, dogs, otters, bears, sea lions, and walruses are in the carnivore group.
- Horses, zebras, pigs, deer, rhinoceroses, and giraffes are hoofed mammals.
- Elephants are trunk-nosed mammals.
- Whales and porpoises are cetaceans.
- Manatees and dugongs are large, slow mammals that live in the water.
- Prosimians, monkeys, apes, and humans are primates.

Using Key Terms

1. Use the following terms in the same sentence: *placental mammal* and *gestation period*.

Understanding Key Ideas

2. Which mammals live entirely in the water?
   a. manatees, dugongs, cetaceans, and pinnipeds
   b. only manatees and dugongs
   c. only cetaceans
   d. manatees, dugongs, and cetaceans

3. A placental mammal's embryo
   a. develops in the uterus.
   b. develops in the placenta.
   c. develops in a pouch.
   d. develops in a leathery egg.

4. Could you tell a horse from a deer just by looking at their feet? Explain.

5. Give one example of each type of placental mammal described in the section.

Critical Thinking

6. **Making Inferences** What is a gestation period? Why do you think elephants have a longer gestation period than mice do?

7. **Identifying Relationships** Manatees may look a little like pinnipeds, but they are more closely related to elephants. In what ways is a manatee more like an elephant than like a pinniped?

Interpreting Graphics

Use the picture of the animal below to answer the questions that follow.

8. To which placental mammal group does this animal belong? How can you tell?

9. Why can't this animal be a rodent?

10. Why can't this animal be a primate?

SC*i*LINKS®

NS**TA**
Developed and maintained by the
National Science Teachers Association

For a variety of links related to this chapter, go to www.scilinks.org

Topic: Kinds of Mammals
SciLinks code: HSM0832

Monotremes and Marsupials

Did you know that some mammals hatch from eggs and that others spend the first months of life in a mother's pouch? Only a few kinds of mammals develop this way.

Placental mammals are born as well-developed young. But monotremes hatch from eggs. And newborn marsupials still need months of development in a mother's pouch.

Monotremes

A **monotreme** (MAHN oh TREEM) is a mammal that lays eggs. Monotremes have all the traits of mammals, including mammary glands, a diaphragm, and hair. And like other mammals, they keep their body temperature constant.

A female monotreme lays eggs with thick, leathery shells. She uses her body's energy to keep the eggs warm. After the young hatch, the mother takes care of them and feeds them milk. Monotremes do not have nipples as other mammals do. Baby monotremes lick milk from the skin and hair around their mother's mammary glands.

Echidnas

There are only three living species of monotremes. Two of these species are echidnas (ee KID nuhz). Echidnas are about the size of a house cat. Their large claws and long snouts help them dig ants and termites out of insect nests. **Figure 1** shows the two species of echidnas.

monotreme a mammal that lays eggs

Figure 1   Echidnas

The **long-beaked echidna** lives in New Guinea.

The **short-beaked echidna** lives in Australia and New Guinea.

Figure 2 *When underwater, a duckbill platypus closes its eyes and ears. It uses its bill to find food.*

The Platypus

The only other living monotreme is the platypus. Only one species of platypus lives today. This animal lives in Australia. It looks very different from other mammals. In fact, when scientists outside Australia were first sent the remains of a platypus, they thought they were the victims of a practical joke. **Figure 2** shows a platypus.

The platypus is a swimming mammal that lives and feeds in rivers and ponds. It has webbed feet and a flat tail to help it move through the water. It uses its flat, rubbery bill to search for food. It uses its claws to dig tunnels in riverbanks. The platypus lays its eggs in these tunnels.

✓ **Reading Check** How does a platypus use its bill? (*See Appendix for answers to Reading Checks.*)

Marsupials

You probably know that kangaroos carry their young in a pouch. Kangaroos and other mammals with pouches are **marsupials** (mahr SOO pee uhlz). Like all mammals, marsupials have mammary glands, hair, and specialized teeth. Unlike monotremes, marsupials give birth to live young. Marsupial development is unique because newborn marsupials continue their development in a mother's pouch. The newborns stay in the pouch for several months.

There are about 280 species of marsupials living today. Most of them live in Australia, New Guinea, and South America. The only living marsupial native to North America is the opossum (uh PAHS uhm).

CONNECTION TO Environmental Science

Pouches in Peril Australia's marsupials are in danger. Many other species have been artificially introduced into Australia's unique ecosystems. These new species are competing with native marsupials for food and living space. One way to stop the introduction of new species into Australia is to educate people about the dangers of species introduction. Make a poster that explains why people should be careful not to release pets or foreign animals into the wild.

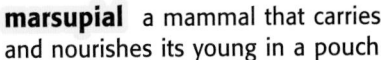

marsupial a mammal that carries and nourishes its young in a pouch

The Pouch

Marsupials are born at an early stage of development. They are born just days or weeks after fertilization. At birth, kangaroos are as small as bumblebees. **Figure 3** shows a newborn kangaroo. Newborn marsupials are hairless, and only their front limbs are well developed. They use these limbs to drag themselves through their mother's fur to the pouch on her belly. Many do this without any help from their parents. Inside the pouch are mammary glands. The newborn climbs in, latches onto a nipple, and starts drinking milk. Young kangaroos, called *joeys,* stay in the mother's pouch for several months. When joeys first leave the pouch, they do so for only short periods of time.

✓ Reading Check How big is a newborn kangaroo?

Figure 3 *This newborn kangaroo will stay in its mother's pouch for several months as it continues developing.*

Kinds of Marsupials

You may be familiar with the well-known marsupials shown in **Figure 4.** But many marsupials are not as familiar. Have you heard of wallabies, bettongs, and numbats? Most marsupials live in and around Australia. Tasmanian devils, which are marsupials that eat other animals, live on the island of Tasmania. Tree kangaroos, which spend much of their time in trees, live in the rain forests of Queensland and New Guinea.

Figure 4 **Kinds of Marsupials**

▼ **Koalas** sleep for about 18 hours each day. They eat eucalyptus leaves.

◀ Young **kangaroos** that no longer live in their mother's pouch return to the pouch if there is any sign of danger.

When in danger, an ▶ **opossum** will lie perfectly still. It "plays dead" so predators will ignore it.

Endangered and Extinct Marsupials

The number of living marsupial species is decreasing. At least 22 of Australia's native mammal species have become extinct in the last 400 years. Many more are currently in danger. When Europeans came to Australia in the 18th and 19th centuries, they brought animals such as rabbits, cats, and foxes. Many of these species escaped into the wild. Some, such as rabbits, now compete with marsupials for food. Others, such as foxes, now prey on marsupials. The marsupials have no adaptations to protect themselves from these exotic species.

Exotic species are not the only threat to marsupials in Australia. Habitat destruction also threatens marsupials. And the Tasmanian tiger, shown in **Figure 5,** was hunted by people who saw it as a threat to their livestock. Today, conservation efforts across Australia are helping to protect the unique marsupials that live there.

Figure 5 *The Tasmanian tiger, a marsupial carnivore, is probably extinct. There have been no official sightings since 1936.*

SECTION Review

Summary

- Monotremes lay eggs instead of bearing live young. They produce milk but do not have nipples.
- The three living species of monotremes are two kinds of echidnas and the platypus.
- Marsupials give birth to live young, but the young are not fully developed when born. They finish developing in a mother's pouch.
- Many marsupials are endangered or extinct.

Using Key Terms

1. Use each of the following terms in a separate sentence: *monotreme* and *marsupial.*

Understanding Key Ideas

2. Which of the following characteristics is shared by monotremes and marsupials?

   a. The young hatch from eggs.

   b. Some species of both live in South America.

   c. Females have no nipples.

   d. Females produce milk.

3. What are the two kinds of monotremes?

4. Name three kinds of marsupials.

5. What has caused many marsupials in Australia to become endangered or extinct?

6. How are monotremes different from all other mammals? How are they similar?

Math Skills

7. What percentage of the approximately 5,000 known species of mammals are monotremes?

Critical Thinking

8. **Making Comparisons** How are monotremes similar to birds? How are they different?

9. **Making Inferences** Why do you think opossums play dead when they are in danger?

SC*L*INKS.

Developed and maintained by the National Science Teachers Association

For a variety of links related to this chapter, go to www.scilinks.org

Topic: Monotremes and Marsupials
SciLinks code: HSM0990

Model-Making Lab

What? No Dentist Bills?

When you and I eat, we must chew our food well. Chewing food into small bits is the first part of digestion. But birds don't have teeth. How do birds make big chunks of food small enough to begin digestion? In this activity, you will develop a hypothesis about how birds digest their food. Then, you will build a model of a bird's digestive system to test your hypothesis.

Ask a Question

1 Formulate a question about how a bird's digestive system can break down food even though the bird has no teeth. Your question may be something such as, "How are birds able to begin digestion without using teeth?"

Form a Hypothesis

2 Look at the diagram below of a bird's digestive system. Form a hypothesis about how birds digest their food without using teeth.

OBJECTIVES

Make a model of a bird's digestive system.

Test your model, using birdseed.

MATERIALS

- bags, plastic, sealable, various sizes (several)
- birdseed
- gravel, aquarium
- scissors (or other materials as needed)
- straw, plastic drinking
- string
- tape, transparent
- water

SAFETY

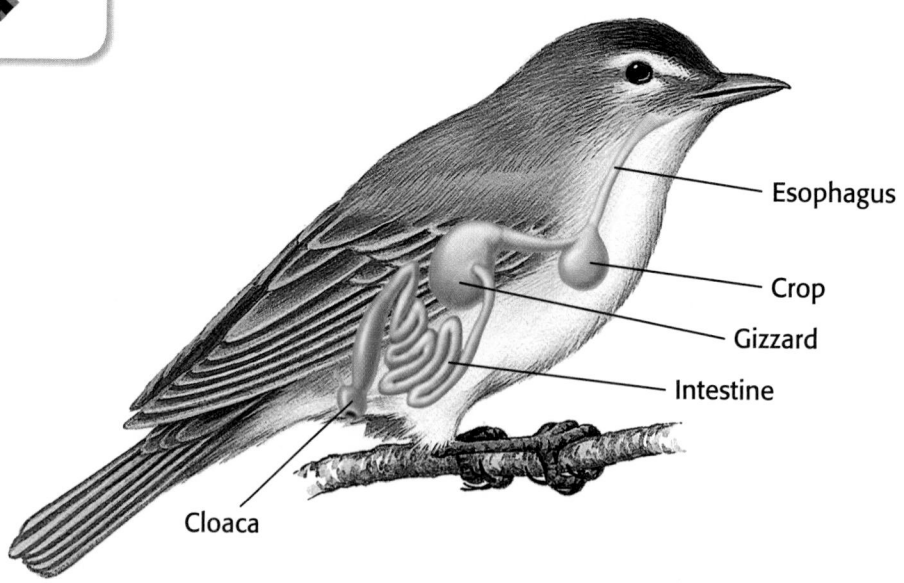

Esophagus

Crop

Gizzard

Intestine

Cloaca

Test the Hypothesis

3 Design a model of a bird's digestive system. Include in your design as many of the following parts as possible: esophagus, crop, gizzard, intestine, and cloaca.

4 Obtain a plastic bag and the other materials you need from your teacher. Build your model.

5 Test your hypothesis by sending birdseed through your model digestive system.

Analyze the Results

1 **Describing Events** Did your model digestive system grind the birdseed? Describe what happened to the birdseed as it moved through the system.

2 **Analyzing Results** Which part of your model was most helpful in grinding? Which part of a real bird's digestive system is represented by this part of your model?

3 **Recognizing Patterns** Does the amount of material added to your model gizzard change the gizzard's ability to work effectively? Explain your answer.

Draw Conclusions

4 **Drawing Conclusions** Birds can break down food without using teeth. What conclusions can you draw about how they do this?

5 **Evaluating Results** Analyze the strengths and weaknesses of your hypothesis based on your results. Was your hypothesis correct? Explain your answer.

6 **Evaluating Models** What are some limitations of your model? How do you think you could improve it?

Applying Your Data

Did you know that scientists have found "gizzard stones" with fossilized dinosaur skeletons? Look in the library or on the Internet for information about the evolutionary relationship between dinosaurs and birds. List the similarities you find between the two types of animals.

Chapter Review

USING KEY TERMS

1 Use the following terms in the same sentence: *mammary gland, placental mammal, marsupial,* and *monotreme*.

Complete each of the following sentences by choosing the correct term from the word bank.

brooding   gestation period
contour feathers lift
diaphragm   molting
down feathers   preening

2 The ___ is a muscle that helps animals breathe.

3 The embryos of placental mammals develop during a ___.

4 Birds grow new feathers as a part of the ___ process.

5 ___ help keep birds warm by trapping air near the body.

6 Birds use the ___ process to keep their eggs warm.

7 ___ form a streamlined surface that helps birds fly.

UNDERSTANDING KEY IDEAS

Multiple Choice

8 Both birds and reptiles
  a. lay eggs.
  b. brood their young.
  c. have air sacs.
  d. have feathers.

9 Only mammals
  a. use internal fertilization.
  b. nurse their young.
  c. lay eggs.
  d. have teeth.

10 Which of the following is NOT a primate?
  a. a lemur
  b. a human
  c. a pika
  d. a chimpanzee

11 Monotremes do NOT
  a. have mammary glands.
  b. care for their young.
  c. give birth to live young.
  d. have hair.

12 What is lift?
  a. air that travels over the top of a wing
  b. a force provided by a bird's air sacs
  c. the upward force on a wing that keeps a bird in the air
  d. a force created by pressure from the diaphragm

Short Answer

13 How are contour feathers and down feathers helpful to birds?

14 How do flightless birds, water birds, perching birds, and birds of prey differ from each other?

15 Which trait allowed early mammals to look for food at night?

16 Describe two ways that animals introduced to Australia threaten its native marsupials.

17 Which kind of marsupial lives in North America?

18 Which group of placental mammals includes the pinnipeds?

19 How is a bird's digestive system related to its ability to fly?

20 How can mammalian milks differ?

CRITICAL THINKING

21 **Concept Mapping** Use the following terms to create a concept map: *monotremes, endotherms, birds, mammals, mammary glands, placental mammals, marsupials, feathers,* and *hair*.

22 **Making Comparisons** The embryos of birds and monotremes get energy from the yolk of the egg. How do developing embryos of marsupials and placental mammals get the nutrition they need?

23 **Making Inferences** Most bats and cetaceans use echolocation. Why don't these mammals rely solely on sight to hunt and sense their surroundings?

24 **Applying Concepts** Suppose you are making a museum display of bird skeletons, but the skeletons have lost their labels. How can you separate the skeletons of flightless birds from those of birds that fly? Will you be able to tell which birds flew rapidly and which birds could soar? Explain your answer.

25 **Making Inferences** Suppose that you saw a bird flying above you. The bird has long, skinny legs and a long, sharp beak. To which group of birds do you think this bird probably belongs? Explain your answer.

INTERPRETING GRAPHICS

The illustrations below show three different kinds of bird feet. Use these illustrations to answer the questions that follow.

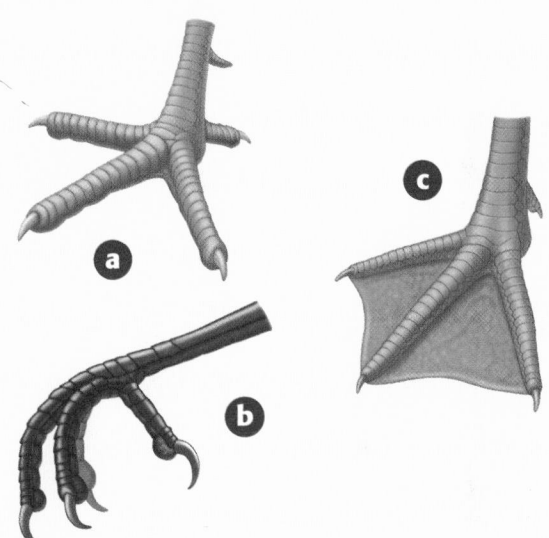

26 Which foot most likely belongs to a water bird? Explain your choice.

27 Which foot most likely belongs to a perching bird? Explain your choice.

28 To what kind of bird do you think the remaining foot could belong? Explain your answer.

Standardized Test Preparation

Read each of the passages below. Then, answer the questions that follow the passage.

Passage 1 A naked mole rat is a rodent that looks like an overcooked hot dog. This nearly blind mammal is 7 cm long and lives in hot, dry regions of Kenya, Ethiopia, and Somalia. This animal has some strange characteristics. Its grayish pink skin hangs loosely on its body. The loose skin allows the naked mole rat to move easily through its home of narrow underground tunnels. At first glance, a naked mole rat appears to be hairless. Though the naked mole rat doesn't have fur, it does have hair. Its sensitive whiskers guide it through the dark tunnels. Hair between its toes acts as tiny brooms to sweep up loose dirt. The naked mole rat even has hair on its lips that keeps dirt from getting into its mouth while it digs.

1. Why does the naked mole rat have hair on its lips?
   A to sweep loose dirt from its tunnels
   B to find its way through the tunnels
   C to keep dirt from getting into its mouth
   D to move easily through its tunnels

2. Which of the following is a characteristic of naked mole rats?
   F thick fur
   G poor eyesight
   H large toes
   I hairless bodies

3. How do naked mole rats navigate through their tunnels?
   A strong sense of hearing
   B sensitive grayish pink skin
   C tasting the dirt along their tunnel walls
   D sensitive whiskers

Passage 2 For centuries, people have tried to imitate a spectacular feat that birds perfected millions of years ago—flight. The Wright brothers were not able to fly in a heavier-than-air flying machine until 1903. Their first flight lasted only 12 s, and they traveled only 37 m. Although modern airplanes are much more sophisticated, they still rely on the same principles of flight. The sleek body of a jet is shaped to battle drag, while the wings are shaped to battle Earth's gravity. In order to take off, airplanes must pull upward with a force greater than gravitational force. This upward force is called lift.

1. According to the passage, how are modern airplanes similar to the flying machine invented by the Wright brothers?
   A Both look like birds.
   B Both rely on the same principles of flight.
   C Both are sophisticated.
   D Both have sleek body shapes.

2. Which part of a jet's design works against Earth's gravity?
   F the sleek shape
   G the wings
   H the heavier-than-air weight
   I the tail

3. Based on the passage, which of the following statements is a fact?
   A The Wright brothers were the first people to try building a flying machine.
   B Modern airplanes can fly more easily than birds can fly.
   C The Wright brothers' first flight lasted for only 12 s.
   D Overcoming gravity with lift is the only force needed to fly an airplane.

The graph below shows how many Calories a small dog uses while running at different speeds. Use this graph to answer the questions that follow.

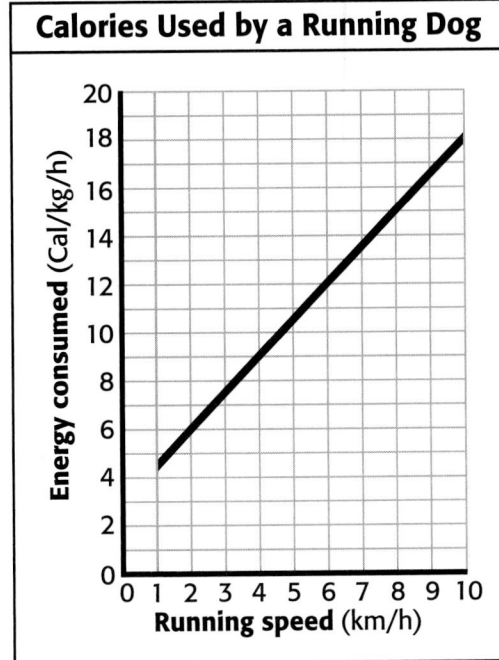

Calories Used by a Running Dog

1. As the dog runs faster, how does the amount of energy it consumes per hour change?
   A The energy consumed increases.
   B The energy consumed decreases.
   C The energy consumed remains the same.
   D Changes in the energy consumed are not related to changes in the dog's speed.

2. How much energy per hour will this dog consume if it is running at 4 km/h?
   F 1 Cal/kg/h
   G 6 Cal/kg/h
   H 9 Cal/kg/h
   I 10 Cal/kg/h

3. How much energy per hour will this dog consume if it is running at 9 km/h?
   A 4 Cal/kg/h
   B 16 Cal/kg/h
   C 16.5 Cal/kg/h
   D 18 Cal/kg/h

4. Energy consumed is given in Calories per kilogram of body mass per hour. If the dog has a mass of 6 kg and is running at 7 km/h, how many Calories per hour will it use?
   F 2.25 Cal/h
   G 19.5 Cal/h
   H 72 Cal/h
   I 81 Cal/h

MATH

Read each question below, and choose the best answer.

1. A bird flying at 35 km/h consumes 60 Cal per gram of body mass per hour. If the bird has a mass of 50 g, how many Calories will it use if it flies for 30 min at this speed?
   A 1,050 Cal
   B 1,500 Cal
   C 1,750 Cal
   D 3,000 Cal

2. Cecilia's kitten weighed 2 lb when she got him. The kitten gained about 0.5 lb each month for the next 11 months. How much did the kitten weigh at the end of the 11 months?
   F less than 6 lb
   G between 6 lb and 7 lb
   H between 7 lb and 8 lb
   I more than 8 lb

3. Gina bought two birds for $31.96, a box of birdseed for $1.69, and some bird treats for $3.98. What is the best estimate of the total cost of Gina's purchase?
   A between $35 and $36
   B between $36 and $37
   C between $37 and $38
   D more than $38

4. On each of 5 days, Leo saw 5 rabbits. He saw 3 rabbits on each of 2 other days. How could you find C, the total number of rabbits he saw?
   F $C = (5 \times 5) + (2 \times 3)$
   G $C = (5 + 5) \times (2 + 3)$
   H $C = 5 + 5 + 2 + 3$
   I $C = (5 \times 5) - (2 \times 3)$

Science in Action

Science, Technology, and Society

Dolphins in the Navy

Did you know that some dolphins work for the Navy? One way that dolphins help the Navy's Marine Mammal Program is by detecting underwater mines, which are bombs that drift underwater. Most mines explode when a large object bumps into them. Dolphins can find mines safely by using a natural sonar system, called *echolocation,* which allows them to sense their surroundings even in murky waters. When dolphin finds a mine and alerts a person, experts can deactivate the mine.

Math ACTIVITY

Suppose that each dolphin in the Navy's program is trained for 5 years and each trained dolphin works for 25 years. If 10 dolphins began training each year for 10 years, how many would be working at the end of those 10 years? How many would still be in training?

Weird Science

Sounds of the Lyrebird

Imagine that you are hiking in an Australian forest. You hear many different bird calls, beaks snapping, and wings rustling. There must be many species of birds around, right? Not if a lyrebird is nearby—all those sounds could be coming from just one bird! The lyrebird imitates the songs of other birds. In fact, lyrebirds can imitate just about any sound they hear. Many Australians have heard lyrebirds singing the sounds of chainsaws, car engines, and dog barks. Supposedly, a lyrebird once confused timber-mill workers when it sang the sound of the mill's whistle, causing the workers to quit for the day.

Language Arts ACTIVITY

WRITING SKILL A lyrebird's ability to imitate noises could lead to a lot of humorous confusion for people who hear its songs. Think about how lyrebirds could mimic human-made sounds, causing confusion for the people nearby, and then write a short story about the situation.

Irene Pepperberg

Bird Brains Dr. Irene Pepperberg studies bird brains. She works with a little African Grey parrot named Alex. Pepperberg began her work with Alex because she wanted to see if birds that could talk could also understand what they were saying.

Pepperberg developed a new kind of communication training, with Alex as her pupil. First, Alex was rewarded with the object that he identified—not with food. This reinforced that the word represented the object. Next, two trainers acted out a kind of play to teach Alex words. One trainer would ask a question, and the other would respond with the right or wrong answer. The first trainer would reward the second for a right answer but take the object away for a wrong answer. This training showed Alex what would happen when he gave an answer.

Pepperberg's experiment has been very successful. Not only can Alex say the names of objects but he can tell you what they are made of, what their shape is, and how one object is different from another. Pepperberg has shown that at least one parrot can pass intelligence tests at the same level as some nonhuman primates and marine mammals. She has discovered that with the right training, animals can teach us a lot about themselves.

Social Studies ACTiViTY

WRITING SKILL People train pets all the time. See if you can train your pet or a friend's pet to learn a simple behavior, such as following a command. Write up your results in a report.

To learn more about these Science in Action topics, visit **go.hrw.com** and type in the keyword **HL5VR2F.**

Current Science

Check out Current Science® articles related to this chapter by visiting go.hrw.com. Just type in the keyword HL5CS17.

Skills Practice Lab

Wet, Wiggly Worms!

Earthworms have been digging in the Earth for more than 100 million years! Earthworms fertilize the soil with their waste and loosen the soil when they tunnel through the moist dirt of a garden or lawn. Worms are food for many animals, such as birds, frogs, snakes, rodents, and fish. Some say they are good food for people, too!

In this activity, you will observe the behavior of a live earthworm. Remember that earthworms are living animals that deserve to be handled gently. Be sure to keep your earthworm moist during this activity. The skin of the earthworm must stay moist so that the worm can get oxygen. If the earthworm's skin dries out, the worm will suffocate and die. Use a spray bottle to moisten the earthworm with water.

- celery leaves
- clock
- dissecting pan
- earthworm, live
- flashlight
- paper towels
- probe
- ruler, metric
- shoe box, with lid
- soil
- spray bottle
- water

SAFETY

Procedure

1. Place a wet paper towel in the bottom of a dissecting pan. Put a live earthworm on the paper towel, and observe how the earthworm moves. Record your observations.

2. Use the probe to carefully touch the anterior end (head) of the worm. Gently touch other areas of the worm's body with the probe. Record the kinds of responses you observe.

3. Place celery leaves at one end of the pan. Record how the earthworm responds to the presence of food.

4. Shine a flashlight on the anterior end of the earthworm. Record the earthworm's reaction to the light.

5. Line the bottom of the shoe box with a damp paper towel. Cover half of the shoe box with the box top.

6. Place the worm on the uncovered side of the shoe box in the light. Record your observations of the worm's behavior for 3 min.

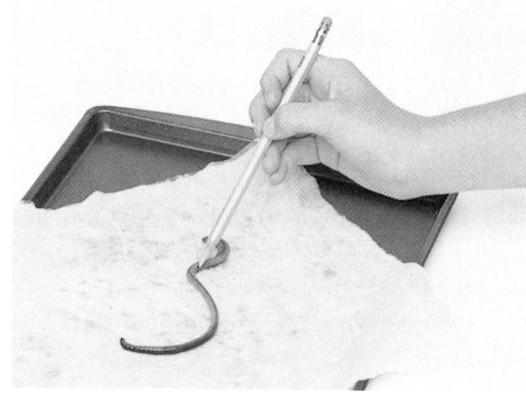

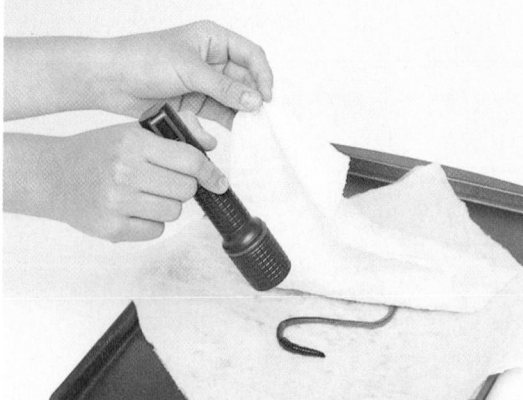

7. Place the worm in the covered side of the box. Record your observations for 3 min.

8. Repeat steps 6–7 three times.

9. Spread some loose soil evenly in the bottom of the shoe box so that the soil is about 4 cm deep. Place the earthworm on top of the soil. Observe and record the earthworm's behavior for 3 min.

10. Dampen the soil on one side of the box, and leave the other side dry. Place the earthworm in the center of the box between the wet and dry soil. Cover the box, and wait 3 min. Uncover the box, and record your observations. Repeat this procedure three times. (You may need to search for the worm!)

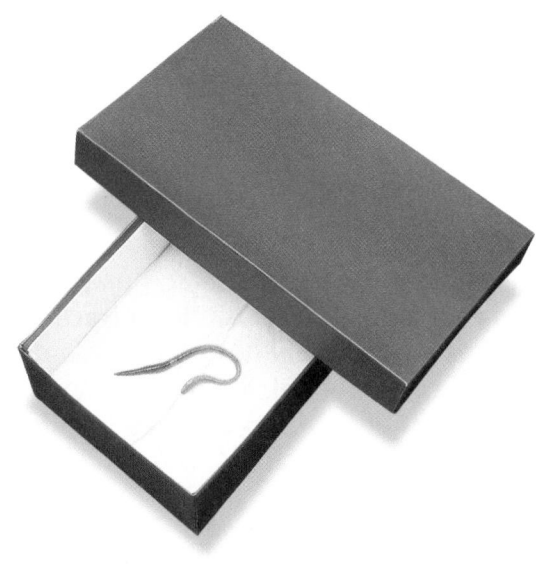

Analyze the Results

1. How did the earthworm respond to being touched? Were some areas more sensitive than others?

2. How did the earthworm respond to the presence of food?

Draw Conclusions

3. How is the earthworm's behavior influenced by light? Based on your observations, describe how an animal's response to a stimulus might provide protection for the animal.

4. When the worm was given a choice of wet or dry soil, which did it choose? Explain this result.

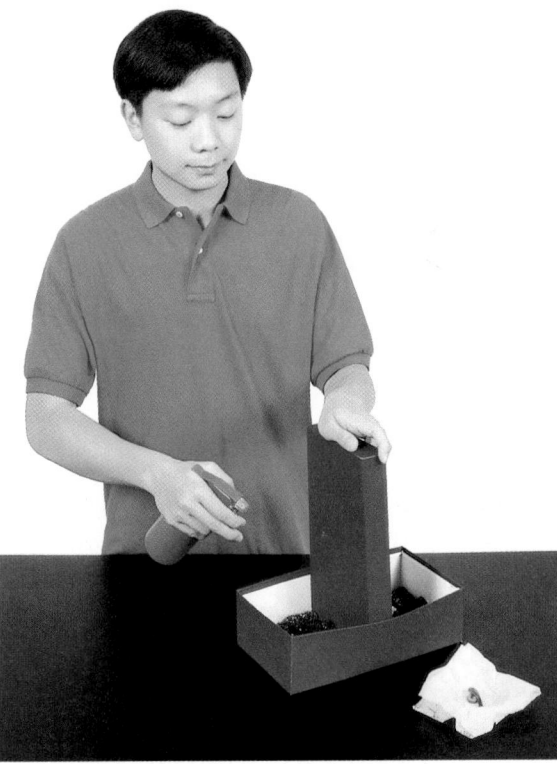

Communicating Your Data

Based on your observations of an earthworm's behavior, prepare a poster showing where you might expect to find earthworms. Draw a picture with colored markers, or cut out pictures from magazines. Include all the variables that you used in your experiment, such as soil or no soil, wet or dry soil, light or dark, and food. Write a caption at the bottom of your poster describing where earthworms might be found in nature.

Skills Practice Lab

The Cricket Caper

Insects are a special class of invertebrates with more than 750,000 known species. Insects may be the most successful group of animals on Earth. In this activity you will observe a cricket's structure and the simple adaptive behaviors that help make it so successful. Remember, you will be handling a living animal that deserves to be treated with care.

MATERIALS

- aluminum foil
- apple
- bags, plastic, sealable (2)
- beaker, 600 mL (2)
- cricket (2)
- hand lens (optional)
- ice, crushed
- lamp
- plastic wrap
- tape, masking
- water, tap, hot

SAFETY

Procedure

1. Place a cricket in a clean 600 mL beaker, and quickly cover the beaker with plastic wrap. The supply of oxygen in the container is enough for the cricket to breathe while you complete your work.

2. While the cricket is getting used to the container, make a data table similar to the one below. Be sure to allow enough space to write your descriptions.

Cricket Body Structures	
Number	**Description**
Body segments	
Antennae	DO NOT WRITE IN BOOK
Eyes	
Wings	

3. Without making much movement, begin to examine the cricket. Fill in your data table with your observations of the cricket's structure.

4. Place a small piece of apple in the beaker. Set the beaker on a table. Sit quietly for several minutes and observe the cricket. Any movement may cause the cricket to stop what it is doing. Record your observations.

5. Remove the plastic wrap from the beaker, remove the apple, and quickly attach a second beaker. Join the two beakers together at the mouths with masking tape. Handle the beakers carefully. Remember, there is a living animal inside.

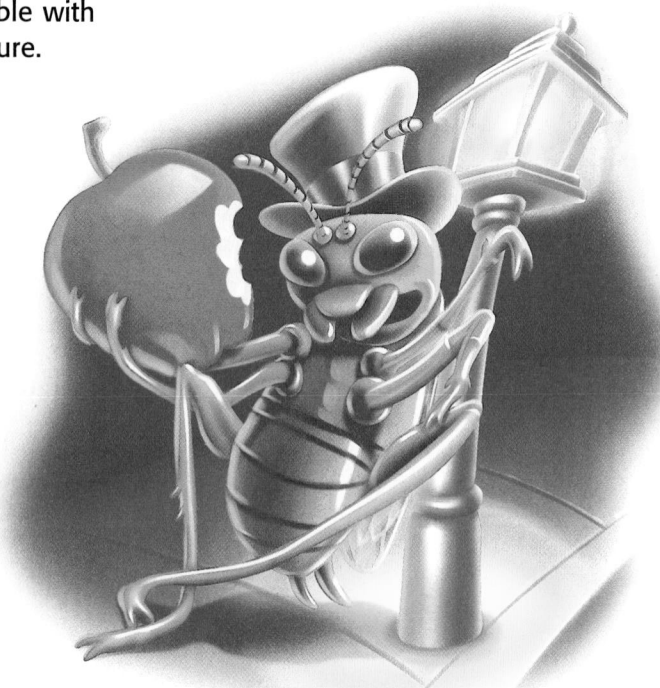

6 Wrap one of the joined beakers with aluminum foil.

7 If the cricket is hiding under the aluminum foil, gently tap the sides of the beaker until the cricket is exposed. Lay the joined beakers on their sides, and shine a lamp on the uncovered side. Record the cricket's location.

8 Record the cricket's location after 5 min. Without disturbing the cricket, carefully move the aluminum foil to the other beaker. After 5 min, record the cricket's location. Repeat this process one more time to see if you get the same result.

9 Fill a sealable plastic bag halfway with crushed ice. Fill another bag halfway with hot tap water. Seal each bag, and arrange them side by side on the table.

10 Remove the aluminum foil from the beakers. Gently rock the joined beakers from side to side until the cricket is in the center. Place the beakers on the plastic bags, as shown below.

11 Observe the cricket's behavior for 5 min. Record your observations.

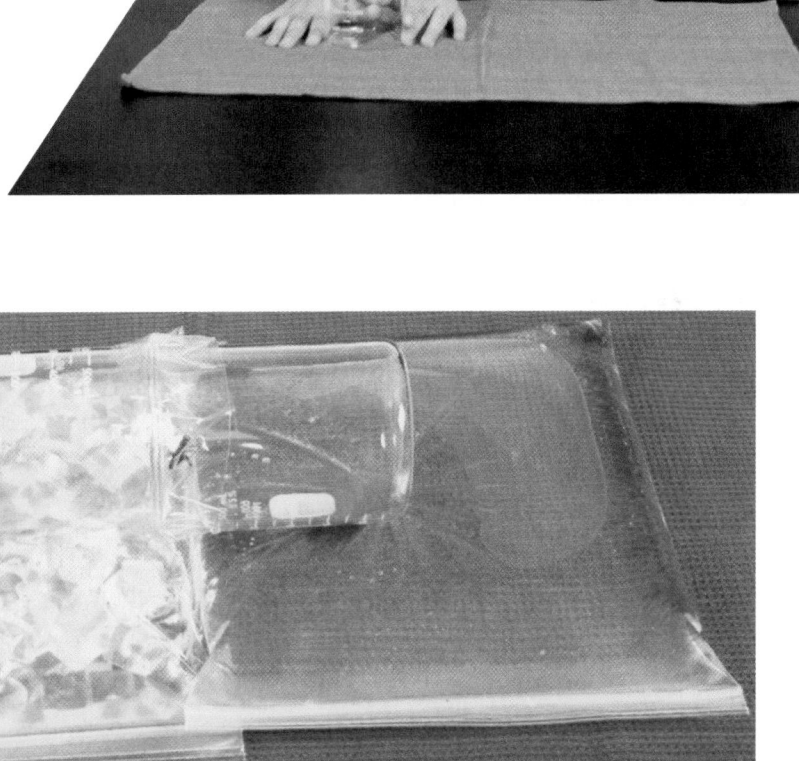

12 Set the beakers on one end for several minutes to allow them to return to room temperature. Repeat steps 10–12 three times. (Why do you think it is necessary to allow the beakers to return to room temperature each time?)

13 Set the beakers on one end. Carefully remove the masking tape, and separate the beakers. Quickly replace the plastic wrap over the beaker containing the cricket. Allow your cricket to rest while you make two data tables similar to those at right.

14 Observe the cricket's movement in the beaker every 15 seconds for 3 min. Fill in the Cricket (alone) data table using the following codes: 0 = no movement, 1 = slight movement, and 2 = rapid movement.

15 Obtain a second cricket from your teacher, and place this cricket in the container with the first cricket. Every 15 seconds, record the movement of each cricket in the Cricket A and Cricket B data table using the codes given in step 14.

Analyze the Results

1 Describe crickets' feeding behavior. Are they lappers, suckers, or chewers?

2 Do crickets prefer light or darkness? Explain.

3 From your observations, what can you infer about a cricket's temperature preferences?

Draw Conclusions

4 Based on your observations of Cricket A and Cricket B, what general statements can you make about the social behavior of crickets?

Applying Your Data

Make a third data table titled "Cricket and Another Species of Insect." Introduce another insect, such as a grasshopper, into the beaker. Record your observations for 3 min. Write a short summary of the cricket's reaction to another species.

Cricket (alone)	
15 s	
30 s	
45 s	
60 s	
75 s	
90 s	DO NOT WRITE IN BOOK
105 s	
120 s	
135 s	
150 s	
165 s	
180 s	

Cricket A and Cricket B		
	A	B
15 s		
30 s		
45 s		
60 s		
75 s		
90 s	DO NOT WRITE IN BOOK	
105 s		
120 s		
135 s		
150 s		
165 s		
180 s		

Skills Practice Lab

A Prince of a Frog

Imagine that you are a scientist interested in amphibians. You have heard in the news about amphibians disappearing all over the world. What a great loss it will be to the environment if all amphibians become extinct! Your job is to learn as much as possible about how frogs normally behave so that you can act as a resource for other scientists who are studying the problem. In this activity, you will observe a normal frog in a dry container and in water.

MATERIALS

- beaker, 600 mL
- container half-filled with dechlorinated water
- crickets, live
- frog, live, in a dry container
- gloves, protective
- rock, large (optional)

SAFETY

Procedure

1. Make a table similar to the one below to note all of your observations of the frog in this investigation.

Observations of a Live Frog	
Characteristic	**Observation**
Breathing	
Eyes	
Legs	
Response to food	DO NOT WRITE IN BOOK
Skin texture	
Swimming behavior	
Skin coloration	

2. Observe a live frog in a dry container. Draw a picture of the frog. Label the eyes, nostrils, front legs, and hind legs.

3. Watch the frog's movements as it breathes air with its lungs. Write a description of the frog's breathing.

4. Look closely at the frog's eyes, and note their location. Examine the upper and lower eyelids as well as the transparent third eyelid. Which of these three eyelids actually moves over the eye?

5. Study the frog's legs. Note in your data table the difference between the front and hind legs

6. Place a live insect, such as a cricket, in the container. Observe and record how the frog reacts.

7. Carefully pick up the frog, and examine its skin. How does it feel?
Caution: Remember that a frog is a living thing and deserves to be handled gently and with respect.

8. Place a 600 mL beaker in the container. Place the frog in the beaker. Cover the beaker with your hand, and carry it to a container of dechlorinated water. Tilt the beaker and gently submerge it in the water until the frog swims out of the beaker.

9. Watch the frog float and swim in the water. How does the frog use its legs to swim? Notice the position of the frog's head.

10. As the frog swims, bend down and look up into the water so that you can see the underside of the frog. Then look down on the frog from above. Compare the color on the top and the underneath sides of the frog. Record your observations in your data table.

Analyze the Results

1. From the position of the frog's eyes, what can you infer about the frog's field of vision? How might the position of the frog's eyes benefit the frog while it is swimming?

2. How can a frog "breathe" while it is swimming in water?

3. How are the hind legs of a frog adapted for life on land and in water?

4. What differences did you notice in coloration on the frog's top side and its underneath side? What advantage might these color differences provide?

5. How does the frog eat? What senses are involved in helping the frog catch its prey?

Applying Your Data

Observe another type of amphibian, such as a salamander. How do the adaptations of other types of amphibians compare with those of the frog you observed in this investigation?

Contents

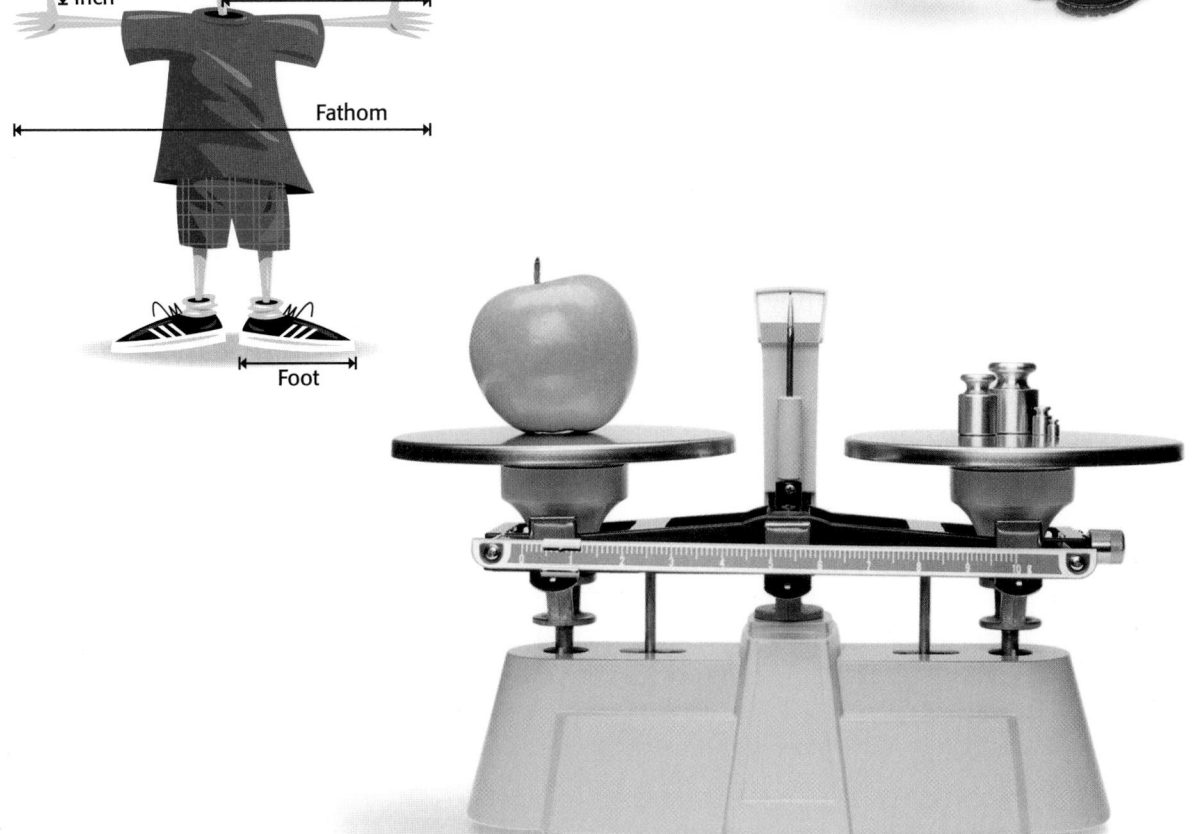

Appendix

✓ Reading Check Answers

Chapter 1   Animals and Behavior

Section 1
Page 5:   vertebrates

Page 6:   heart, lung, and kidneys

Section 2
Page 9:   A predator hunts prey as its food.

Page 10:   A rabbit can "freeze" to hide from predators, or it can try to outrun predators.

Page 12:   mice, squirrels, and skunks

Section 3
Page 14:   defend a territory, find food, warn others of danger, identify family, frighten predators, and find mates

Page 16:   They use body language to communicate where to find food sources.

Chapter 2   Invertebrates

Section 1
Page 29:   The coelom is the space in the body that surrounds the gut.

Page 30:   Water enters a sponge's body through pores.

Page 33:   planarians, flukes, and tapeworms

Page 34:   pinworms, hookworms, and *Trichinella spiralis*

Section 2
Page 37:   An open circulatory system has a heart that pumps blood through blood vessels that empty into sinuses. A closed circulatory system has a heart that pumps blood through a closed loop of blood vessels.

Page 39:   Doctors use leeches to prevent swelling and to prevent and break down blood clots.

Section 3
Page 41:   Both an exoskeleton and an internal skeleton support an animal's body and allow the animal to move.

Page 43:   Spiders are helpful because they catch small insects that are pests to humans.

Page 45:   egg, nymph, and adult

Section 4
Page 47:   Radial nerves control the movements of a sea star's arms.

Page 49:   A sea lily's body is at the end of a long stalk, while a feather star does not have a stalk.

Chapter 3 Fishes, Amphibians, and Reptiles

Section 1
Page 61: cartilage

Page 62: Because most fishes are ectotherms, the body temperature of most fishes would increase as the temperature of their environment increased.

Page 64: Hagfish eat dead fishes on the ocean floor. Lampreys suck other animals' blood and flesh through a toothed suction cup–like mouth.

Page 66: Bony fishes have skeletons made of bone, have bodies covered in bony scales, and can rest in one place without swimming.

Section 2
Page 68: Most amphibians get oxygen through lungs.

Page 71: Most salamanders lose gills and grow lungs but do not go through a tadpole stage.

Page 72: Frogs use vocal sacs to sing, which helps frogs mark territories and attract mates.

Section 3
Page 75: Reptile eggs have a shell that keeps the embryo from drying out on land.

Page 76: turtles and tortoises, crocodiles and alligators, lizards and snakes, and tuataras

Page 79: Tuataras are most active at low temperatures, and they have no visible ear openings on the outside of the body.

Chapter 4 Birds and Mammals

Section 1
Page 91: Down feathers help birds stay warm.

Page 92: The heart beats rapidly so that it can pump enough blood to power the flight muscles.

Page 94: A bird's body heat warms the eggs.

Section 2
Page 97: rounded, flat beaks and long, sharp beaks

Page 98: The perching bird's feet will remain closed around the branch.

Section 3
Page 101: water, protein, fat, and sugar

Page 103: until the young mammal is grown

Section 4
Page 105: They gnaw and chew.

Page 106: Rabbits have two sets of sharp front teeth in their upper jaw, and they have a short tail.

Page 109: all of their time

Page 110: large brains, grasping hands and feet, flexible shoulder joints, and forward-facing eyes

Section 5
Page 113: A platypus uses its bill to dig for food and dig tunnels in the riverbanks where it can lay its eggs.

Page 114: as small as a bumblebee

Appendix

Study Skills

FoldNote Instructions

Have you ever tried to study for a test or quiz but didn't know where to start? Or have you read a chapter and found that you can remember only a few ideas? Well, FoldNotes are a fun and exciting way to help you learn and remember the ideas you encounter as you learn science!

FoldNotes are tools that you can use to organize concepts. By focusing on a few main concepts, FoldNotes help you learn and remember how the concepts fit together. They can help you see the "big picture." Below you will find instructions for building 10 different FoldNotes.

Pyramid

1. Place a sheet of paper in front of you. Fold the lower left-hand corner of the paper diagonally to the opposite edge of the paper.

2. Cut off the tab of paper created by the fold (at the top).

3. Open the paper so that it is a square. Fold the lower right-hand corner of the paper diagonally to the opposite corner to form a triangle.

4. Open the paper. The creases of the two folds will have created an X.

5. Using scissors, cut along one of the creases. Start from any corner, and stop at the center point to create two flaps. Use tape or glue to attach one of the flaps on top of the other flap.

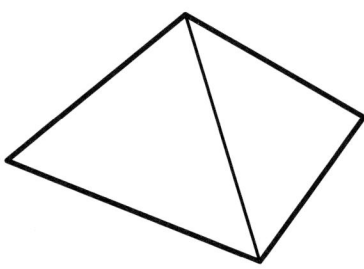

Double Door

1. Fold a sheet of paper in half from the top to the bottom. Then, unfold the paper.

2. Fold the top and bottom edges of the paper to the crease.

Booklet

1. Fold a sheet of paper in half from left to right. Then, unfold the paper.

2. Fold the sheet of paper in half again from the top to the bottom. Then, unfold the paper.

3. Refold the sheet of paper in half from left to right.

4. Fold the top and bottom edges to the center crease.

5. Completely unfold the paper.

6. Refold the paper from top to bottom.

7. Using scissors, cut a slit along the center crease of the sheet from the folded edge to the creases made in step 4. Do not cut the entire sheet in half.

8. Fold the sheet of paper in half from left to right. While holding the bottom and top edges of the paper, push the bottom and top edges together so that the center collapses at the center slit. Fold the four flaps to form a four-page book.

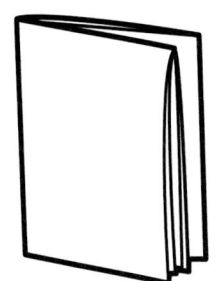

Layered Book

1. Lay one sheet of paper on top of another sheet. Slide the top sheet up so that 2 cm of the bottom sheet is showing.

2. Hold the two sheets together, fold down the top of the two sheets so that you see four 2 cm tabs along the bottom.

3. Using a stapler, staple the top of the FoldNote.

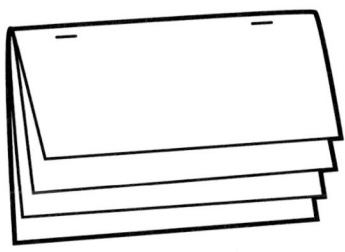

Key-Term Fold

1. Fold a sheet of lined notebook paper in half from left to right.

2. Using scissors, cut along every third line from the right edge of the paper to the center fold to make tabs.

Four-Corner Fold

1. Fold a sheet of paper in half from left to right. Then, unfold the paper.

2. Fold each side of the paper to the crease in the center of the paper.

3. Fold the paper in half from the top to the bottom. Then, unfold the paper.

4. Using scissors, cut the top flap creases made in step 3 to form four flaps.

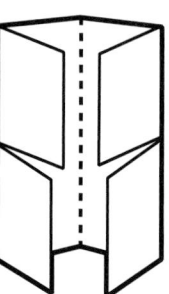

Three-Panel Flip Chart

1. Fold a piece of paper in half from the top to the bottom.

2. Fold the paper in thirds from side to side. Then, unfold the paper so that you can see the three sections.

3. From the top of the paper, cut along each of the vertical fold lines to the fold in the middle of the paper. You will now have three flaps.

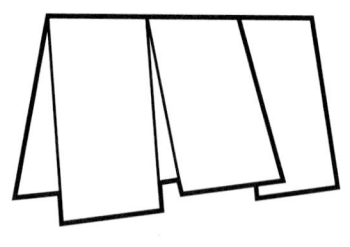

Appendix

Table Fold

1. Fold a piece of paper in half from the top to the bottom. Then, fold the paper in half again.

2. Fold the paper in thirds from side to side.

3. Unfold the paper completely. Carefully trace the fold lines by using a pen or pencil.

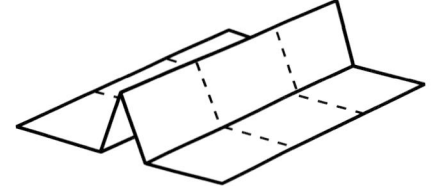

Two-Panel Flip Chart

1. Fold a piece of paper in half from the top to the bottom.

2. Fold the paper in half from side to side. Then, unfold the paper so that you can see the two sections.

3. From the top of the paper, cut along the vertical fold line to the fold in the middle of the paper. You will now have two flaps.

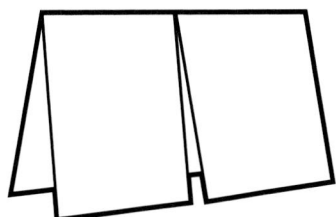

Tri-Fold

1. Fold a piece a paper in thirds from the top to the bottom.

2. Unfold the paper so that you can see the three sections. Then, turn the paper sideways so that the three sections form vertical columns.

3. Trace the fold lines by using a pen or pencil. Label the columns "Know," "Want," and "Learn."

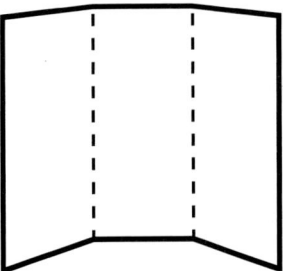

Appendix

Graphic Organizer Instructions

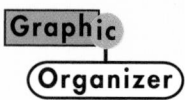 Have you ever wished that you could "draw out" the many concepts you learn in your science class? Sometimes, being able to *see* how concepts are related really helps you remember what you've learned. Graphic Organizers do just that! They give you a way to draw or map out concepts.

All you need to make a Graphic Organizer is a piece of paper and a pencil. Below you will find instructions for four different Graphic Organizers designed to help you organize the concepts you'll learn in this book.

Spider Map

1. Draw a diagram like the one shown. In the circle, write the main topic.

2. From the circle, draw legs to represent different categories of the main topic. You can have as many categories as you want.

3. From the category legs, draw horizontal lines. As you read the chapter, write details about each category on the horizontal lines.

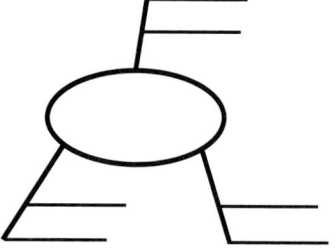

Comparison Table

1. Draw a chart like the one shown. Your chart can have as many columns and rows as you want.

2. In the top row, write the topics that you want to compare.

3. In the left column, write characteristics of the topics that you want to compare. As you read the chapter, fill in the characteristics for each topic in the appropriate boxes.

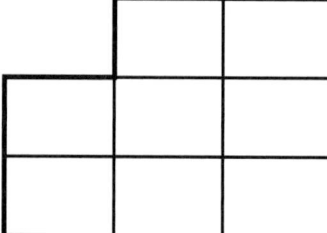

Chain-of-Events-Chart

1. Draw a box. In the box, write the first step of a process or the first event of a timeline.

2. Under the box, draw another box, and use an arrow to connect the two boxes. In the second box, write the next step of the process or the next event in the timeline.

3. Continue adding boxes until the process or timeline is finished.

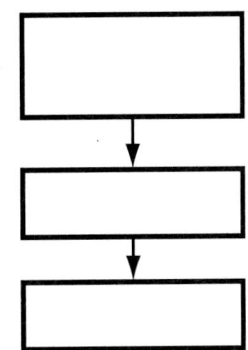

Concept Map

1. Draw a circle in the center of a piece of paper. Write the main idea of the chapter in the center of the circle.

2. From the circle, draw other circles. In those circles, write characteristics of the main idea. Draw arrows from the center circle to the circles that contain the characteristics.

3. From each circle that contains a characteristic, draw other circles. In those circles, write specific details about the characteristic. Draw arrows from each circle that contains a characteristic to the circles that contain specific details. You may draw as many circles as you want.

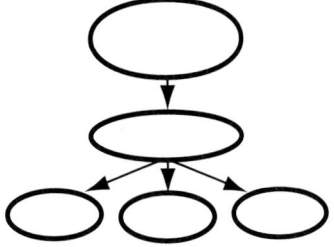

SI Measurement

The International System of Units, or SI, is the standard system of measurement used by many scientists. Using the same standards of measurement makes it easier for scientists to communicate with one another.

SI works by combining prefixes and base units. Each base unit can be used with different prefixes to define smaller and larger quantities. The table below lists common SI prefixes.

SI Prefixes

Prefix	Symbol	Factor	Example
kilo-	k	1,000	kilogram, 1 kg = 1,000 g
hecto-	h	100	hectoliter, 1 hL = 100 L
deka-	da	10	dekameter, 1 dam = 10 m
		1	meter, liter, gram
deci-	d	0.1	decigram, 1 dg = 0.1 g
centi-	c	0.01	centimeter, 1 cm = 0.01 m
milli-	m	0.001	milliliter, 1 mL = 0.001 L
micro-	μ	0.000 001	micrometer, 1 μm = 0.000 001 m

SI Conversion Table

SI units	From SI to English	From English to SI
Length		
kilometer (km) = 1,000 m	1 km = 0.621 mi	1 mi = 1.609 km
meter (m) = 100 cm	1 m = 3.281 ft	1 ft = 0.305 m
centimeter (cm) = 0.01 m	1 cm = 0.394 in.	1 in. = 2.540 cm
millimeter (mm) = 0.001 m	1 mm = 0.039 in.	
micrometer (μm) = 0.000 001 m		
nanometer (nm) = 0.000 000 001 m		
Area		
square kilometer (km^2) = 100 hectares	1 km^2 = 0.386 mi^2	1 mi^2 = 2.590 km^2
hectare (ha) = 10,000 m^2	1 ha = 2.471 acres	1 acre = 0.405 ha
square meter (m^2) = 10,000 cm^2	1 m^2 = 10.764 ft^2	1 ft^2 = 0.093 m^2
square centimeter (cm^2) = 100 mm^2	1 cm^2 = 0.155 in.^{2}	1 in.^{2} = 6.452 cm^2
Volume		
liter (L) = 1,000 mL = 1 dm^3	1 L = 1.057 fl qt	1 fl qt = 0.946 L
milliliter (mL) = 0.001 L = 1 cm^3	1 mL = 0.034 fl oz	1 fl oz = 29.574 mL
microliter (μL) = 0.000 001 L		
Mass		
kilogram (kg) = 1,000 g	1 kg = 2.205 lb	1 lb = 0.454 kg
gram (g) = 1,000 mg	1 g = 0.035 oz	1 oz = 28.350 g
milligram (mg) = 0.001 g		
microgram (μg) = 0.000 001 g		

Appendix

Measuring Skills

Using a Graduated Cylinder

When using a graduated cylinder to measure volume, keep the following procedures in mind:

1 Place the cylinder on a flat, level surface before measuring liquid.

2 Move your head so that your eye is level with the surface of the liquid.

3 Read the mark closest to the liquid level. On glass graduated cylinders, read the mark closest to the center of the curve in the liquid's surface.

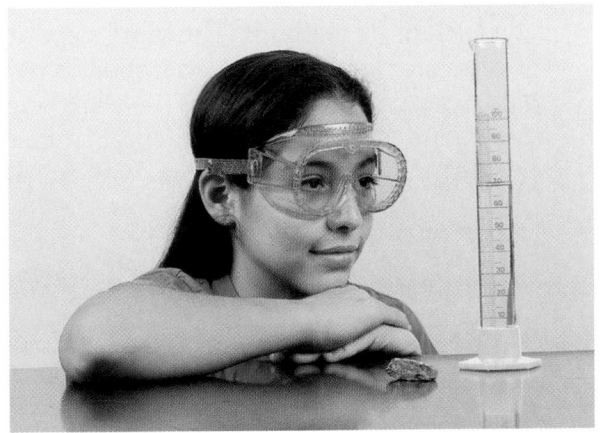

Using a Meterstick or Metric Ruler

When using a meterstick or metric ruler to measure length, keep the following procedures in mind:

1 Place the ruler firmly against the object that you are measuring.

2 Align one edge of the object exactly with the 0 end of the ruler.

3 Look at the other edge of the object to see which of the marks on the ruler is closest to that edge. (Note: Each small slash between the centimeters represents a millimeter, which is one-tenth of a centimeter.)

Using a Triple-Beam Balance

When using a triple-beam balance to measure mass, keep the following procedures in mind:

1 Make sure the balance is on a level surface.

2 Place all of the countermasses at 0. Adjust the balancing knob until the pointer rests at 0.

3 Place the object you wish to measure on the pan. **Caution:** Do not place hot objects or chemicals directly on the balance pan.

4 Move the largest countermass along the beam to the right until it is at the last notch that does not tip the balance. Follow the same procedure with the next-largest countermass. Then, move the smallest countermass until the pointer rests at 0.

5 Add the readings from the three beams together to determine the mass of the object.

6 When determining the mass of crystals or powders, first find the mass of a piece of filter paper. Then, add the crystals or powder to the paper, and remeasure. The actual mass of the crystals or powder is the total mass minus the mass of the paper. When finding the mass of liquids, first find the mass of the empty container. Then, find the combined mass of the liquid and container. The mass of the liquid is the total mass minus the mass of the container.

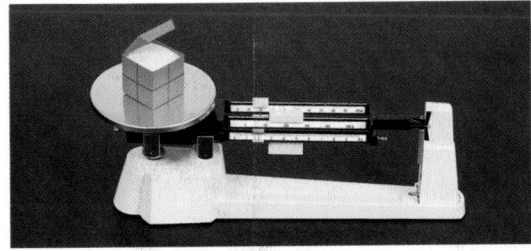

Scientific Methods

The ways in which scientists answer questions and solve problems are called **scientific methods.** The same steps are often used by scientists as they look for answers. However, there is more than one way to use these steps. Scientists may use all of the steps or just some of the steps during an investigation. They may even repeat some of the steps. The goal of using scientific methods is to come up with reliable answers and solutions.

Six Steps of Scientific Methods

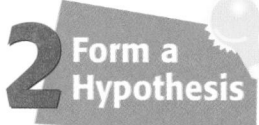

1 Ask a Question

Good questions come from careful **observations.** You make observations by using your senses to gather information. Sometimes, you may use instruments, such as microscopes and telescopes, to extend the range of your senses. As you observe the natural world, you will discover that you have many more questions than answers. These questions drive investigations.

Questions beginning with *what, why, how,* and *when* are important in focusing an investigation. Here is an example of a question that could lead to an investigation.

Question: How does acid rain affect plant growth?

2 Form a Hypothesis

After you ask a question, you need to form a **hypothesis.** A hypothesis is a clear statement of what you expect the answer to your question to be. Your hypothesis will represent your best "educated guess" based on what you have observed and what you already know. A good hypothesis is testable. Otherwise, the investigation can go no further. Here is a hypothesis based on the question, "How does acid rain affect plant growth?"

Hypothesis: Acid rain slows plant growth.

The hypothesis can lead to predictions. A prediction is what you think the outcome of your experiment or data collection will be. Predictions are usually stated in an if-then format. Here is a sample prediction for the hypothesis that acid rain slows plant growth.

Prediction: If a plant is watered with only acid rain (which has a pH of 4), then the plant will grow at half its normal rate.

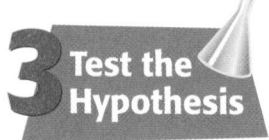

3 Test the Hypothesis

After you have formed a hypothesis and made a prediction, your hypothesis should be tested. One way to test a hypothesis is with a controlled experiment. A **controlled experiment** tests only one factor at a time. In an experiment to test the effect of acid rain on plant growth, the **control group** would be watered with normal rain water. The **experimental group** would be watered with acid rain. All of the plants should receive the same amount of sunlight and water each day. The air temperature should be the same for all groups. However, the acidity of the water will be a variable. In fact, any factor that is different from one group to another is a **variable.** If your hypothesis is correct, then the acidity of the water and plant growth are *dependant variables.* The amount a plant grows is dependent on the acidity of the water. However, the amount of water each plant receives and the amount of sunlight each plant receives are *independent variables.* Either of these factors could change without affecting the other factor.

Sometimes, the nature of an investigation makes a controlled experiment impossible. For example, the Earth's core is surrounded by thousands of meters of rock. Under such circumstances, a hypothesis may be tested by making detailed observations.

4 Analyze the Results

After you have completed your experiments, made your observations, and collected your data, you must analyze all the information you have gathered. Tables and graphs are often used in this step to organize the data.

5 Draw Conclusions

After analyzing your data, you can determine if your results support your hypothesis. If your hypothesis is supported, you (or others) might want to repeat the observations or experiments to verify your results. If your hypothesis is not supported by the data, you may have to check your procedure for errors. You may even have to reject your hypothesis and make a new one. If you cannot draw a conclusion from your results, you may have to try the investigation again or carry out further observations or experiments.

6 Communicate Results

After any scientific investigation, you should report your results. By preparing a written or oral report, you let others know what you have learned. They may repeat your investigation to see if they get the same results. Your report may even lead to another question and then to another investigation.

Scientific Methods in Action

Scientific methods contain loops in which several steps may be repeated over and over again. In some cases, certain steps are unnecessary. Thus, there is not a "straight line" of steps. For example, sometimes scientists find that testing one hypothesis raises new questions and new hypotheses to be tested. And sometimes, testing the hypothesis leads directly to a conclusion. Furthermore, the steps in scientific methods are not always used in the same order. Follow the steps in the diagram, and see how many different directions scientific methods can take you.

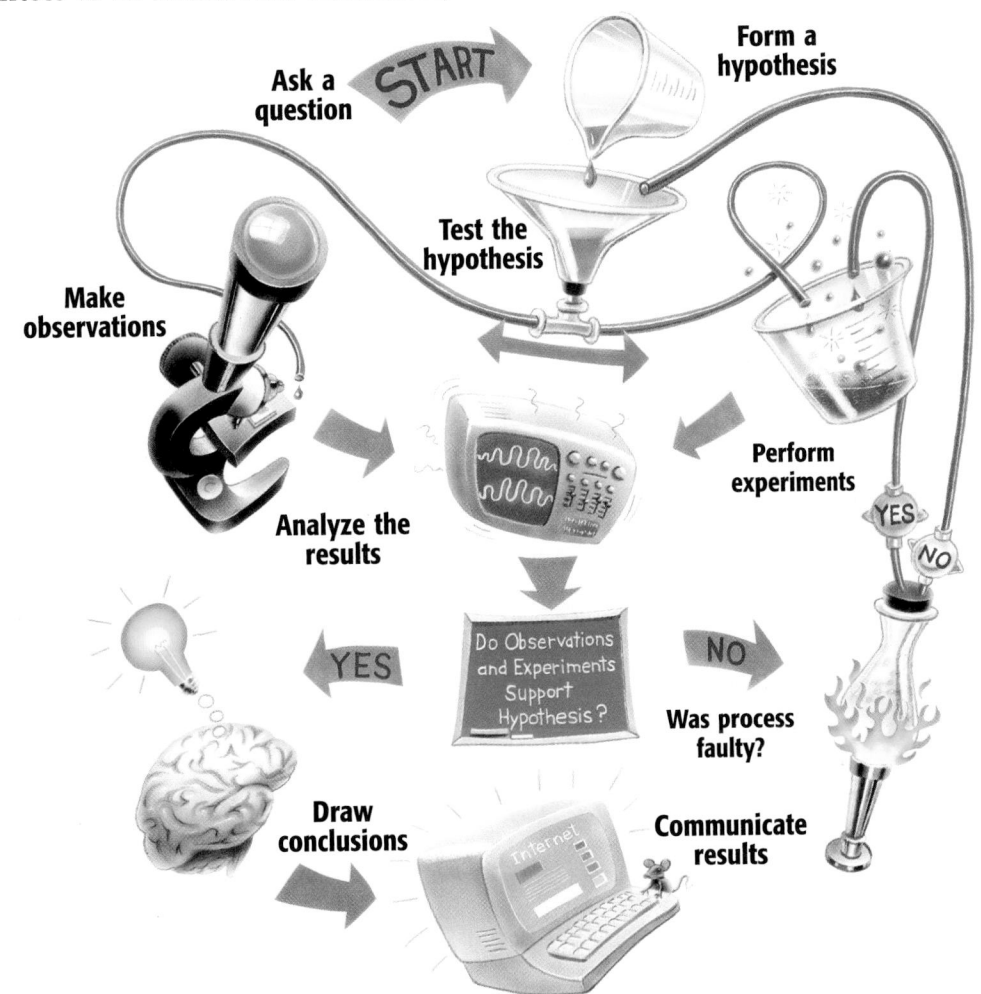

Temperature Scales

Temperature can be expressed by using three different scales: Fahrenheit, Celsius, and Kelvin. The SI unit for temperature is the kelvin (K).

Although 0 K is much colder than 0°C, a change of 1 K is equal to a change of 1°C.

Three Temperature Scales

	Fahrenheit	Celsius	Kelvin
Water boils	212°	100°	373
Body temperature	98.6°	37°	310
Room temperature	68°	20°	293
Water freezes	32°	0°	273

Temperature Conversions Table

To convert	Use this equation:	Example
Celsius to Fahrenheit °C → °F	$°F = \left(\dfrac{9}{5} \times °C\right) + 32$	Convert 45°C to °F. $°F = \left(\dfrac{9}{5} \times 45°C\right) + 32 = 113°F$
Fahrenheit to Celsius °F → °C	$°C = \dfrac{5}{9} \times (°F - 32)$	Convert 68°F to °C. $°C = \dfrac{5}{9} \times (68°F - 32) = 20°C$
Celsius to Kelvin °C → K	$K = °C + 273$	Convert 45°C to K. $K = 45°C + 273 = 318 \ K$
Kelvin to Celsius K → °C	$°C = K - 273$	Convert 32 K to °C. $°C = 32K - 273 = -241°C$

Making Charts and Graphs

Pie Charts

A pie chart shows how each group of data relates to all of the data. Each part of the circle forming the chart represents a category of the data. The entire circle represents all of the data. For example, a biologist studying a hardwood forest in Wisconsin found that there were five different types of trees. The data table at right summarizes the biologist's findings.

Wisconsin Hardwood Trees	
Type of tree	**Number found**
Oak	600
Maple	750
Beech	300
Birch	1,200
Hickory	150
Total	3,000

How to Make a Pie Chart

1 To make a pie chart of these data, first find the percentage of each type of tree. Divide the number of trees of each type by the total number of trees, and multiply by 100.

$$\frac{600 \text{ oak}}{3,000 \text{ trees}} \times 100 = 20\%$$

$$\frac{750 \text{ maple}}{3,000 \text{ trees}} \times 100 = 25\%$$

$$\frac{300 \text{ beech}}{3,000 \text{ trees}} \times 100 = 10\%$$

$$\frac{1,200 \text{ birch}}{3,000 \text{ trees}} \times 100 = 40\%$$

$$\frac{150 \text{ hickory}}{3,000 \text{ trees}} \times 100 = 5\%$$

2 Now, determine the size of the wedges that make up the pie chart. Multiply each percentage by 360°. Remember that a circle contains 360°.

$20\% \times 360° = 72°$ $25\% \times 360° = 90°$
$10\% \times 360° = 36°$ $40\% \times 360° = 144°$
$5\% \times 360° = 18°$

3 Check that the sum of the percentages is 100 and the sum of the degrees is 360.

$20\% + 25\% + 10\% + 40\% + 5\% = 100\%$
$72° + 90° + 36° + 144° + 18° = 360°$

4 Use a compass to draw a circle and mark the center of the circle.

5 Then, use a protractor to draw angles of 72°, 90°, 36°, 144°, and 18° in the circle.

6 Finally, label each part of the chart, and choose an appropriate title.

A Community of Wisconsin Hardwood Trees

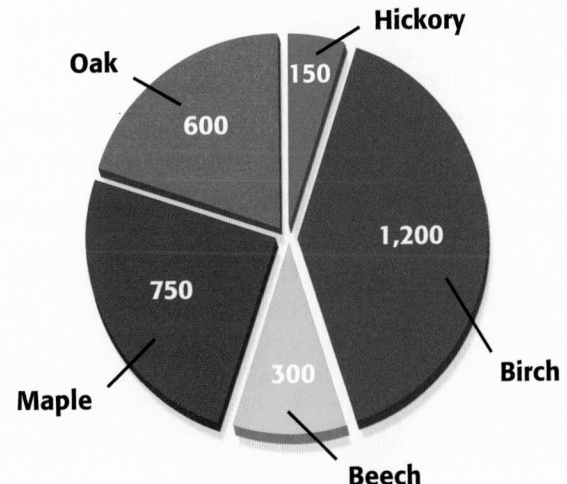

Line Graphs

Line graphs are most often used to demonstrate continuous change. For example, Mr. Smith's students analyzed the population records for their hometown, Appleton, between 1900 and 2000. Examine the data at right.

Because the year and the population change, they are the *variables*. The population is determined by, or dependent on, the year. Therefore, the population is called the **dependent variable,** and the year is called the **independent variable.** Each set of data is called a **data pair.** To prepare a line graph, you must first organize data pairs into a table like the one at right.

Population of Appleton, 1900–2000	
Year	**Population**
1900	1,800
1920	2,500
1940	3,200
1960	3,900
1980	4,600
2000	5,300

How to Make a Line Graph

1 Place the independent variable along the horizontal (*x*) axis. Place the dependent variable along the vertical (*y*) axis.

2 Label the *x*-axis "Year" and the *y*-axis "Population." Look at your largest and smallest values for the population. For the *y*-axis, determine a scale that will provide enough space to show these values. You must use the same scale for the entire length of the axis. Next, find an appropriate scale for the *x*-axis.

3 Choose reasonable starting points for each axis.

4 Plot the data pairs as accurately as possible.

5 Choose a title that accurately represents the data.

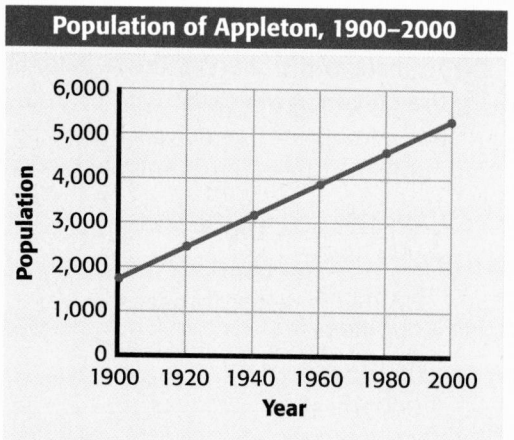

How to Determine Slope

Slope is the ratio of the change in the *y*-value to the change in the *x*-value, or "rise over run."

1 Choose two points on the line graph. For example, the population of Appleton in 2000 was 5,300 people. Therefore, you can define point *a* as (2000, 5,300). In 1900, the population was 1,800 people. You can define point *b* as (1900, 1,800).

2 Find the change in the *y*-value.
(*y* at point *a*) − (*y* at point *b*) =
5,300 people − 1,800 people =
3,500 people

3 Find the change in the *x*-value.
(*x* at point *a*) − (*x* at point *b*) =
2000 − 1900 = 100 years

4 Calculate the slope of the graph by dividing the change in *y* by the change in *x*.

$$slope = \frac{change\ in\ y}{change\ in\ x}$$

$$slope = \frac{3,500\ people}{100\ years}$$

$$slope = 35\ people\ per\ year$$

In this example, the population in Appleton increased by a fixed amount each year. The graph of these data is a straight line. Therefore, the relationship is **linear.** When the graph of a set of data is not a straight line, the relationship is **nonlinear.**

Using Algebra to Determine Slope

The equation in step 4 may also be arranged to be

$$y = kx$$

where y represents the change in the y-value, k represents the slope, and x represents the change in the x-value.

$$slope = \frac{change\ in\ y}{change\ in\ x}$$

$$k = \frac{y}{x}$$

$$k \times x = \frac{y \times x}{x}$$

$$kx = y$$

Bar Graphs

Bar graphs are used to demonstrate change that is not continuous. These graphs can be used to indicate trends when the data cover a long period of time. A meteorologist gathered the precipitation data shown here for Hartford, Connecticut, for April 1–15, 1996, and used a bar graph to represent the data.

Precipitation in Hartford, Connecticut April 1–15, 1996			
Date	Precipitation (cm)	Date	Precipitation (cm)
April 1	0.5	April 9	0.25
April 2	1.25	April 10	0.0
April 3	0.0	April 11	1.0
April 4	0.0	April 12	0.0
April 5	0.0	April 13	0.25
April 6	0.0	April 14	0.0
April 7	0.0	April 15	6.50
April 8	1.75		

How to Make a Bar Graph

1. Use an appropriate scale and a reasonable starting point for each axis.

2. Label the axes, and plot the data.

3. Choose a title that accurately represents the data.

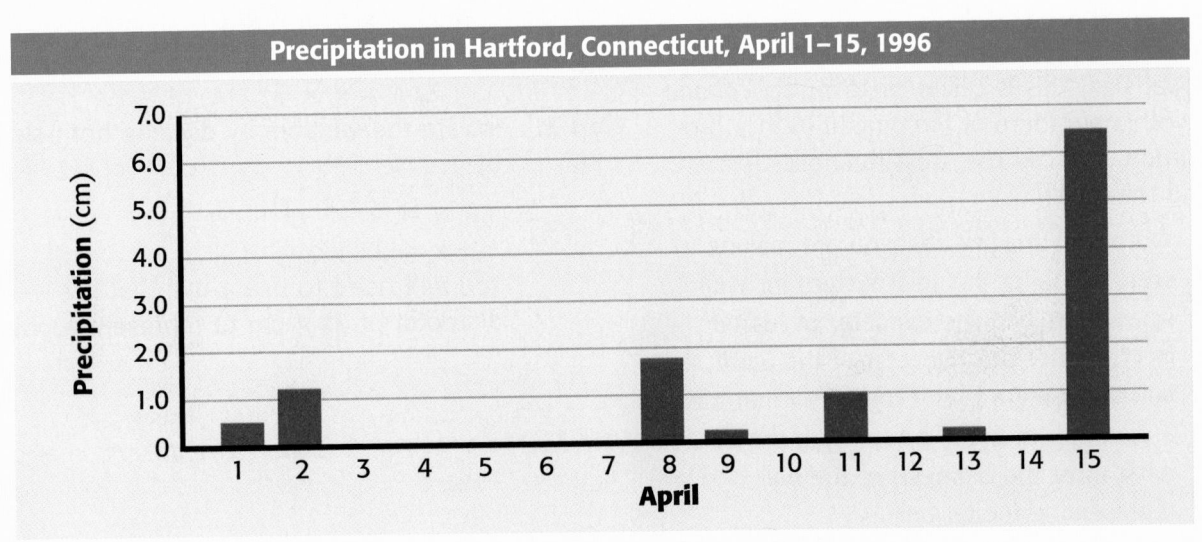

Math Refresher

Science requires an understanding of many math concepts. The following pages will help you review some important math skills.

Averages

An **average,** or **mean,** simplifies a set of numbers into a single number that *approximates* the value of the set.

> **Example:** Find the average of the following set of numbers: 5, 4, 7, and 8.

Step 1: Find the sum.

$$5 + 4 + 7 + 8 = 24$$

Step 2: Divide the sum by the number of numbers in your set. Because there are four numbers in this example, divide the sum by 4.

$$\frac{24}{4} = 6$$

The average, or mean, is **6.**

Ratios

A **ratio** is a comparison between numbers, and it is usually written as a fraction.

> **Example:** Find the ratio of thermometers to students if you have 36 thermometers and 48 students in your class.

Step 1: Make the ratio.

$$\frac{36 \text{ thermometers}}{48 \text{ students}}$$

Step 2: Reduce the fraction to its simplest form.

$$\frac{36}{48} = \frac{36 \div 12}{48 \div 12} = \frac{3}{4}$$

The ratio of thermometers to students is **3 to 4,** or $\frac{3}{4}$. The ratio may also be written in the form 3:4.

Proportions

A **proportion** is an equation that states that two ratios are equal.

$$\frac{3}{1} = \frac{12}{4}$$

To solve a proportion, first multiply across the equal sign. This is called *cross-multiplication.* If you know three of the quantities in a proportion, you can use cross-multiplication to find the fourth.

> **Example:** Imagine that you are making a scale model of the solar system for your science project. The diameter of Jupiter is 11.2 times the diameter of the Earth. If you are using a plastic-foam ball that has a diameter of 2 cm to represent the Earth, what must the diameter of the ball representing Jupiter be?
>
> $$\frac{11.2}{1} = \frac{x}{2 \text{ cm}}$$

Step 1: Cross-multiply.

$$\frac{11.2}{1} \diagdown\!\!\!\!\!\diagup \frac{x}{2}$$

$$11.2 \times 2 = x \times 1$$

Step 2: Multiply.

$$22.4 = x \times 1$$

Step 3: Isolate the variable by dividing both sides by 1.

$$x = \frac{22.4}{1}$$

$$x = 22.4 \text{ cm}$$

You will need to use a ball that has a diameter of **22.4** cm to represent Jupiter.

Percentages

A **percentage** is a ratio of a given number to 100.

    Example: What is 85% of 40?

Step 1: Rewrite the percentage by moving the decimal point two places to the left.

$$0.\overset{\frown}{85}$$

Step 2: Multiply the decimal by the number that you are calculating the percentage of.

$$0.85 \times 40 = 34$$

85% of 40 is **34.**

Decimals

To **add** or **subtract decimals,** line up the digits vertically so that the decimal points line up. Then, add or subtract the columns from right to left. Carry or borrow numbers as necessary.

    Example: Add the following numbers: 3.1415 and 2.96.

Step 1: Line up the digits vertically so that the decimal points line up.

$$\begin{array}{r} 3.1415 \\ + \ 2.96 \\ \hline \end{array}$$

Step 2: Add the columns from right to left, and carry when necessary.

$$\begin{array}{r} {}^{1\ 1} \\ 3.1415 \\ + \ 2.96 \\ \hline 6.1015 \end{array}$$

The sum is **6.1015.**

Fractions

Numbers tell you how many; **fractions** tell you *how much of a whole*.

    Example: Your class has 24 plants. Your teacher instructs you to put 5 plants in a shady spot. What fraction of the plants in your class will you put in a shady spot?

Step 1: In the denominator, write the total number of parts in the whole.

$$\frac{?}{24}$$

Step 2: In the numerator, write the number of parts of the whole that are being considered.

$$\frac{5}{24}$$

So, $\frac{5}{24}$ of the plants will be in the shade.

Reducing Fractions

It is usually best to express a fraction in its simplest form. Expressing a fraction in its simplest form is called *reducing* a fraction.

    Example: Reduce the fraction $\frac{30}{45}$ to its simplest form.

Step 1: Find the largest whole number that will divide evenly into both the numerator and denominator. This number is called the *greatest common factor* (GCF).

Factors of the numerator 30:

    1, 2, 3, 5, 6, 10, **15,** 30

Factors of the denominator 45:

    1, 3, 5, 9, **15,** 45

Step 2: Divide both the numerator and the denominator by the GCF, which in this case is 15.

$$\frac{30}{45} = \frac{30 \div 15}{45 \div 15} = \frac{2}{3}$$

Thus, $\frac{30}{45}$ reduced to its simplest form is $\frac{2}{3}$.

Adding and Subtracting Fractions

To **add** or **subtract fractions** that have the **same denominator,** simply add or subtract the numerators.

Examples:

$$\frac{3}{5} + \frac{1}{5} = ? \text{ and } \frac{3}{4} - \frac{1}{4} = ?$$

Step 1: Add or subtract the numerators.

$$\frac{3}{5} + \frac{1}{5} = \frac{4}{} \text{ and } \frac{3}{4} - \frac{1}{4} = \frac{2}{}$$

Step 2: Write the sum or difference over the denominator.

$$\frac{3}{5} + \frac{1}{5} = \frac{4}{5} \text{ and } \frac{3}{4} - \frac{1}{4} = \frac{2}{4}$$

Step 3: If necessary, reduce the fraction to its simplest form.

$\frac{4}{5}$ cannot be reduced, and $\frac{2}{4} = \frac{1}{2}$.

To **add** or **subtract fractions** that have **different denominators,** first find the least common denominator (LCD).

Examples:

$$\frac{1}{2} + \frac{1}{6} = ? \text{ and } \frac{3}{4} - \frac{2}{3} = ?$$

Step 1: Write the equivalent fractions that have a common denominator.

$$\frac{3}{6} + \frac{1}{6} = ? \text{ and } \frac{9}{12} - \frac{8}{12} = ?$$

Step 2: Add or subtract the fractions.

$$\frac{3}{6} + \frac{1}{6} = \frac{4}{6} \text{ and } \frac{9}{12} - \frac{8}{12} = \frac{1}{12}$$

Step 3: If necessary, reduce the fraction to its simplest form.

The fraction $\frac{4}{6} = \frac{2}{3}$, and $\frac{1}{12}$ cannot be reduced.

Multiplying Fractions

To **multiply fractions,** multiply the numerators and the denominators together, and then reduce the fraction to its simplest form.

Example:

$$\frac{5}{9} \times \frac{7}{10} = ?$$

Step 1: Multiply the numerators and denominators.

$$\frac{5}{9} \times \frac{7}{10} = \frac{5 \times 7}{9 \times 10} = \frac{35}{90}$$

Step 2: Reduce the fraction.

$$\frac{35}{90} = \frac{35 \div 5}{90 \div 5} = \frac{7}{18}$$

Dividing Fractions

To **divide fractions,** first rewrite the divisor (the number you divide by) upside down. This number is called the *reciprocal* of the divisor. Then multiply and reduce if necessary.

Example:

$$\frac{5}{8} \div \frac{3}{2} = ?$$

Step 1: Rewrite the divisor as its reciprocal.

$$\frac{3}{2} \rightarrow \frac{2}{3}$$

Step 2: Multiply the fractions.

$$\frac{5}{8} \times \frac{2}{3} = \frac{5 \times 2}{8 \times 3} = \frac{10}{24}$$

Step 3: Reduce the fraction.

$$\frac{10}{24} = \frac{10 \div 2}{24 \div 2} = \frac{5}{12}$$

Appendix

Scientific Notation

Scientific notation is a short way of representing very large and very small numbers without writing all of the place-holding zeros.

Example: Write 653,000,000 in scientific notation.

Step 1: Write the number without the place-holding zeros.

653

Step 2: Place the decimal point after the first digit.

6.53

Step 3: Find the exponent by counting the number of places that you moved the decimal point.

6.53000000

The decimal point was moved eight places to the left. Therefore, the exponent of 10 is positive 8. If you had moved the decimal point to the right, the exponent would be negative.

Step 4: Write the number in scientific notation.

$$6.53 \times 10^8$$

Area

Area is the number of square units needed to cover the surface of an object.

Formulas:

area of a square = side × side
area of a rectangle = length × width
area of a triangle = $\frac{1}{2}$ × base × height

Examples: Find the areas.

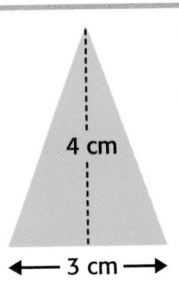

Triangle

area = $\frac{1}{2}$ × base × height
area = $\frac{1}{2}$ × 3 cm × 4 cm
area = **6 cm²**

4 cm

3 cm

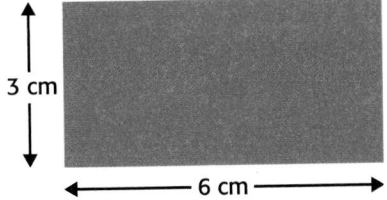

3 cm

6 cm

Rectangle
area = length × width
area = 6 cm × 3 cm
area = **18 cm²**

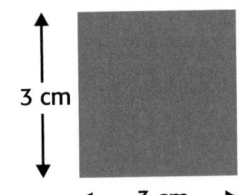

3 cm

3 cm

Square
area = side × side
area = 3 cm × 3 cm
area = **9 cm²**

Volume

Volume is the amount of space that something occupies.

Formulas:

volume of a cube =
side × side × side

volume of a prism =
area of base × height

Examples:

Find the volume of the solids.

Cube
volume = side × side × side
volume = 4 cm × 4 cm × 4 cm
volume = **64 cm³**

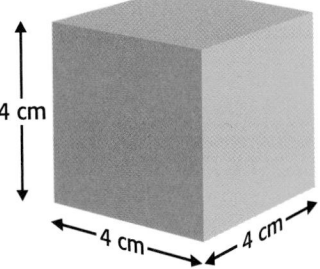

4 cm

4 cm

4 cm

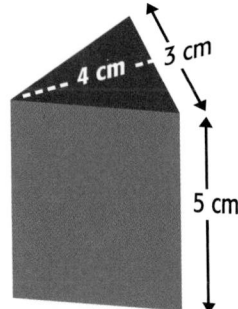

4 cm

3 cm

5 cm

Prism
volume = area of base × height
volume = (area of triangle) × height
volume = ($\frac{1}{2}$ × 3 cm × 4 cm) × 5 cm
volume = 6 cm² × 5 cm
volume = **30 cm³**

Appendix   **151**

Glossary

A

amniotic egg (AM nee AHT ik EG) a type of egg that is surrounded by a membrane, the amnion, and that in reptiles, birds, and egg-laying mammals contains a large amount of yolk and is surrounded by a shell (75)

antenna a feeler that is on the head of an invertebrate, such as a crustacean or an insect, and that senses touch, taste, or smell (42)

B

brooding to sit on and cover eggs to keep them warm until they hatch; to incubate (94)

C

circadian rhythm a biological daily cycle (12)

closed circulatory system a circulatory system in which the heart circulates blood through a network of vessels that form a closed loop; the blood does not leave the blood vessels, and materials diffuse across the walls of the vessels (37)

coelom (SEE luhm) a body cavity that contains the internal organs (29)

communication a transfer of a signal or message from one animal to another that results in some type of response (14)

compound eye an eye composed of many light detectors (41)

consumer an organism that eats other organisms or organic matter (7)

contour feather one of the most external feathers that cover a bird and that help determine its shape (91)

D

diaphragm (DIE uh FRAM) a dome-shaped muscle that is attached to the lower ribs and that functions as the main muscle in respiration (101)

down feather a soft feather that covers the body of young birds and provides insulation to adult birds (91)

E

ectotherm (EK toh thuhrm) an organism that needs sources of heat outside of itself (62)

embryo (EM bree OH) a plant or an animal in an early stage of development (6)

endoskeleton (EN doh SKEL uh tuhn) an internal skeleton made of bone and cartilage (46)

endotherm (EN doh THUHRM) an animal that can use body heat from chemical reactions in the body's cells to maintain a constant body temperature (62)

estivation a period of inactivity and lowered body temperature that some animals undergo in summer as a protection against hot weather and lack of food (12)

exoskeleton a hard, external, supporting structure (41)

G

ganglion (GANG glee uhn) a mass of nerve cells (29)

gestation period (jes TAY shuhn PIR ee uhd) in mammals, the length of time between fertilization and birth (104)

gill a respiratory organ in which oxygen from the water is exchanged with carbon dioxide from the blood (63)

gut the digestive tract (29)

H

hibernation a period of inactivity and lowered body temperature that some animals undergo in winter as a protection against cold weather and lack of food (12)

I

innate behavior an inherited behavior that does not depend on the environment or experience (8)

invertebrate (in VUHR tuh brit) an animal that does not have a backbone (28)

L

lateral line a faint line visible on both sides of a fish's body that runs the length of the body and marks the location of sense organs that detect vibrations in water (63)

learned behavior a behavior that has been learned from experience (8)

lift an upward force on an object that moves in a fluid (94)

lung a respiratory organ in which oxygen from the air is exchanged with carbon dioxide from the blood (68)

M

mammary gland in a female mammal, a gland that secretes milk (101)

marsupial (mahr SOO pee uhl) a mammal that carries and nourishes its young in a pouch (113)

metamorphosis (MET uh MAWR fuh sis) a phase in the life cycle of many animals during which a rapid change from the immature form of an organism to the adult form takes place (44, 70)

molting the shedding of an exoskeleton, skin, feathers, or hair to be replaced by new parts (90)

monotreme (MAHN oh TREEM) a mammal that lays eggs (112)

O

open circulatory system a circulatory system in which the circulatory fluid is not contained entirely within vessels; a heart pumps fluid through vessels that empty into spaces called *sinuses* (37)

P

pheromone (FER uh MOHN) a substance that is released by the body and that causes another individual of the same species to react in a predictable way (15)

placenta (pluh SEN tuh) the structure that attaches a developing fetus to the uterus and that enables the exchange of nutrients, wastes, and gases between the mother and the fetus

placental mammal a mammal that nourishes its unborn offspring through a placenta inside its uterus (104)

preening in birds, the act of grooming and maintaining their feathers (90)

S

segment any part of a larger structure, such as the body of an organism, that is set off by natural or arbitrary boundaries (38)

social behavior the interaction between animals of the same species (14)

swim bladder in bony fishes, a gas-filled sac that is used to control buoyancy; also known as a *gas bladder* (66)

T

tadpole the aquatic, fish-shaped larva of a frog or toad (70)

territory an area that is occupied by one animal or a group of animals that do not allow other members of the species to enter (9)

V

vertebrate (VUHR tuh brit) an animal that has a backbone (60)

W

water vascular system a system of canals filled with a watery fluid that circulates throughout the body of an echinoderm (46)

Glossary

Spanish Glossary

A

amniotic egg/huevo amniótico un tipo de huevo que está rodeado por una membrana, el amnios, y que en los reptiles, las aves y los mamíferos que ponen huevos contiene una gran cantidad de yema y está rodeado por una cáscara (75)

antenna/antena una estructura ubicada en la cabeza de un invertebrado, como por ejemplo, un crustáceo o un insecto, que percibe sensaciones de tacto, gusto u olor (42)

B

brooding/empollar sentarse y cubrir los huevos para mantenerlos calientes hasta que las crías salgan del cascarón; incubar (94)

C

circadian rhythm/ritmo circadiano un ciclo biológico diario (12)

closed circulatory system/aparato circulatorio cerrado un aparato circulatorio en el que el corazón hace que la sangre circule a través de una red de vasos que forman un circuito cerrado; la sangre no sale de los vasos sanguíneos y los materiales pasan a través de las paredes de los vasos por difusión (37)

coelom/celoma una cavidad del cuerpo que contiene los órganos internos (29)

communication/comunicación la transferencia de una señal o mensaje de un animal a otro, la cual resulta en algún tipo de respuesta (14)

compound eye/ojo compuesto un ojo compuesto por muchos detectores de luz (41)

consumer/consumidor un organismo que se alimenta de otros organismos o de materia orgánica (7)

contour feather/pluma de contorno una las plumas más externas que cubren a un ave y que sirven para determinar su forma (91)

D

diaphragm/diafragma un músculo en forma de cúpula que está unido a las costillas inferiores y que es el músculo principal de la respiración (101)

down feather/plumón una pluma suave que cubre el cuerpo de las crías de las aves y sirve como aislante en las aves adultas (91)

E

ectotherm/ectotermo un organismo que necesita fuentes de calor fuera de sí mismo (62)

embryo/embrión una planta o un animal en una de las primeras etapas de su desarrollo (358); un ser humano desde la fecundación hasta las primeras 8 semanas de desarrollo (décima semana del embarazo) (6)

endoskeleton/endoesqueleto un esqueleto interno hecho de hueso y cartílago (46)

endotherm/endotermo un animal que puede utilizar el calor del cuerpo producido por las reacciones químicas de sus células para mantener una temperatura corporal constante (62)

estivation/estivación un período de inactividad y menor temperatura corporal por el que pasan algunos animales durante el verano para protegerse del calor y la falta de alimento (12)

exoskeleton/exoesqueleto una estructura de soporte, dura y externa (41)

G

ganglion/ganglio una masa de células nerviosas (29)

gestation period/período de gestación en los mamíferos, el tiempo que transcurre entre la fecundación y el nacimiento (104)

gill/branquiaen un órgano respiratorio en el que el oxígeno del agua se intercambia con el dióxido de carbono de la sangre (63)

gut/tripa el tracto digestivo (29)

H

hibernation/hibernación un período de inactividad y disminución de la temperatura del cuerpo que algunos animales experimentan en invierno como protección contra el tiempo frío y la escasez de comida (12)

I

innate behavior/conducta innata una conducta heredada que no depende del ambiente ni de la experiencia (8)

invertebrate/invertebrado un animal que no tiene columna vertebral (28)

L

lateral line/línea lateral una línea apenas visible que se encuentra a ambos lados del cuerpo de unpez y que recorre la longitud del cuerpo, marcando la ubicación de los órganos de los sentidos que detectan vibraciones en el agua (63)

learned behavior/conducta aprendida una conducta que se ha aprendido por experiencia (8)

lift/propulsión una fuerza hacia arriba en un objeto que se mueve en un fluido (94)

lung/pulmón un órgano respiratorio en el que el oxígeno del aire se intercambia con el dióxido de carbono de la sangre (68)

M

mammary gland/glándula mamaria en los mamíferos hembra, una glándula que secreta leche (101)

marsupial/marsupial un mamífero que lleva y alimenta a sus crías en una bolsa (113)

metamorphosis/metamorfosis una fase del ciclo de vida de muchos animales durante la cual ocurre un cambio rápido de la forma inmadura del organismo a la adulta (44, 70)

molting/pelechar la muda de un exoesqueleto, piel, plumas o pelo, los cuales son reemplazados por partes nuevas (90)

monotreme/monotrema un mamífero que pone-huevos (112)

O

open circulatory system/aparato circulatorio abierto un aparato circulatorio en el que el fluido circulatorio no está totalmente contenido en los vasos sanguíneos; un corazón bombea fluido por los vasos sanguíneos, los cuales se vacían en espacios llamados *senos* (37)

P

pheromone/feromona una substancia que el cuerpo libera y que hace que otro individuo de la misma especia reaccione de un modo predecible (15)

placenta/placenta la estructura que une al feto en desarrollo con el útero y que permite el intercambio de nutrientes, desechos y gases entre la madre y el feto

placental mammal/mamífero placentario un mamífero que nutre a sus crías aún no nacidas a través de una placenta que se encuentra dentro de su útero (104)

preening/acicalamiento en las aves, el acto de limpiar y mantener saludables las plumas (90)

S

segment/segmento cualquier parte de una estructura más grande, como el cuerpo de un organismo, que se determina por límites naturales o arbitrarios (38)

social behavior/comportamiento social la interacción entre animales de la misma especie (14)

swim bladder/vejiga natatoria en los peces óseos, una bolsa llena de gas que se usa para controlar la flotabilidad; también se llama *vejiga de aire* (66)

T

tadpole/renacuajo la larva acuática, parecida a un pez, de una rana o sapo (70)

territory/territorio un área que está ocupada por un animal o por un grupo de animales que no permiten que entren otros miembros de la especie (9)

V

vertebrate/vertebrado un animal que tiene columna vertebral (60)

W

water vascular system/sistema vascular acuoso un sistema de canales que están llenos de un fluido acuoso que circula por todo el cuerpo de los equinodermos (46)

Spanish Glossary

Index

Index

Index

graphs, 145–147, **145, 146, 147**
grasshoppers, 45, **45**
great blue herons, **90**
greatest common factor (GCF), 149
Green Iguana Foundation, 87
green sea turtles, **77**
ground squirrels, 17, **17**
guide horses, 24
guts, in invertebrates, 29, **29**

H

habitats, destruction of, 115
hagfish, 64, **64**
hair, 102
hammerhead sharks, **65**
heart, in birds, **92**
hedgehogs, **105**
hibernation, 12, **12**
hollow nerve chords, **61**
hoofed mammals, 108, **108**
horses, 24, **102,** 108
hummingbirds, **90**
humpback whales, 15, 109, **109**
hydras, 6, 31–32, **32**
hypotheses, 142–143

I

iguanas, 87
imprinting, 25
incisors, 102, **102**
innate behavior, 8, **8, 9**
insectivores, 105, **105**
insects, 43–45, **43, 44, 45**
internal fertilization, 63
International System of Units (SI),
    140, **140**
invertebrates, 28–49, **29**
    abundance of, 5
    annelid worms, 38–39, **38, 39**
    arthropods, 40–45, **40, 41, 42,
        43, 44**
    characteristics of, 28–29, **29**
    cnidarians, 31–32, **31, 32**
    ctenophores, 57
    echinoderms, 46–49, **46, 47, 48,
        49**
    flatworms, 33–34, **33, 34**
    lab on, 50–51
    metamorphosis, 44–45, **44, 45,**
        70, **70**
    mollusks, 36–37, **36, 37**
    roundworms, 34, **34**
    simple, 28–35
    sponges, 29–31, 29, **30, 31**
    symmetry in, 28, **28**

J

Japanese ground cranes, **10**
jawless fishes, 64, **64**
jellyfish, 31–32, **31, 32**
joeys, 114, **114**
joints, 41

K

kangaroos, 113–115, **114**
Kanzi, 24
keels, in birds, **93**
kelvins (units), 144, **144**
key-term fold instructions
    (FoldNote), 136, **136**
killer whales, **11**
kilograms (kg), **140**
kiwi birds, **96**
koalas, **114**
Komodo dragons, 78

L

lampreys, 64, **64**
lancelets, 60, **60**
landmarks, 11
larvae, **44, 46**
lateral lines, 63, **63**
layered book instructions
    (FoldNote), 135, **135**
LCD (least common denominator),
    150
leafy sea dragons, **62**
learned behavior, 8, **8, 9**
least common denominator (LCD),
    150
leeches, 39, **39,** 56
length, **140,** 141
life cycle of amphibians, 70, **70**
lift, 94, **94**
line graphs, 146–147, **146**
lions, 16–17
liters (L), **140**
livers, 65
lizards, 78, **78,** 87
lobe-finned fishes, 66
lobsters, 42, **42**
loons, **97**
lungfishes, 66, **66,** 68
lungs, 68
Lyme disease, 43
lyrebirds, 122

M

macaques, **110**
mammals, 100–111. *See also*
        names of individual mammals
anteaters, armadillos, and sloths,
    104, **104**
carnivores, 107, **107**
cetaceans, 109, **109**
characteristics of, 101–103, **101,
    102, 103**
evolution of, 100
flying, 106, **106**
hoofed, 108, **108**
insectivores, 105, **105**
manatees and dugongs, 109,
    109
marsupials, 113–115, **113, 114,
    115**
monotremes, 112–113, **112, 113**
number of species, **5**
placental, 104, **104** (*see also*
    placental mammals)
primates, **9,** 110, **110**
rabbits, hares, and pikas, 106,
    106
rodents, 105, **105**
sexual reproduction in, 103–104,
    113 (*see also* sexual
    reproduction)
trunk-nosed, 15, **15,** 107, **107**
mammary glands, 101, **101**
manatees, 109, **109**
mandibles, 42
mandrill baboons, **100**
mantis shrimps, 56
mantles, **37**
marbled salamanders, **71**
marine biologists, 57
marine worms, 38, **38**
marking territory, 9
marsupials, 113–115, **113, 114, 115**
masked butterfly fish, **66**
mass, **140,** 141
math refresher, 148–150
Matsumoto, George, 57
measurement, 141, **141**
medusa form, 31, **31**
metamorphosis, 44–45, **44, 45,** 70,
    70
meters (m), **140**
metersticks, 141, **141**
metric rulers, 141, **141**
metric system, 140, **140**
micrometers (μm), **140**
migration, 11, **11**
milk, 101, **101**
milliliters (mL), **140**
millimeters (mm), **140**
millipedes, 42, **42**
molars, 102, **102**
moles, **105**
mollusks, 36–37, **36, 37**
molting, **44,** 45, 90, **90**
monkeys, 110, **110**

Index

Credits

PHOTOGRAPHY

Front Cover Chris Johns/Getty Images

Skills Practice Lab Teens Sam Dudgeon/HRW

Connection to Astronomy Corbis Images; **Connection to Biology** David M. Phillips/Visuals Unlimited; **Connection to Chemistry** Digital Image copyright © 2005 PhotoDisc; **Connection to Environment** Digital Image copyright © 2005 PhotoDisc; **Connection to Geology** Letraset Phototone; **Connection to Language Arts** Digital Image copyright © 2005 PhotoDisc; **Connection to Meteorology** Digital Image copyright © 2005 PhotoDisc; **Connection to Oceanography** © ICONOTEC; **Connection to Physics** Digital Image copyright © 2005 PhotoDisc

Table of Contents iv (tl), Ron Kimball; iv (b), © Jeffrey L. Rotman/CORBIS; v (tl), © Kevin Schafer/CORBIS; v (bc), Sylvain Cordier/Photo Researchers; vi–vii, Victoria Smith/HRW; x (bl), Sam Dudgeon/HRW; xi (tl), John Langford/HRW; xi (b), Sam Dudgeon/HRW; xii (tl), Victoria Smith/HRW; xii (bl), Stephanie Morris/HRW; xii (br), Sam Dudgeon/HRW; xiii (tl), Patti Murray/Animals, Animals; xiii (tr), Jana Birchum/HRW; xiii (b), Peter Van Steen/HRW

Chapter One 2–3 Bruce Coleman, Ltd./Natural Selection; 4 © David B. Fleetham/Getty Images/FPG International; 5 (bc), Digital Image copyright © 2005 Artville; 5 (bl), Digital Image copyright © 2005 Artville; 5 (br), Digital Image copyright © 2005 Artville; 5 (tl), Digital Image copyright © 2005 Artville; 5 (tr), Digital Image copyright © 2005 Artville; 6 (t), Visuals Unlimited/Fred Hossler ; 7 (t), © Keren Su/Getty Images/Stone; 7 (b), Digital Image copyright © 2005 Artville; 8 © Michael & Patricia Fogden/CORBIS; 9 © Tim Davis/Getty Images/Stone; 10 (r), Fernandez & Peck/Adventure Photo & Film; 10 (l), © Tom Brakefield/CORBIS; 11 (t), Gerard Lacz/Peter Arnold; 11 (b), © George D. Lepp/Getty Images/Stone; 12 © Ralph A. Clevenger/CORBIS; 13 Brian Kenney; 14 Peter Weimann/Animals Animals; 15 (t), Johnny Johnson/Animals Animals; 15 (b), Kenneth G. Ross; 16 (b), Ron Kimball; 17 Richard R. Hansen/Photo Researchers, Inc.; 20 (t), Digital Image copyright © 2005 Artville; 20 (b), Richard R. Hansen/Photo Researchers, Inc.; 24 (r), Todd Sumlin/© The Charlotte Observer; 24 (l), © National Geographic Image Collection/Michael K. Nichols; 25 Photo courtesy The International Crane Foundation

Chapter Two 26–27 W. Gregory Brown/Animals Animals; 29 (b), © Keith Philpott/Getty Images/The Image Bank; 31 (tr), Jeffrey L. Rotman/Peter Arnold, Inc.; 31 (cr), © Jeffrey L. Rotman/CORBIS; 32 (cl), Randy Morse/Tom Stack & Associates; 32 (cl), Biophoto Associates/Science Source/Photo Researchers; 32 (bc), © Lee Foster/Getty Images/FPG International; 32 (bl), David B. Fleetham/Visuals Unlimited; 33 (t), Visuals Unlimited/T. E. Adams; 33 (b), CNRI/Science Photo Library/Photo Researchers; 34 (t), Visuals Unlimited/R. Calentine; 34 (b), Visuals Unlimited/A. M. Siegelman; 35 (t), Randy Morse/Tom Stack & Associates; 36 (l), Nigel Cattlin/Holt Studios International/Photo Researchers; 36 (r), Visuals Unlimited/David M. Phillips; 37 (t), © David Fleetham/Getty Images/FPG International; 38 (t), Milton Rand/Tom Stack & Associates; 38 (b), Mary Beth Angelo/Photo Researchers; 39 (t), St. Bartholomew's Hospital/Science Photo Library/Photo Researchers; 40 Leroy Simon/Visuals Unlimited; 41 (b), CNRI/Science Photo Library/Photo Researchers; 41 (t), © M. H. Sharp/Photo Researchers, Inc.; 42 (tl), Visuals Unlimited/A. Kerstitch; 42 (cl), Dr. E.R. Degginger, FPSA; 42 (b), Daniel Gotshall/Visuals Unlimited; 42 (inset), © M. i. Walker/Photo Researchers, Inc.; 43 (brc), Uniphoto; 43 (tc), Stephen Dalton/NHPA; 43 (bl), © Gail Shumway/Getty Images/FPG International; 44 (t), Leroy Simon/Visuals Unlimited; 46 (br), © Paul McCormick/Getty Images/The Image Bank; 46 (bl), Visuals Unlimited/Cabisco; 48 (br), Visuals Unlimited/Marty Snyderman; 48 (tl), Andrew J. Martinez/Photo Researchers; 48 (tr), Robert Dunne/Photo Researchers; 48 (bl), Flip Nicklin/Minden Pictures; 49 (l), Visuals Unlimited/Daniel W. Gotshall; 49 (r), Chesher/Photo Researchers; 50 (c), Digital imagery® copyright 2002 PhotoDisc, Inc.; 51 Victoria Smith/HRW; 52 (b), © David Fleetham/Getty Images/FPG International; 53 (b), Leroy Simon/Visuals Unlimited; 53 (t), © Paul McCormick/Getty Images/The Image Bank; 56 (r), © Tim Rock/Lonely Planet Images; 56 (l), © Bill Beatty/Visuals Unlimited; 57 (r), Ed Seibel ©2000 MBARI; 57 (b), © 2005 Norbert Wu/www.norbertwu.com

Chapter Three 58–59 (t), MARTIN WENDLER/NHPA; 60 (tr), Randy Morse/Tom Stack; 60 (bl), Brian Parker/Tom Stack; 60 (br), G.I. Bernard OSF/Animals Animals; 61 (b), Grant Heilman; 62 (t), ©James Watt/Animals Animals/Earth Scenes; 64 (r), Hans Reinhard/Bruce Coleman; 64 (l), Steinhart Aquarium/Photo Researchers, Inc.; 65 (b), Index Stock; 65 (tr), © Martin Barraud/Getty Images/Stone; 65 (tl), ©2000 Norbert Wu/www.norbertwu.com; 66 (br), Bruce Coleman; 66 (bl), Steinhart Aquarium/Tom McHugh/Photo Researchers; 66 (bc), Ron & Valerie Taylor/Bruce Coleman, Inc.; 67 Doug Perrine/DRK Photo; 68 (l), Michael Fogden/DRK Photo; 68 (r), Visuals Unlimited/Nathan W. Cohen; 69 (t), David M. Dennis/Tom Stack & Associates; 69 (b), C.K. Lorenz/Photo Researchers; 70 (b), Michael and Patricia Fogden; 71 (t), M.P.L. Fogden/Bruce Coleman; 71 (br), Stephen Dalton/NHPA; 71 (bl), Richard Thom/Visuals Unlimited; 72 (tl), Leonard Lee Rue/Photo Researchers; 72 (tr), Breck P. Kent; 72 (b), Telegraph Color Library/Getty Images/FPG International; 73 ©Michael & Patricia Fogden/Minden Pictures; 74 (bl), Visuals Unlimited; 74 (br), Kenneth Fink/Bruce Coleman, Inc.; 74 (t), Danilo B. Donadoni/Bruce Coleman; 75 (t), © Gail Shumway/Getty Images/FPG International; 75 (bl), Stanley Breeden/DRK Photo; 75 (br), Visuals Unlimited/Joe McDonald; 76 (b), Visuals Unlimited/Rob & Ann Simpson; 77 (tl), © Mike Severns/Getty Images/Stone; 77 (br), Kevin Schafer/Peter Arnold; 77 (bl), Wayne Lynch/DRK Photo; 77 (tr), Carl Ernst; 78 (bl), C. E. Schmida/F.P./Bruce Coleman, Inc.; 78 (tl), E. R. Degginger/Bruce Coleman, Inc.; 78 (br), © Uhlenhut, Klaus/Animals Animals/Earth Scenes; 78 (tr), © Unknown PhotographerAnimals Animals/Earth Scenes; 79 © Kevin Schafer/CORBIS; 80 Peter Van Steen/HRW; 82 (b), Steinhart Aquarium/Tom McHugh/Photo Researchers; 82 (t), Visuals Unlimited/Rob & Ann Simpson; 83 (t), Brian Parker/Tom Stack; 83 (b), Leonard Lee Rue/Photo Researchers; 86 (r), Rick Bowmer/AP/Wide World Photos; 86 (tl), Victoria Smith/HRW; 87 (t), Karen M. Allen; 87 (b), Karen Allen

Chapter Four 88–89 Bianca Lavies/National Geographic Society Image Collection; 90 (tr), © Stan Osolinski; 90 (br), © Gail Shumway/Getty Images/FPG International; 90 (l), G.C. Kelley/Photo Researchers; 94 (b), D. Cavagnaro/DRK Photo; 95 Hal H. Harrison/Grant Heilman; 96 (c), © Gavriel Jecan/Getty Images/Stone; 96 (r), APL/J. Carnemolla/Westlight; 96 (l), © Kevin Schafer/Getty Images/Stone; 97 (tl), Tui De Roy/Minden Pictures; 97 (b), Wayne Lankinen/Bruce Coleman; 97 (tr), S. Nielsen/DRK Photo; 98 (t), Stephen J. Krasemann/DRK Photo; 98 (b), Visuals Unlimited/S. Maslowski; 98 (cl), Frans Lanting/Minden Pictures; 99 (l), © Greg Vaughn/Getty Images/Stone; 99 (r), Fritz Polking/Bruce Coleman; 100 (l), Gerard Lacz/Animals Animals; 100 (r), Tim Davis/Photo Researchers; 100 (bl), Nigel Dennis/Photo Researchers; 101 Hans Reinhard/Bruce Coleman; 102 (t), © David E. Myers/Getty Images/Stone; 102 (bl), © Tom Tietz/Getty Images/Stone; 102 (br), Sylvain Cordier/Photo Researchers; 103 © Kathy Bushue/Getty Images/Stone; 104 (l), Wayne Lynch/DRK Photo; 104 (r), John D. Cunningham/Visuals Unlimited; 105 (tr), © Gail Shumway/Getty Images/FPG International; 105 (tl), D. R. Kuhn/Bruce Coleman; 105 (br), Frans Lanting/Minden Pictures; 105 (bl), Gerry Ellis/Minden Pictures; 106 (tl), David Cavagnaro/Peter Arnold; 106 (tr), John Cancalosi; 106 (bl), Art Wolfe/Stone; 106 (br), Merlin D. Tuttle/Bat Conservation International; 107 (tl), © Gail Shumway/Getty Images/FPG International; 107 (tr), Arthur C. Smith III/Grant Heilman; 107 (bl), © Art Wolfe/Getty Images/Stone; 107 (br), Manoi Shah/Stone; 108 (br), © Scott Daniel Peterson/Liaison/Getty News Images; 108 (tl), © Gail Shumway/Getty Images/FPG International; 108 (bl), Roberto Arakaki/International Stock; 109 (tl), Flip Nicklin/Minden Pictures; 109 (b), Tom & Therisa Stack; 109 (tr), Pete Atkinson/NHPA; 110 (c), J. & P. Wegner/Animals Animals; 110 (b), Inga Spence/Tom Stack; 110 (br), Martin Harvey/NHPA; 111 (b), Joe McDonald/Bruce Coleman; 111 (t), © Scott Daniel Peterson/Liaison/Getty News Images; 112 (r), Edwin & Peggy Bauer/Bruce Coleman; 112 (l), © Pavel German/NHPA; 113 Dave Watts/Nature Picture Library; 114 (bc), Jean–Paul Ferrero/AUSCAPE; 114 (r), Hans Reinhard/Bruce Coleman; 114 (bl), © Art Wolfe/Getty Images/Stone; 114 (t), © Mitsuaki Iwago/Minden Pictures; 115 (t), © Photo Researchers, Inc.; 117 (b), Sam Dudgeon/HRW; 118 Tui De Roy/Minden Pictures; 118 (b), Merlin D. Tuttle/Bat Conservation International; 119 (t), © Stan Osolinski/Getty Images/FPG International; 122 (l), U.S. Navy, Brien Aho, HO/AP/Wide World Photos; 122 (r), Dave Watts/Nature Picture Library; 123 (r), William Munoz; 123 (l), William Munoz

Lab Book/Appendix "LabBook Header", "L", Corbis Images; "a", Letraset Phototone; "b", and "B", HRW; "o", and "k", images ©2006 PhotoDisc/HRW; 124 (t), John Langford/HRW Photo; 124 (b), John Langford/HRW Photo; 125 (t), Sam Dudgeon/HRW; 125 (c), Sam Dudgeon/HRW; 127 (t), Sam Dudgeon/HRW; 127 (b), Sam Dudgeon/HRW; 129 Rod Planck/Photo Researchers; 130 Peter Van Steen/HRW; 135 Sam Dudgeon/HRW; 136 Sam Dudgeon/HRW; 141 (t), Peter Van Steen/HRW; 141 (b), Sam Dudgeon/HRW

Credits